THE ART *of* CHEATING

THE ART *of* CHEATING

A Nasty Little Book for Tricky
Little Schemers and Their Hapless Victims

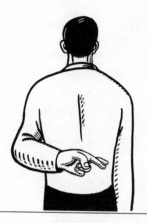

Jessica Dorfman Jones

With Illustrations by Alison Seiffer

POCKET BOOKS

NEW YORK   LONDON   TORONTO   SYDNEY

Pocket Books
A Division of Simon & Schuster, Inc.
1230 Avenue of the Americas
New York, NY 10020

Text copyright © 2007 Jessica Dorfman Jones
Compilation copyright © 2007 by D&J Book Packaging and Media
Cover design by D&J Book Packaging and Media © 2007

First Pocket Books trade paperback edition October 2007

POCKET and colophon are registered trademarks of Simon & Schuster, Inc.

For information about special discounts for bulk purchases,
please contact Simon & Schuster Special Sales at
1-800-456-6798 or business@simonandschuster.com

Designed by Jan Pisciotta

Manufactured in the United States of America

10   9   8   7   6   5   4   3   2   1

Library of Congress Cataloging-in-Publication Data

Jones, Jessica Dorfman.
    The art of cheating : a nasty little book for tricky little schemers and their hapless victims / Jessica Dorfman Jones.—1st Pocket Books trade paperback ed.
        p. cm.
    1. Truthfulness and falsehood—Humor.   2. Deception—Humor.   I. Title.
PN6231.T74J66 2007
818'.607—dc22   2007021161

ISBN-13: 978-1-4165-4913-0
ISBN-10:   1-4165-4913-7

For Jim

CONTENTS

Whether we want to admit it or not, cheating is an inescapable part of the human condition. Some of us are more comfortable than others acknowledging this fact, but it's still a fact, plain and simple.

There's no shortage of people who like to claim that they lead lives above reproach. You know the type: God fearing, seemingly honest, quick to tell others when they're straying off the path, certainly not likely to identify themselves as cheaters. But they are. We all are. Everyone is guilty of telling little white lies or devising secret ways to get ahead when the right moment arises. It doesn't matter if you're fibbing a little so that your wall-eyed colleague doesn't feel bad ("No, really, no one can tell"), or if you stole a recipe to win the county bake-off just once. Even if you're usually on the up-and-up, those little lapses land you squarely in cheater country. Despite our best efforts, we're all cheaters in our own ways.

Still think you're not a creepy little cheater? Are you shaking your head as you read this and saying "Oh, no, I'd never do that!" Think again. Remember when you got your college roommate to write that homework assignment for you? How about when you weren't really cheating on your significant other because you were "on a break"? That's right, folks, you were cheating. And don't even get started trying to justify that time you claimed your dog as a dependent on your tax return. That was cheating too. Getting away with it, whatever "it" may be, is cheating.

Even though you're cheating a little bit every day, chances are you could be doing it better. Why settle for a minor promotion when you could have the corner office? Why bother taking the loose change out of your friend's couch when you could be making the big bucks forging checks? If your answer is that you just don't know how, look no further. This is the book for you.

In the pages of this little tome, you'll find a guide to grifting, a sourcebook of sophistry, and a bible of bunco. Everything the modern mountebank needs to know to pull off the most essential cheats can be found in these pages. Every cheat has been numbered for your easy reference and reading pleasure. You will, however, notice that they are in no easily discernible order. This is much like life, as the ways in which we cheat and the reasons we decide to do so don't follow any particular patterns either. As you leaf through this book, let the myriad ways in which you can get one over on the other guy surprise and entertain you as you stumble on them, just as you will stumble on opportunities to exercise your new shady talents after reading this book. You'll also find that the information in each chapter has been neatly laid out in an easy step-by-step format so you can be up and running in no time with your new and improved life of chicanery. Feel free to mix and match your cheats at will. A life without artful cheating isn't a life worth living.

If the above statement fills you with horror, and you're truly one of the few people left on earth who shun sharp practice, don't despair. You'll be glad to know that every cheat in this book includes a section on protecting yourself from that particular type of flimflammery. Read carefully, lest you leave yourself open to the wily ways of your fellow readers.

Now that you're fully briefed on what this guide to skulduggery has in store for you, dearest con artists and marks alike, read on. And don't forget to keep looking over your shoulder. There's always someone a little sharper and a little cagier right behind you.

FAKING AN ORGASM

BABY, YOU'RE THE GREATEST

Rules of etiquette apply in all sorts of situations, and while Emily Post may never have weighed in on this particular topic, bedroom activity is no exception to the rule. Egos can be particularly fragile and emotions can run high while couples are in the throes of passion, and most people know that it's just as important to make your partner feel good emotionally as well as physically.

This is easy to do when you've got the lover of the century who can be a relentless sex machine while simultaneously delivering sweet nothings in your ear. Sweet nothings that are a delicious melange of *Penthouse Forum* smut and Hallmark sentiment. Of course you'll affirm someone who's hitting the mark perfectly on a regular basis. It's like playing tennis with a player who's better than you. You feed off their game, they feed off yours, and so on and so on. What happens, however, when your lover is a dud? What's a right-thinking person to do when his or her sweetie is so lackluster in the sack as to be yawn inducing? Even worse, what do you do when they know they're a snore and keep trying (dear God) and trying and trying and trying? You get them to stop. And there's one sure way to get anyone to simmer down and call it a night: fake that orgasm and beg for rest.

Sure, you could keep trying until you actually reach the final denouement, but if your lover is truly awful, it's not likely that this is going to happen. You could try to show him or her what needs to be done, but if you've been going at it so long that the opportunity for the usual moment for release has come and gone, it's best to relax and live to fight another day.

So go to it, people. It doesn't matter if you're a man or a woman, where there's a will there's a way. Learn to fake it and get on with your life.

THE UPSIDE

Cheating of any kind can be a moral dilemma for most people. Even so, it's much easier to rationalize small lies or lies of convenience, while the big ones can eat away at you. Faking an orgasm, for most people, falls squarely in the "little white lie" category. It can be argued that faking an orgasm is tantamount to saying that you love someone's new acid-washed jeans, or that their poetry is the best you've ever heard. It makes the other person feel good and doesn't really add any negative karma to the world—it's a small kindness that greases the wheels of social (and sexual) intercourse.

Although a bit less altruistic, there are a handful of other (no less valuable) bonuses to cheating your way through a particularly un-satisfying sexual encounter. Getting some much needed sleep is gen-erally the most popular response (and actually trumps the desire to spare a lousy lover's feelings). Considering that at last count 62 per-cent of Americans are sleep deprived, calling it quits when the going gets too tough is a fairly sensible thing to do.

Reclaiming your valuable time and spending it well is another good reason to pull the plug when your libido isn't showing any signs of life. Although Woody Allen once professed that "even my worst orgasm was right on the money," many people these days beg to differ. Living in a nonstop world of work and family obligations has made most people value their time and keep an eye on the clock in a more serious way than ever before. So, at the end of the day, no sex can be better than bad sex. Given the choice of letting someone pull out all his or her lackluster stops, or catch up on a little reading (even watching a rerun of *CSI*), go for the reading. You'll get more out of it in the end.

Finally, it's time to call it quits when you're so sore that you just can't go on. Going numb from the waist down is a surefire sign that it's time to gear up with your performance so that you can let your lover down easy. It's great to know when you've had enough not only so that you can move on with your life, but you'll also avoid a lot of discomfort down the road. So what's the upside, exactly? Escaping the indignities of pulled groin muscles, rampant chafing, urinary tract infections, and emotional meltdowns, to name a few horrors that can come (or not come) from a night of fruitless tugging and rubbing. These are all avoidable perils for the covert faker.

THE DOWNSIDE

Obviously, anytime you tell a lie, you are potentially driving a wedge between yourself and your loved one. Honesty is the cornerstone of any good relationship, and any lie, no matter how small, could wind up biting you in the behind (and we know that's probably what you wish your misguided lover was doing). Essentially, once your lover finds out that you've been faking it in bed, it opens the door for his or her imagination to run wild with other potential lies you may or may not have told. Why was the mailman so happy to see you this morning? What was up with that dental hygienist winking like that? The possibilities are endless. What seems like a good idea at the time (no more pulling, please!!) may wind up requiring more explaining and reparations than you're willing to dish out in the long run.

Your attempt to save your partner's ego could backfire. If you're constantly faking orgasms to get out of going-nowhere sex, your partner will catch on. You'll slip up somehow, and they'll know that the last so many months spent in bed together have been less pleasure party and more your audition for a SAG card. What was initially designed to save your partner's ego and alleviate all the aforementioned indignities of tolerating a bothersome boink will just make your honey sad and depressed and leave you in the doghouse.

The end result of all this? You'll wind up alone again (perhaps not the worst fate if the sex was so awful), or, even worse, you'll get dragged to sex seminars and couple's therapy. Either way, sex should be fun, and the agita resulting from your little white lie will most certainly not be worth all the trouble. Unless you can pull it off.

TOOLS OF THE TRADE

There are very few props necessary to pull this off. All you really need is a few acting chops and a little chutzpah. You should, however, try to get your hands on:

1. Mirror
2. Ex-boyfriend or girlfriend

3. Condom
4. Kegel exercises

WAYS AND MEANS: HOW TO PULL IT OFF

1. GETTING YOUR GAME FACE ON—First things first. Do you know what you look like when you're getting down and dirty? Be honest. Thought not—most people don't. Unless you're a happily self-aware narcissist or exhibitionist, and you've got a mirror installed in the perfect spot to check yourself out mid-*shtup,* you can't even begin to think about pulling this cheat off successfully. As with all method acting (start to think of yourself as the Brando of the bedroom), you have to be as true to life in your actions as possible if anyone's going to buy your performance. Assuming that you've had an orgasm at least once in front of your lover (even if you had to produce it yourself), you've established a baseline understanding of what you look like when you're experiencing *le petit mort.* Any deviation from this will be a tip-off that you're being less than honest about how much you're enjoying yourself. So a mirror and a self-pleasuring session in the bathroom (time to pull out the Rabbit, ladies?) will clue you in to what grimaces, sexy pouts, or vacant stares you should be trying to replicate at the big anticlimactic moment.

2. THE GIFT OF GAB—Not only are people distinctive in the way they look during sex, but what they say is rather telling as well. There are legions of shouters, screamers, babblers, announcers, and criers out there who can shake your bedroom walls, not to mention the nerves of your neighbors. Then again, there are the silent types. These people could get it on behind enemy lines, and no one would ever be the wiser. Which one are you? Have you ever paid attention? Have you gotten feedback from former lovers ("Why can't you just be quiet?" "Speak up—I don't know what you like!") that can guide you? Think about it, as a sudden

shift from meowing to mute will tip off your bed partner to the fact that something's afoot. You must remember to remain consistent.

3. A SPECIAL "HEADS-UP" FOR THE GUYS—As we all know, unprotected sex with a man will result in certain evidence of whether or not he's had a satisfactory ending. Unprotected sex in this day and age is a bad idea to begin with, but it's a particularly bad situation to be in if you've got to fake an orgasm. When you're trying to get an unsatisfactory sexual partner off your junk and out of your bed, it's absolutely possible to fake an orgasm using the right grimaces and vocalizations. But you'll really seal the deal if the moment you've "finished" you race to the bathroom to pull off the condom, thus protecting your lover from the shattering news that your Trojan is as empty as the day is long. If you can't manage this swift sprint from bed to bathroom, or aren't using condoms, you do have one other possible excuse for your lack of spooge. Thanks to Sting and the constant flaunting of his tantric sex life, those in the know are clued in to the fact that men practicing tantric sex can redirect the flow of their genetic matter and actually avoid ejaculating altogether. If you happen to be a fast talker or particularly cool under pressure, go ahead and tell your lover that he or she was a participant in the most mind-blowing tantric sex session of your life. *Of course* there's no evidence of your orgasm! You've internalized it for energy conservation and future hot loving!

4. LOVE LIFTS US UP WHERE WE BELONG—The wondrous effects of Kegel exercises have been touted by women for years. Having problems with incontinence? Do Kegels. Want to have an easier time giving birth? Do Kegels. Kegel exercises (aka pelvic floor exercises) consist of the regular lifting/clenching and lowering/unclenching of the muscles of the pelvic floor, resulting in a tighter hoo-ha and less likelihood that you'll pee on yourself when you sneeze. Another fabulous

by-product of doing your fifty Kegels a day, ladies, is that you can become a blue-ribbon orgasm faker. When a woman has an orgasm, there are internal indicators that coincide with all the external goings-on. That rhythmic inner clenching is a definite signal to whoever's going spelunking in your lady bits that you're having a swell time. If your benighted love monkey isn't making that happen naturally, a few well-timed Kegels will convince him or her that the smile on your face is genuine and all is right with the world.

MOST LIKELY TO SUCCEED

If you don't give a fig for the person you're in bed with, chances are you won't bother faking it. If it's a one-night stand who's boring you to tears, it's easier to just give them the boot and let a warm TV lull you to sleep. The best fakers are those who really care for the person they're treating to this Oscar-worthy performance. These cheaters are motivated to keep their honey's ego intact. Extra points go to those who have had a few acting classes (even workshop at theater camp counts), as they've probably worked on their technique a little. Not suffering from shame or embarrassment helps too. Once again, theater camp or talent show experience comes in handy. If you've ever had to tap dance in a leotard and bow tie to "Puttin' On the Ritz" in front of a few hundred other middle schoolers, you'll be able to writhe around a little for the good of your relationship.

CATCHING ORGASM FAKERS AT THEIR OWN GAME

Look into your lover's eyes. Deeply. Does he or she seem just a little bored? Does that faraway look turn out to be, at closer inspection, an inventory of your ceiling tiles? Is your loved one's passion for you still white-hot, or does it just seem, well, a little clammy? As "The Shoop Shoop Song" tells us, "it's in his[/her] kiss." You can check the bed for telltale stains, you can search for a full-body flush or deep inner clenches, but the only way to know for sure is if you're in tune with your partner. If your sweetie seems bored, disinterested, impatient, frustrated, finicky, tolerant, or, even worse, bemused, it's because they're not getting what they came for (so to speak). How to solve this dilemma? Be brave and ask what's wrong—then ask for instructions.

❧ *Would I Lie?* ❧

1

Researchers at the University of Groningen in the Netherlands conducted a neurological experiment on orgasms in 2005 with thirteen heterosexual couples aged nineteen to forty-nine. One person lay down with his or her head in a scanner while their partner manually stimulated them, and the doctors took brain scans of each individual while they had an orgasm. They also had the women fake orgasms, so they could compare the scans. The results showed that in a fake orgasm, the brain's motor cortex was very active, whereas during a genuine orgasm, the portions of the brain that control fear and anxiety were deactivated along with the motor cortex—meaning that actual orgasms are not conscious. For men, the most highly active areas of the brain were those that interpret touch.

2

Some orgasm-faking stats: According to the 2000 Orgasm Survey, 72 percent of women and 26 percent of men have faked an orgasm at least once, and 55 percent of men say that they can tell if their partner is faking. In a survey on Queen dom.com (answered by more than fifteen thousand people), 70 percent of women and 25 percent of men admitted to faking it at least once. Seventy-three percent of women say that they can tell if their lover is faking an orgasm, and 61 percent of men think that women can tell. While 55 percent of men claim to be able to tell if their partner is faking it or not, only 23 percent of women thought that their partners could tell the difference between their real and fake orgasms.

·················· (3) ··················

In a study about female orgasms, researchers Richard Alexander and Katharine Noonan argue that female orgasm is less necessary than the external sign of an orgasm, or "faking it." The reasoning for this is based on a theory by William Bernds and David Barash (published in 1979), which correlates the rate of orgasm to spontaneous abortion and claims that the female orgasm was developed as an evolutionary strategy in order to kill the unborn infants of men from other tribes or invading countries who raped the local women. According to Alexander and Noonan, the woman's gasps and moans are enough to alert her suspicious mate that she is carrying another man's baby, so he will pleasure her to climax in order to induce an abortion. Hence, faking an orgasm is the only thing that makes evolutionary sense. Perhaps Noonan just needs to have real orgasms more often!

TAKING CREDIT FOR YOUR COLLEAGUES' WORK

I LOVE YOUR WORK

Working hard to achieve your goals is, of course, the honest and upstanding way to go about that particular task. Toiling away for long hours and missing out on all the fun you could be having is, however, a less than appealing prospect. Finding a happy medium between these two approaches would solve the age-old question of how to work less but achieve more.

One way to accomplish this lofty goal is to take credit for others' work at the office. If you happen to be a manager and have a rising star on your team, why bother burning the midnight oil if you know your personal workhorse is going to be pulling the project together with or without you? Let him or her do all the heavy lifting; you'll just get in the way.

Taking credit for other people's work may not be nice, but remember that nice guys tend to finish last. Being polite and getting out of the eight-hundred-pound gorilla's way may be the way to behave if you want people to like you, but on the job it pays to *be* the eight-hundred-pound gorilla. The rules of polite society do not apply at the office, and what you might do on your off-hours to win friends and influence people will only get you run over in the rat race.

So go ahead, be a workplace bully, take credit for your colleagues' work. Give *no* credit where credit is due, and put your name on every successful product you can. If you're loud enough and obnoxious enough, no one lower on the totem pole than you will ever challenge you. You can thank them for their jobs well done and for their silence when you move on to a new (and better) company and position.

THE UPSIDE

By stealing colleagues' work, you can claim to have skills and insights that are far above your own meager talents. This can lead to more recognition and, consequently, faster advancement in the company.

At most companies, advancement leads to better pay, more perks, and better bonuses. Better pay and the easier lifestyle it brings can lead to a happier home life, which in turn can make you feel more confident and productive on the job. It's a cycle of well-being that you can create by cheating someone else out of their own on-the-job recognition and slice of the pie.

No one ever said office politics are easy.

THE DRAWBACK

Even if you don't get caught, the pressure of having to seem like you can perform as well as the person you're ripping off can be an unbelievable strain. It's hard enough to do good work legitimately, but constantly tap dancing to cover your tracks when you're lying to your manager and colleagues can wear you out fast. If you don't have an outlet to release the stress, which could be anything from a therapist to a weekly basketball game, you'll freak out. If that happens while you're at work, all the cred you've built up by taking credit for others' work will be for naught. This is no cycle of joy, but a chain of pain. Stress can kill.

If you *do* get caught, you'll have to find another job. If you don't get fired for your duplicity, you'll still have a hard time because no one will want to work with you. Everyone will be too savvy to agree to cooperate with you on any project, and you'll always be the odd person out, left holding the bag if something goes wrong. Have the good sense to move on with as little hubbub as possible. It's also important to do it quickly before news about your actions leaks into your industry.

TOOLS OF THE TRADE

There aren't any tools that are absolutely essential to pulling off taking credit for a colleague's work. The only tool that you must have is your coworker's report, charts, or spreadsheets that you intend to claim as your own. Other than that essential element, there are a few items you'd do well to get your hands on, as they'll make your task a bit easier. They are:

1. Access to employees' email
2. Printer
3. Golf clubs

WAYS AND MEANS: HOW TO PULL IT OFF

Now you're ready to act like the shark you are. You've got your victim in your sights and your tools at the ready. Here's how you can become the star of the office without breaking a sweat:

1. HAND IT IN—If you've got to hand in a printed report, be sure to be the one to do the handoff. If the document has to be emailed, make sure you're the one to hit "send." By taking control of information that needs to be submitted to your boss or manager, you can remove your team members' names and substitute yours. If that isn't possible, you could attach a cover letter that strongly and clearly implies that you're the creative force behind the work.

2. FRONT MAN—Always give presentations for your team and do the talking for the group if you can. Anyone who takes the role of mouthpiece for the group will be perceived as the one who came up with the lion's share of the work and is the innovator in the group. This is not so hard to do, as most people aren't too eager to speak in public.

3. DON'T ASK, DON'T TELL—Another way to ensure your star status on the team is to be careful never to mention your colleagues by name. This also holds true if you are a manager, and you're claiming credit for the group's efforts. By keeping everyone as anonymous as possible in the eyes of upper management, you have a much stronger chance of being singled out for glory. The deserving employees can't be singled out if no one knows who they are.

4. MANAGE UP—Not only should you keep others in the shadows, but you should definitely thrust yourself into the spotlight. The key to "managing up" is making friends with anyone in upper management who can suggest you for promotion or champion your cause if you get caught for any shady activities as you claw your way up the corporate ladder. This is where golf clubs (or similar sports equipment) come in handy. Find a hobby that you share with someone in management and work it until you're best buddies. The people who get promoted first are usually the ones who shower with the boss at the club.

5. SCARE TACTICS—Start rumors and gossip among your colleagues and people who report to you about how difficult management is. If everyone is afraid of the upper-level staff, they'll be less likely to try to create their own alliances. They'll also be too nervous to report you if they clue in to the fact that you're copping the credit.

6. NO WHINING ALLOWED—Another way to use the threat of difficult upper management to your advantage is to convince your colleagues that complainers are viewed with suspicion. It's not unheard of for people in higher-level jobs to be wary of upstarts who are jockeying for their jobs. Use this fact to persuade those around you that anyone who reports a grievance will be dismissed as a troublemaker. Even worse, they might be thought of as a liar.

7. CONSTANT CRITICISM—Never, ever speak well of any colleague or anyone who reports to you in front of the people you want to impress. It doesn't pay to incessantly bad-mouth everyone you work with, but kind words stick just as much as harsh ones do, and there's no need to burnish anyone's reputation but your own. A slow chipping away at your colleagues' reputations won't necessarily make you look great on your own, but you could look better by comparison.

MOST LIKELY TO SUCCEED

If you're the kind who could sell your grandma down the river to win just about anything, from a game of Monopoly to the corner office, you're going to do well at this cheat. You've got to have major drive and a cutthroat sensibility to lie, cheat, and steal your way to the top. This is not for the faint of heart. The stakes can actually be really high when you're trying to get a promotion, particularly when you're not doing it in the most honest way possible. You've got to be ready to do the cheat and then stand by what you did if anyone tries to call you on it. This frequently requires bald-faced lying and denial. If you can carry it off, you'll be in the office of your dreams, complete with huge windows, administrative assistant right outside, and expensively framed inspirational posters in no time.

CATCHING WORKPLACE CHEATS AT THEIR OWN GAME

How do you know if one of your employees is a snake? How can you tell if a manager who should be championing his or her team is stealing the credit? Even if no one comes to complain, there are telltale signs that all is not right with the world:

First off, if there's one person the staff avoids, it is usually because he or she doesn't "have their backs." At the office, the most important assets anyone can bring to the table are reliability and trustworthiness. If you don't have those traits, you'll soon have the stink of your colleagues' distaste and distrust all over you. Whoever stinks is usually the rat.

If things get bad enough with a manager or employee stealing others' credit (which is almost the same as stealing advancement—ergo, money—from them), complaints will start rolling in. Enough complaints about the same person for the same transgression—in this case claiming wrongful authorship of a work product—usually add up to the truth.

The next stage in knowing that someone is wrongfully taking credit, or just being generally unsupportive, is a high turnover rate. No one wants to work someplace that has no opportunity for advancement. Constant credit blocking leaves no room for growth.

If you suspect someone of stealing credit for work, simply document everything you do through email or memos that get circulated to someone below you, someone at your level, someone at your boss's level, and someone above him or her. Even if you have to blind copy them, make sure that these people know what you've been doing. If you're management, require this behavior from everyone who's making complaints. The offender will get flushed out soon enough.

The best way to catch someone red-handed at this cheat, if you think they're up to no good, is to sabotage their sabotage. People who steal their coworkers' work are, at their core, lazy. They probably won't take the time to carefully review whatever it is they're going to submit as their own work. In their view, it's usually good enough that the project has been completed and they have an opportunity to curry favor with some mucky-muck of their choosing. If you're on the team that's getting shafted by this slippery character, create a horrible mistake or embarrassing typo in the work that will cast a pall on whoever is responsible for the work. After your credit thief has told everyone that the work is his, he can't very easily take it back. He'll have to take the blame for what you did. This scenario unmistakably screams "scene stealer" to anyone who counts, and your office nightmare might very well be a distant memory before too long.

❧ *Would I Lie?* ❧

In 1998 a Cornell University graduate student named Antonia Demas sued the university on allegations that a professor who served on her thesis committee had stolen her ideas and passed them off as his own. Demas formulated her thesis upon starting at Cornell, and she put together a team of professors to work with her. Professor David Levitsky was not chosen, but he joined the team later upon a recommendation from another professor. Demas later discovered that Levitsky had been speaking about her research at his lectures and professional seminars, referring to it as "our research" but not mentioning Demas by name at all. He also applied to the U.S. Department of Agriculture for a grant to continue the research that Demas had started, but did not list her name as a co-PI (co–principal investigator) on the grant. The case finally concluded in 2003, with Levitsky being charged with fraud and breach of contract.

In 1997 Dr. Carolyn Phinney, a University of Michigan researcher, was awarded $1.67 million in a lawsuit against the university stating that her supervisor had stolen her work. Her case began ten years earlier when her supervisor, Dr. Marion Perlmutter, suggested that she write up her research results in order to obtain a grant. She promised

(continued)

Dr. Phinney that she would be credited as the author of the research and offered her a job, but instead Dr. Perlmutter passed off Dr. Phinney's research as her own. When Dr. Phinney tried to report her supervisor's misconduct, she was threatened by Dr. Richard Adelman, the institute's director, to keep her mouth shut or lose her position. The court found Dr. Perlmutter guilty of fraud and Dr. Adelman guilty of retaliation against Dr. Phinney.

.... **3** ....

In 2003 Deborah C. Kogan, a photojournalist, accused veteran combat photojournalist James Nachtwey of taking credit for her research into orphanages in Romania. Nachtwey had conducted research of his own and had showed it to editors in New York prior to meeting Kogan. The editors sent him back to Romania for further research, and upon his arrival, he met Kogan. She gave him a roll of film (which was hard to find in the area) and told him about an orphanage she had visited. He went there and took photos, which, along with his others, were eventually published in articles. Kogan later published a book in which she accused Nachtwey of stealing the entire story from her. Her claims were never proven.

FORGING HANDWRITING

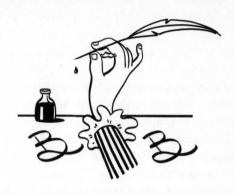

PUT YOUR JOHN HANCOCK
RIGHT HERE

There are several ways to cheat people or companies out of their money, and forging documents is one of the classics. Forgery is the act of claiming that one person's signature, document, or effort is in fact another's. The goal of this cheat is to get your hands on someone's checkbook, credit card number, will, or deed. If you can't find one of these items (or any other document that entitles one to money or property), you could create it yourself. In that case, just falsely sign the other person's name, and you're home free with new goods, property, or funds to show for your trouble.

It takes a bit of skill to do this cheat expertly, but a lot of people become forgers because they stumble into it. A wallet found in a parking lot, a single check blowing across the street, a credit card receipt left on a table in a restaurant—these are all scenarios that prove to be too tempting for the average person. The promise of easy money staring you in the face can easily outweigh the possible consequences of falsely assuming someone else's identity and claiming what is rightfully theirs.

You might also make your initial foray into forgery out of rage and indignation. Heirs and assigns who are left out of wills, or grants of money or land, can find themselves doing the strangest things. That includes creating an alternate document that reflects the way they feel things ought to have gone and signing the rightful grantor's name to the instrument.

Then there's the full commitment to fake documents and false signatures for the professional forger. For those who really want to delve into grifterhood whole hog, no need to target individuals. Forging a private citizen's signature can take you only so far for so long. Career forgers go for corporations that will sustain their shenanigans much longer by not noticing the problem at first and then taking awhile to get organized to fight it. By then, the forger can move on to the next bloated target.

Financial gain is the name of the game. You can make big bucks by siphoning money out of a huge corporation or keep yourself afloat by taking little old ladies' checkbooks. You might even be able to forge a famous autograph and sell it for a decent profit. Whatever it is you choose to do, forgery is all about getting paid.

Forgery is an appealing cheat because you can see the money you're going to make before you make it. It's already out there waiting for you to claim it. Why generate your own legitimate income when someone else already made it for you? The formula for being a successful handwriting forger is as follows: Figure out how to make your mark's mark, get what's coming to you, and keep moving.

THE UPSIDE

Some people just don't deserve what they've got. Did the great-uncle you've been taking care of your whole life finally die and leave everything to his cat? No fair. That estate should be yours, and, thankfully, there's a way to claim it. Forgery is a time-honored way to right the financial wrongs of the world.

This cheat can also provide you with a means to earn way above your normal earning potential with a few strokes of a pen. If you never finished grade school and have no trade skills, the world can seem like a pretty bleak place. How can you possibly make enough money to create a comfortable existence? If you've got a little artistic talent and drive, you can rake in the big bucks with just a little training. Let the business school experience of the chump you've targeted work for you.

One of the major advantages of the forger's lifestyle is that your time is your own. No nine-to-five grind, no corporate retreats; you're the ultimate entrepreneur. You can decide how much you want to make, what kind of patsy you want to target, and how much time you'll spend doing it. Your days are your own, and you're your own boss. Forgery can buy you freedom.

THE DRAWBACK

Unless you're forging your parents' handwriting for a note to get out of gym class (which is not a bad training ground for future escapades), this is a serious offense. This cheat will earn you a nice vacation in prison should you get caught. Don't get caught.

If you do use this skill at school, you'll get reprimanded at school and at home. If you do it too frequently, you'll get detention or suspension. If you're doing this cheat to avoid dodgeball or having to shower with other people, your cause is admirable, but you probably won't win in the long run. It's more advisable to use this cheat on a more selective basis and use your careful forgeries for bigger and better reasons such as a doctor's note to leave school right before a test you haven't studied for. You might still get suspended if you're caught, but it's for a better reason than not getting hit with a red rubber ball.

TOOLS OF THE TRADE

The tools of the trade for forgers are pretty standard. Advances in technology are constantly making the forger's job easier, but they also provide for more ways to be detected. Stay on top of new developments in computer imaging, but sometimes the old ways are the best ways. You'll need:

1. Pens
2. Pencils
3. Photocopier
4. Light box
5. Tracing paper
6. Photoshop or similar computer program
7. Handwriting samples

WAYS AND MEANS: HOW TO PULL IT OFF

Now that you've got your tools lined up, here's the methodology to follow to make the cheat really come together:

1. FIND YOUR TARGET—First off, you need to find someone you're going to cheat out of their money or belongings. People who are care-

less and leave their wallet or checkbook lying around are easy targets. You can find signed receipts inside a wallet or carbon copies of signed checks in a checkbook. That's an easy score. You can also look for an older person who may not properly remember what documents they've signed, or a signature scribbler. Signature scribblers are an interesting breed, as they think their illegible scrawl is insurance against forgers. Quite the opposite. The more indecipherable and random the scrawl, the easier it is to copy.

2. STUDY THE SIGNATURE—Whether you've got a scribbler or not, it's time to study the handwriting you're going to copy. It's best to think of the signature as an image you're copying so that you can break it down into its elements to replicate more easily. Once your confidence is up, practice writing it over and over, as a real signature is a flowing line with speed and motion behind it.

3. TRACING A SIGNATURE—If you don't have great hand-eye coordination and lack artistic skill, you can always use a photographer's light table to trace your mark's handwriting. Just backlight the original document and place your new document on top of it. Trace what you see coming through the paper, and you're finished in a flash.

4. PHOTOSHOP—Another method for forgers with no artistic acumen is to specialize in digital documents. You can scan whatever you want to replicate into your computer and place it wherever you think it needs to go. Save and send.

5. SAMPLE SIGNATURE—A wily forger can get his or her victim to sign a blank sheet of paper and then apply that signature to any chosen document. You can ask someone for their contact information or even to show you how they write their name in cursive (after enough cock-

tails and friendly banter about penmanship), and they'll probably un-wittingly hand over exactly what you need to cheat them out of their savings. You can trace, scan, or photocopy that signature anywhere you like.

6. ALTER THE DOCUMENT IN YOUR FAVOR—You don't always have to forge a signature, you can also alter a document. If you have reason to get anyone to sign a contract of any kind that commits them to a payment, all you need to do is find a way to change the amount owed in the contract: $5,000 can become $15,000 in the blink of an eye. If you think about it ahead of time, remember to leave room for extra digits!

7. BE REASONABLE—If you're going to attach a signature to a will, deed, or contract that you concoct, don't go crazy and make the document too far-fetched. If you're trying to get Great-aunt Irma's vintage jewelry collection, and you're the only living woman in the family, you've got a fighting chance. If Irma had ten other nieces and nephews she liked much more than you, had a good will, and everyone knew she hated you, you're going to have a hard time convincing anyone that your newly discovered will has any merit.

MOST LIKELY TO SUCCEED

Artists, accountants, lawyers, and computer-graphics experts are tai-lor-made for this cheat. They either know the rules of granting money and rights, so they can avoid detection, or they can simulate great replicas of handwriting and signatures.

Storytellers who think fast on their feet are suited to this cheat as well. They can invent innumerable reasons why they should get whatever they're going after and can create scenarios that others might find plausible. They'll also be able to defend at the drop of a hat whatever tall tale they've come up with.

CATCHING FORGERS AT THEIR OWN GAME

The best and most energy efficient way to catch a forger in the act is to hire a handwriting expert and let him or her do all the work. If that isn't possible, and you find yourself stuck with having to finger the cheat, here are a few methods for identifying your forger:

1. SPATIAL RELATIONS—All handwriting has its own unique spacing between words, particularly if you're looking at cursive writing. If the spacing between words is inconsistent with your sample, or the relation of words to one another is wrong, you've caught your cheater.

2. RHYTHM AND FLOW—Anyone's handwriting has an identifiable flow. Every word stops and starts in a unique way. A forgery will have words and letters stop and start in the wrong spots and have a cramped look and feel, like someone who's trying to color inside the lines.

3. MATCH GAME—If someone traced a signature, you've caught him if you can find the original. Since no one can reproduce their own signature exactly from day to day, an identical signature to that of a previous date is not only unlikely, it's impossible. This method of catching the cheater is also applicable to photocopied signatures and those that are digitally reproduced.

4. PIXILATION—If your forger doesn't spend enough time digitally manipulating the signature or handwriting sample he or she scanned, the image will be pixilated. This is a major giveaway. An original signature is like any other piece of artwork; it has smooth edges, not little boxes on the outer part of the line.

5. TIME WILL TELL—Handwriting and signatures evolve over time. The way you sign your name when you're fifteen isn't the same as you do when you're fifty. A careless forger will base their handiwork on an out-of-date handwriting or signature sample, effectively making a younger version of the person being cheated sign a document prepared for an older version. Time is, indeed, on your side.

Would I Lie?

1

Photographer John Rutter was recently convicted of forgery after trying to sell topless photos of actress Cameron Diaz back to her for $3.5 million. Diaz had posed for Rutter when she was nineteen and never signed a release form to allow him to use the photos for commercial use. He said she did. She took him to court, where two different forensic document examiners testified that the signature on Rutter's release form was a forgery. They used samples of Diaz's handwriting to compare against the signature and found that the signature was slanted differently. Rutter was charged with forgery, perjury, and attempted grand theft.

2

Mark Hofmann was an antiques dealer who began his practice of deceit by forging signatures on currency and other items to increase their value. He then began forging documents, specifically ones related to the Church of Jesus Christ of Latter-day Saints (of which he had been a member). He claimed that he had discovered these documents through his interest in antiques. Before he was exposed, he sold or donated over four hundred such documents to the Mormon Church. He also forged many literary works, two of which were purported to be by Emily Dickinson and Walt Whitman.

··· **3** ···

Konrad Kujau was a Nazi document collector in Germany who claimed to have been given Adolf Hitler's diaries and a third volume of *Mein Kampf* by a former World War II general. Supposedly the notebooks had been aboard a plane that crashed, and this unnamed general had retrieved them. Kujau took the works to *Stern* magazine, which began publishing diary entries every week. Upon comparing the handwriting in the diaries to known samples of Hitler's handwriting, three different experts declared that the handwriting was a match. Next came the forensics tests on the paper and ink. Kujau couldn't cheat on these tests. Forensic scientists discovered that the paper and ink were only a few years old, even though Kujau had stained the paper with tea to make it look older. Kujau tried to run but was caught in Hamburg, Germany, and tried in 1984. The most amazing part of this story is that the handwriting samples the "experts" had used to compare against Kujau's forgeries were *also* forgeries written by Kujau!

CHEATING ON A DIET

DON'T MIND ME, I'LL JUST PICK

There are few things on the planet more horrific than going on a diet. It doesn't matter if you're trying to lose ten pounds, a hundred pounds, or more, dieting is a depressing and debilitating endeavor. The more you can do to distance yourself from the experience, the better.

Why is dieting such a bummer? Not only do we all need to eat to survive, thus making total abstinence from food an unrealistic choice, but eating is also a basic sensual pleasure. Let's be honest. It feels good to sit down to a well-prepared meal, inhale the delicious aromas, appreciate the lovely presentation, and then dive into belly-bursting indulgence. There's a reason that people feast when they're happy or want to celebrate good fortune: Eating is fun, it's essential, and a particularly good meal can be said to be even better than sex. Particularly when chocolate is involved.

Refraining from the pleasures of food is clearly something we are not programmed to do. Then again, swallowing multiple buckets of Kentucky Fried Chicken in a single sitting isn't what we're programmed to do either. In our current culture of limited exercise, fast food, at-home deep fryers, and zero portion control, our girths are increasing, and our incidence of diabetes and heart disease is skyrocketing. Unfortunately, diet and exercise are the only answer.

Even so, there is no need to give up hope entirely. You don't need to live a life of denial and austerity! What to do if you just can't pass by a Krispy Kreme without pressing your nose to the glass and moaning? What if you absolutely need to watch the entire NBC Thursday TV lineup while snacking until you fall over in a bloated heap? What if you just can't bring yourself to watch *The Biggest Loser* and think "what an amazing group of winners"? Then you cheat. You cheat on your diet and find ways to fool your family, friends, and, most importantly, yourself into thinking that you're really trying to slim down and reclaim your health. So what if your clothes don't fit, and your cholesterol is above 350? What counts is that you're making an effort. Sort of.

THE UPSIDE

The upside to cheating on a diet is never having to admit that you're ever really *off* your diet. It's one thing to be on a diet and struggling, but it's another thing entirely to just give up the ghost and indulge however you want to. Unfortunately, morality seems to have snuck into our cultural perspective on weight loss, and anyone who needs to lose a few is looked at askance for not taking better care of themselves. Who needs that?

By retaining the trappings of the true dieter—such as abstaining from obviously calorie-packed foods (at least in public), complaining about your weight, commenting on how everyone who's thin must be anorexic, and conspicuously munching on vegetables—you can create the illusion that you're fighting the good fight. Privately, you can do as you please. In fact, you can also eat as you like in public as long as you follow the basic rules of cheating on your diet.

Another major upside to cheating on your diet is that by keeping true efforts to lose weight at bay, you'll never really know how successful or unsuccessful at dieting you might be. This is the underachiever's syndrome. It would be absolutely galling to really give it your all and find out that you've got a tragically slow metabolism or that you really are the laziest person on earth and just can't make it to the gym. This way, if you don't really try, you won't ever know the awful truth. This is a very comfortable place to be emotionally. Almost as comfortable as a giant sofa. With a bag of Cheetos next to you.

So, yes, you could join a gym, do Weight Watchers, get some therapy, and generally turn your life around. Or you could settle for the status quo. Nothing ventured, nothing gained, nothing risked. And you get to eat chocolate cake.

THE DRAWBACK

You'll stay fat. And your heart will be overtaxed, your cholesterol will be dangerously high, your arches will drop, and you might give yourself a nice little case of diabetes. Oh, yes, and you'll need an extra large cover-up for the beach. Which is annoying, because they're hard to find.

TOOLS OF THE TRADE

Cheating on your diet requires quite a few tools and can be an all-consuming affair that demands a lot of your attention and time. Considering that food is probably already a focal point, finding ways to eat what you want while camouflaging your actions will require more of a commitment than you ever thought possible. A little practice helps, along with the following:

1. Megamart grocery store
2. Friends
3. Child
4. Scale
5. Coffee
6. Cigarettes
7. Diuretics
8. Ipecac

WAYS AND MEANS: HOW TO PULL IT OFF

Even though the tools listed above are of extreme importance, it is essential to mention that delusion plays a large role in this particular cheat. Unlike a lot of the other cheats showcased in this book, cheating on a diet requires not only that you fool others but yourself as well. This can be very difficult and requires that potent cocktail of commitment and desire so frequently found in blue-chip athletes. You have to *know* you want to look like a dieter and that you *absolutely will not* do what it takes to lose weight. The key to fooling others, however, is a convincing performance complete with frustration, guilt, exhaustion, and determination. The only way to achieve this (without studying Stanislavsky) is to believe your own hype. Once you've gotten yourself to believe your own ersatz conviction, you'll have the key to great lying under your belt. You'll have duped yourself.

1. **I'LL HAVE WHAT HE'S HAVING**—Anyone who cheats on his or her diet knows the joy of looking at their dining companion's plate and seeing something they just need to have. That could be anything from a handful of fries to a sliver of chocolate mud cake. Whatever your weakness, go right ahead and claim those goodies for yourself. It's common knowledge that food from someone else's plate has no calories. If you have kids, make sure you're serving them something *you* really want to eat. Kids never finish what's in front of them, and you can freely hoover up anything they don't polish off. Calorie free, guilt free.

2. **STANDING OVER THE SINK**—Another method used to make calories magically disappear is to eat standing up. Interestingly, the energy exerted while standing (and possibly pacing) while you're eating out of the refrigerator or over the kitchen sink counteracts the calories in the food you're eating. Although it has rarely been done, it is possible to eat an entire Thanksgiving dinner over the sink and have nothing to show for it on the scale the next day.

3. **RESET THE SCALE**—As we get older, our minds begin to fail. This is a sad but true fact of life. The good news is that if you reset your scale to five pounds less than your true weight, you will eventually forget that you did it. Although this is not exactly cheating on your diet, it is lying about your weight to yourself—which is very similar to cheating on a diet, and, in fact, works as an enhancement to your established cheating program.

4. **WHAT GOES IN MUST COME OUT**—If you're an experienced dieter and, more to the point, an experienced diet cheater, you know the

value of a good poop. If you can manage to have a superproductive morning before you get on the scale, you can reduce the reading by as much as three pounds. Unfortunately, it's very hard to orchestrate a regular bowel movement every morning pre-weigh-in. This is where coffee and cigarettes come in. Both of these stimulants will have you running to the bathroom for a major bowl clutcher should you indulge in them on an empty stomach. True, coffee can add water weight, but if you wait an extra half hour to pee, all will be right with the world.

5. WHAT'S UP, DOC?—Vegetables are your friends, carrots in particular. Not only do carrots have a ton of fiber and help you feel full quickly, but if you're a smoker, you'll be happy to know that carrots contain naturally occurring nicotine. So if you're not going to be successful with your diet, at least you might stop smoking. As anyone who's watched a single sitcom or movie in their lifetime knows, someone snacking on carrots and celery is on a diet. To get away with this cheat, it's all right if you're secretly eating fourteen Baby Ruth bars while sitting on the floor of your closet. So long as you're carrying around a plastic baggie with your veggies, you're a dieter who's really trying to go the distance.

6. SANS-A-BELT—Don't want to know how fat you are or how fat you're getting? Let the elastic waistband be your friend. If you gain weight while you're supposedly dieting, your supporters' sympathy may very well dry up and leave you feeling terribly alone and more dejected than usual. It's easy to keep your ups and downs hidden from friends, family, and yourself if you have no idea whether or not you're expanding. Elastic waistbands are frequently featured on spandex clothing. Spandex is also your friend.

7. I'VE GOT A GUT FEELING—Surgery is the ultimate last resort for those intent on cheating on a diet. If you really don't feel like denying

yourself food or hauling yourself to the gym, and you're faced with some pretty serious numbers on the scale, you can always opt for bariatric surgery. True, this is an extreme decision, and your stomach will be reduced to the size of a sucking candy, but you won't really be faced with the rigors of dieting again. You will, however, be faced with the rigor of limiting yourself to meals that are appropriately sized for hamsters, lest you run the risk of extreme illness and bodily harm.

8. THAT SUCKS—Another cheater's surgical option is the ever-popular liposuction. It can be performed repeatedly, can remove up to five liters of fat per session, and can provide you with the sculpted look you've always longed for. You will have to wrap your head around the fact that someone will be repeatedly and roughly shoving a hollow tube in an orifice created expressly for this purpose. Then again, some people pay top dollar to have people shove things in their orifices. It's your call.

9. WHEN IN ROME—Finally, there's the old binge and purge. Needless to say, bulimia is a horrible disease that leads to the loss of many lives. With that said, it is true that sometimes, when you realize that you spent a night at home eating multiple pizzas and several boxes of mini egg rolls, you just need to do something. That horrible bloated and roiling feeling in your stomach must be attended to, and the best way to walk away from a disastrous pig-out is to do just that. Walk away from it. Literally leave it in the toilet and walk away. It's well known that in ancient Rome, multiday feasts were helped along by the presence of the vomitorium. The vomitorium was a bowl with a rotted fish (or some other proto-ipecac substance) to sip, which would induce vomiting. More partying would immediately ensue. If it was good enough for the Caesars, it's good enough for you.

MOST LIKELY TO SUCCEED

Anyone who's really not that motivated to change his or her lifestyle and, frankly, doesn't really care what anyone thinks of them. This cheat is for people who want to look like they're aware of what's expected of them and will go along just enough to avoid being annoyed by others' judgment. If you really want to lose weight, care what people think of you, are filled with self-loathing, or want to institute real and lasting change, this is definitely not the cheat for you.

CATCHING DIETING CHEATS AT THEIR OWN GAME

No matter how crafty a cheating dieter thinks he or she is, there's one telltale sign that your friend or loved one hasn't been totally honest. He or she is still overweight. No matter what their excuse is—"I'm big boned," "I've got a slow metabolism," "Everyone in my family is overweight"—the reality is that if you diet and exercise, you lose weight. Yes, of course, there are anomalies, but they constitute about 0.2 percent of the dieters out there. Here's the formula to remember: dieting + complaining + time + no weight loss = cheater. Not that there's anything wrong with that. If someone doesn't want to lose weight, that's his or her own beeswax, and not an opportunity for everyone around them to judge and provide advice. Case closed.

.... **1** ....

A spokeswoman for the American Dietetic Association says to stop feeling guilty about cheating on your diet, because if you're going to do it, you might as well enjoy it. The five rules that you should follow when thinking about cheating are:

- No more guilt—It's bad for your perception of food to feel guilty about cheating, so instead focus on portion control.
- Only cheat in public—It won't feel so illicit if you're not hiding in your closet eating french fries.
- Cheating doesn't mean you have no willpower—You made the decision to eat it, so don't regret it.
- Nobody's perfect—If you're making improvements in your eating habits, it can be enough. Perfection is impossible!
- Don't eat when you're not hungry—If your office party is serving pizza, and you're not hungry, don't feel that you have a social obligation to eat it. Learn to separate physical hunger from emotional hunger.

.... **2** ....

A diet shouldn't be a one-time thing, it should be a way of life. When you improve your eating habits, it's perfectly OK to reward yourself sometimes. It's not going to bring back all your bad habits—on the contrary, when you are too harsh on yourself in your diet, you will feel negatively toward eating healthy and may abandon the idea entirely. In other words, cheating is unavoidable, necessary, and well advised. Outstanding!

························· 3 ·························

Leptin, a hormone that is produced by your fat cells, directly helps control your metabolism. It causes you to burn stored fats and decreases your appetite when produced at normal levels. The problem with very strict dieting is that your leptin levels decrease, and your metabolism slows down. Your appetite also increases the thinner you become. If you "cheat," however, your leptin levels will go up again because your body will try to adapt to the higher food intake. The best way to achieve this is to eat a diet low in calories for several days each week, then have one or two days where you eat more. This will keep your body in constant flux so that your leptin levels will not drop too low.

CHEATING ON YOUR SIGNIFICANT OTHER— THE CLASSIC AFFAIR

ALL'S FAIR IN LOVE AND . . .

Let's face it, the grass is always greener on the other side of the fence. No matter what you have—be it a great job, huge house, racy car, or fabulous wardrobe—it's always easy to look at what your neighbor is enjoying and think, I wish I could have what he's got. Significant others are no exception to this rule. Your husband, wife, girlfriend, boyfriend, or life partner could be as smoking as Brad

Pitt or as sultry as Angelina Jolie-Miller-Thornton, and you'd still think, He/she's all right, but that one over there is incredible! It's human nature. The interesting part is what you decide to do with the impulse.

What most people choose to do, at least at some point in their lives, is cheat on their significant other and have an affair. Why cheat? Simple. Most people are terrified of giving up whatever it is they've got, even if they're deeply dissatisfied. No one likes change, and we tend to do whatever we can to avoid it. That could mean that we stay in dead-end jobs, don't lose weight, don't buy new clothes, or don't do anything to change the status quo. Change leads to the world of the unknown, and as we all know from childhood, a bird in the hand is worth two in the bush—even if the bird sitting in your hand has covered you in poop and is gearing up to dump another load.

So cheating on a loved one is the name of the game. Bored by having sex with the same person all the time? Get a cookie on the side! Afraid of leaving your partner because you might wind up alone forever? Take up philandering! Want to go for a quick swim in the dating pool to see if it's really for you? Go right ahead! And for those gambling types who seek out the ultimate adrenaline rush, having an affair is definitely for you. There are no bigger stakes around than possibly losing the life you've built for yourself all in one fell swoop. The payoff: a little tail on the side.

With all that said, nothing's sweeter than getting away with it. You can get your ya-ya's out without any consequences. Get a second chance at sowing your wild oats without anyone being the wiser. And if you're really unhappy in your relationship and want out, the cheat allows you to segue neatly into a new life without the pain of being alone. Score!

So you can take the responsible route and do a life inventory, figure out what you want to change and what you don't, and possibly leave your partner if things aren't all you'd hoped they would be. Or . . . you can have an affair. Everybody's doing it!

THE UPSIDE

The upside to having an affair is simple: You get to have sex with someone else. Easy enough for anyone to wrap their head around. After enough years of looking at your significant other's pieces and parts, they become as familiar to you as your own goods—which is (unless you're an unbridled narcissist) pretty boring. Of course, there's also the added thrill of the forbidden, which is a rather well-established upside for all human beings (think Eve and that apple, Pandora and her box, and so on). We *love* doing what we've been told not to, and getting away with our bad behavior can be an unparalleled joy.

Having an affair can also afford you a window into what you might be missing out on, thus providing you with the tools to make better life choices. Conversely, you might determine that you aren't missing out on anything and should stay exactly where you are, with exactly who you're with. Just keep your fingers crossed that you don't get busted while you're sampling the goodies on display.

The final upside—and it might seem like a stretch at first—is that you're saving your significant other from staying in a loveless, passionless relationship. Right? Right! This will be hard to convince him or her of at first when your straying has come to light. Give it time. When they've had the chance to build a life that conforms far better to their needs, they'll thank you for it. Really.

THE DRAWBACK

You'll get caught and lose your girlfriend/boyfriend/spouse/life partner. You'll also possibly lose half your assets, your house, custody of your kids, your friends, and all your dignity. Sadly, American culture doesn't have the "live and let live" hands-up, shoulder-shrug attitude that the French do for this sort of thing. Another unfavorable repercussion for some folks is the risk of going to hell. Others may face karma or reincarnation as a sea cucumber or beast of burden. The risk is yours.

TOOLS OF THE TRADE

The tools required for having an affair are rather elaborate and can leave the cheater feeling overwhelmed and confused. Be sure to have a system worked out for keeping track of your tools and methods prior to beginning the affair. Among other things, a lack of organization can be the death knell of your successful philandering. You will need:

1. Credit card(s)
2. Extra cell phone
3. Private email account
4. Job that requires traveling
5. Gym membership
6. Gym bag with change of clothes and condoms
7. Discreet partner

WAYS AND MEANS: HOW TO PULL IT OFF

Now that you've got your tools lined up, let's outline the methodology necessary to make this cheat really come together. Keep in mind that this particular type of deceit can work only if you get everything lined up ahead of time. Some cheats can succeed if you develop your methodology or innovate as you go—this isn't one of them. Here's what you need to make the magic happen:

1. THE ATTITUDE—The first and most essential weapon to have in your arsenal if you're going to undertake this classic cheat is the right mind-set. If you're not mentally prepared to embark on this journey of complicated lies and subterfuge, you'll fail. And rest assured, it will be a spectacular failure. The main ingredients to having the right attitude are threefold:

1. Nerves of steel
2. An innate ability to compartmentalize the elements of your life
3. A strong sense of denial

The denial piece of the puzzle overlaps with the ability to rationalize, but they're too close to really get overly specific. Suffice it to say that if you can rewrite the events of your day to suit your particular perspective, you're in like Flynn.

It boils down to this: If you can lie to your partner and then lie down next to your partner (and still get a good night's sleep), you can pull this off.

At least for a while.

2. A PRIVATE/ALTERNATE EXISTENCE—The successful affair is conducted when the person who's straying has essentially set up an alternate identity for himself or herself that makes the strayer's actions undetectable to their spouse or partner. This means that all payments made to support the affair and all communication made to the partner in crime are invisible. This is actually quite simple to do.

A new credit card used only for the hotel reservations, travel arrangements, gifts, and other miscellaneous affair expenses must be procured, and *no bills can be sent to the philanderer's home address*! Make your office or PO box your billing address. Now it's impossible for the significant other to intercept any suspicious bills.

The same principle applies to having an email address and cell phone that the significant other is unaware of. It is imperative to remember *never to give this information to anyone other than the person with whom you're having an affair.* The moment you slip, it's out there, and it's guaranteed that you'll look suspicious.

3. LOCATION, LOCATION, LOCATION—If you travel for work, you probably already know how easy it is to have illicit sex on the road. Airport bars, hotel bars—any bar, really—are the perfect place to find other transients looking for a no-strings-attached dalliance. If you're looking for something with a little more permanence, you can subscribe to the "girl (or guy) in every port" modus operandi. If you live in Cleveland and travel regularly to Dubuque, well, then it's a pretty sure bet that your honey in Ohio won't run into your Iowa sweetie at the Price Chopper. And that's good.

If you don't travel for work, don't let that stand in your way. It's time to get inventive. Do some research online and find conferences out of town that are relevant to your business (in case your spouse/girlfriend/boyfriend starts to get wise and does a little research of his or her own) to use as a cover for your infidelity. Then just say that you're going out of town for the big event—but the real big event will take place while you're holed up in your lover's apartment for the weekend. Brilliant! So far, at least.

4. LET'S GET PHYSICAL—Having a gym membership is insanely useful when you need to carve out some private time. There's the added bonus that you can shower at the gym, so any telltale odors (cologne, smoke, sex) can be conveniently washed away before you come home. Just be careful that your significant other doesn't try to join the gym with you. If there's a gym in your office building, that's the best way to go. You can also carry a change of clothing in your gym bag along with any accoutrements you might want when meeting up with your part-time lover. If all else fails, you'll have a great body with which to start your new dating life after you've been kicked out of the house.

5. **LOOSE LIPS SINK SHIPS**—No matter what else you do, be discreet. The minute you tell anyone about what you're up to, rest assured that absolutely everyone will know. You may think your best friends will keep their mouths shut and that your business can't possibly be that interesting to others—and you'd be wrong. Everyone loves to gossip, and this is the best kind of gossip there is. The person you're flinging with also has to have a major grasp on keeping your fun on the down-low. Even though your lives may not intersect in any way beyond your affair right now, the minute he or she blabs, your circles will meet, and your doom awaits. One more time in case you missed it: Tell no one.

MOST LIKELY TO SUCCEED

The people most likely to get away with this cheat are those who can believe their own lies. This is the most intimate setting in which to cheat, and you'll certainly fail if you don't believe your own story. It also helps if your significant other is deeply invested in the relationship and will believe your story in order to preserve the status quo. Then again, he or she may not believe it, but still wants to keep life running along as it has been. To review, temerity plus willing prey equals success.

CATCHING ADULTERERS AT THEIR OWN GAME

The key to catching someone who's having an affair is to know that seeing (or smelling or hearing) is believing. If you *think* your loved one is having an affair, and you just know that something is not kosher, have faith in your convictions. We all have radar, and we unfailingly get into trouble when we ignore it. Unless you're paranoid—and a surprisingly high percentage of us are—if you think your spouse is cheating on you, you're probably right.

Nonetheless, there are steps that can be taken to detect the cheater: Hire a private investigator, pick up the phone extension at unlikely times, hang out in local motels (Who knows? You might pick up your own paramour while you're at it.), and generally assume an air of extreme suspicion. Investing in a wardrobe of wigs and dark glasses wouldn't hurt.

Once you've figured out that he or she is playing around, it's up to you to decide what to do. You can stay, you can leave, you can issue ultimatums. Whatever you decide to do, at least you'll know. Catching the cheater is easy if you just poke around online or follow them around a bit. All you need to do is: check credit card, cell phone, and internet bills for odd activity (assuming they weren't clever enough to set up alternate billing practices), call the suspected cheater's office to verify travel plans, follow them (at a discreet distance) when they go to the gym or on errands, and ask his or her friends. Guaranteed someone will eventually feel guilty and spill the beans. Finally, keep your schedule erratic. Your unfaithful love is counting on your routine for opportunities to slip away. Keep him or her on their toes and you'll be in control.

≪ *Would I Lie?* ≫

I

President John F. Kennedy and Marilyn Monroe. While rumors of an affair between JFK and Marilyn Monroe never made it to the mainstream media while they were still alive, biographers of both figures have since routinely reported their affair as fact. The closest that the couple ever came to

(continued)

announcing their relationship was in May 1962, when Marilyn Monroe sang the president her famous (infamous?) rendition of "Happy Birthday to You" at his widely publicized forty-fifth birthday party at Madison Square Garden.

.... **2** ....

President Bill Clinton and Monica Lewinsky. "I did not have sex with that woman" has sadly become the most famous phrase that Bill Clinton ever uttered. According to audiotapes secretly recorded by Linda Tripp, Lewinsky and Clinton allegedly began a sexual relationship in 1995. By 1998 President Clinton was on trial, and the entire country knew about the alleged affair. When Lewinsky gave prosecutors a semen-stained dress in exchange for immunity in July 1998, it was clear that President Clinton had lied.

.... **3** ....

Former New Jersey governor James McGreevey and Golan Cipel. On August 12, 2004, Governor McGreevey announced his resignation after declaring that he was gay and had cheated on his wife with another man. According to McGreevey's memoir, he and a former security aide, Golan Cipel, had a romantic relationship in 2002. Cipel, on the other hand, denied any relationship with the former governor and threatened him with a sexual harassment lawsuit. McGreevey's coming out made him the first openly gay governor in United States history.

.... **4** ....

Woody Allen and Soon-Yi Previn. Woody Allen and Mia Farrow were in a relationship for twelve years. They never married, but they adopted two children together and had one of their own. Farrow had other biological and adopted children, whom Allen never adopted—or at least not in the traditional sense. In 1992 Farrow found nude photos of Soon-Yi, taken by Allen, and he admitted to having a sexual relationship with her. He and Farrow separated, and he continued his relationship with Previn. He was fifty-seven, and she was twenty-two. The couple married in 1997 and adopted two daughters.

CHEATING AT POKER

KNOWING WHEN TO HOLD 'EM AND WHEN TO FOLD 'EM (WITH APOLOGIES TO KENNY ROGERS)

Money makes the world go around—or so the song says. One of the major motivators for much of people's bad behavior is, of course, money. Sex is the other main culprit, and without the unholy trinity of sex, money, and greed, where would modern civilization be? How would the de Medicis ever have made a name for themselves? Sex, greed, and money put those crazy schemers on the map and have made many people's lives that much more interesting, not to mention dangerous. Money can make people lie, steal, cheat, and even kill, and a desire to get more of it leads people to do just those things every day.

Of the myriad ways that someone can go about laying their hands on some major funds, gambling is in the top ten. With casinos doing big business in the United States, not to mention the world, the temptation to try for the big bucks is unceasing. And of all the games you can play to try your luck, poker is one of the most popular. In fact, the sudden proliferation of professional poker tournaments is proof positive that the craze for the game is only on the rise.

But what to do if you're just a lousy card player? How about if you've been on a losing streak for longer than you can remember? How do you ensure that you'll still rake in the dough? Thankfully, cheating at poker is just as long-lived and popular as the game itself. Even so, cheating at poker can cost you your reputation as a gentleman (or gentlewoman), and with its long and bloody history (moment of silence for Wild Bill Hickok, please), it could also cost you life and limb. Proceed at your own peril.

THE UPSIDE

Money. Shall we say this one more time to make it clear? Money. Sure, there's a thrill to winning (or even getting one over on the other players by cheating), but the real reason that anyone gambles or plays cards is to win the pot. So if you're playing, and you're winning, you're getting paid. And that, as Martha Stewart would say, is a good thing.

THE DRAWBACK

As money is the great motivator of some of the most outrageous violence known to man, the big drawback to unfairly getting your mitts on someone else's dough is that you could find yourself in a lot of pain. That is, of course, if you get caught. Sure, there could be emotional or psychic pain because you know you cheated and lied, but pain of the physical variety is the real issue here. If you're playing with some high rollers, goon activity is not unheard of. It is also not unheard of for tire irons, lengths of wire, two-by-fours, lead pipes, or plastic bags to be used for rather untraditional purposes.

If violence is not likely, another drawback to contend with is that if you're found out, you'll probably get banned from any and all games going on in your neighborhood or anywhere else you're known. Your usual poker buddies will give you the cold shoulder, and all your months (or years) of preparation for becoming a master poker cheat will be for naught.

The idea is that no one wants to have anything to do with anyone who would steal their money or stuff. That holds true for poker games just as much as it does for home invasions. No one likes to feel violated.

TOOLS OF THE TRADE

There isn't much that you can bring to a poker table that will help you lie and cheat your way through the game. This is definitely a situation where skill and cunning are going to get you through. Even so, it's helpful to have:

1. Deck of cards
2. Sunglasses
3. Affinity for card tricks

WAYS AND MEANS: HOW TO PULL IT OFF

And now for your foray into cardsharp history. Keep in mind that poker is a game that is not played against the house but against your fellow players. Knowing their weaknesses, strengths, tells, habits, propensity for booze—anything at all—will help you to pull one over on them. Before we go any further, a brief review of how to play poker is probably in order.

A Brief History and Rules of the Game

Poker is supposedly a mix of several games of varied descent, including French, German, English, and even Persian card-related pastimes. Of course, this new and exciting game found its way onto a Mississippi riverboat in the mid-1800s (what didn't?) and joined the ranks of popular activities involving gambling on those floating dens of vice. Soon after the Civil War, an array of types of poker started cropping up, including the draw, stud, straight, and wild-card varieties. No more than one hundred years later, poker had flourished as one of America's favorite professional and amateur card games, no doubt promoted by the addition of beer and potato chips at the crucial moment.

Poker is easy to play and hard to master. The fundamentals are as follows: Get your hands on a standard fifty-two-card deck. Aces can be high or low, number cards' value is the number on the face, and the king, queen, and jack have the highest value, in that order. In some games, jokers can have any value you like (now you know where the name for that TV game show *The Joker's Wild* comes from). The types of hands that you can get in the game are (from highest value to lowest): five of a kind, royal flush, straight flush, four of a kind, full house, flush, straight, three of a kind, two pair, and a pair. Ironically, a pair is of the lowest value. This is the inverse reality for most guys, who are likely to say at some point in their lives, "Hey, dude, check out the pair on her!"

Now that you know how to play, here are the top ways to pull one over on your fellow players:

1. GET EVERYONE ELSE AT THE TABLE BOMBED—True, this is not a particularly sophisticated way to cheat, but it's effective. If your fellow players are guzzling steadily while you nurse a beer or a club soda, chances are that you'll have the upper hand by the end of the night. If ever there was a time to be generous, this is it. Don't skimp on buying the rounds, and keep an eagle eye out for the first person who's having a hard time keeping his or her head off the table.

2. PRACTICE CARD TRICKS—No, this is not so you can be the back-yard David Copperfield (or worse, David Blaine), this is so you can learn to palm a deck and start a career of dirty dealing. Being able to conceal a deck of cards in one hand is the key to dealing "creatively" off that deck and making the odds work in your favor.

3. WHAT'S THE DEAL?—Once you can palm a deck, you can take advantage of being the dealer. Some of the most popular ways to take advantage of dealing for fun and profit are: dealing off the bottom, concealing and dealing extra cards, looking at the cards before you deal them, and finding cards you've marked and dealing them to yourself. This takes lightning fast reflexes, because hesitating will certainly give you away, and you'll look particularly jerky.

4. SAFETY IN NUMBERS—If you have a friend you're willing to share your ill-gotten gains with, you can team up and take down the table together. This manner of cheating is based on deciding (through a se-cret method of communication) who has the better hand. The cheaters then drive the table to a betting frenzy, and then the one with the lower hand drops out, thus increasing the odds for the other player. The trick for the player who didn't take the chips off the table will probably be shaking them out of his or her partner at the end of the night.

5. ACE IN THE HOLE—A truly great cheat, worthy of Old West gun-fights and general shenanigans, is "holding cards out." This consists of secreting an ace up your sleeve before you fold. Later on, when it's convenient and will lead to a bigger take, that ace makes a magical reappearance. If you can pull this off, you're a card-cheating god. If you get caught by fellow players or casino owners, you can bet that your chances of ever playing cards again, not to mention breathing, are slim to none.

6. WHEN THE CHIPS ARE DOWN—If you're no good at shuffling cards around or stuffing them up your sleeve when no one's looking, a more ham-fisted approach is best for you. Shorting the pot is no less devious than any of the cheats listed above, but it requires much less finesse. All you need to do is toss your chips into the center of the table when you're placing your bet with enough vigor to make them dance around a bit. Call out what you're betting, but withhold a chip or two from the actual bet. Skimming like this can save you a bundle and really set you up with what you need when the bet you want to make presents itself. Note to the wise: This technique is easy and common enough that casinos are wise to it and will seriously mess you up if you're caught. This cheat is best left for use on your drunk friends.

MOST LIKELY TO SUCCEED

Depending on who you're trying to cheat, different skills come into play. If you're cheating your pals who are probably wasted and won't drop you over a friendly (or not so friendly) card game, then you don't need much skill. What you do need is timing and the will to cheat your friends. It's one thing to cheat strangers, another thing entirely to bilk your buddies. Frankly, it's cold. But, if you're a cold kind of person, and no one else in your group is a cheater, you'll probably get away with it. Just deny it when someone accuses you, and it'll probably blow over.

If you want to cheat casinos, you need much different skills. Essentially, it wouldn't hurt to be a professional magician. You need to be a master of sleight of hand, you need to possess grace under pressure, and you have to have a flair for performance. It wouldn't hurt to have a few bodyguards and really good running shoes.

For both scenarios, however, whether or not you have a grasp of basic human psychology will indicate your success rate. If you can scan a group, know the nervous types and the braggers at a glance, figure out people's tells, know how to motivate your fellow players or make them edgy, you're a shoo-in. People will tell you everything you need to know about themselves without saying a word. If your antennae are up, you're a born poker cheater.

CATCHING POKER CHEATS AT THEIR OWN GAME

Look around the room. Who's watching you too closely? Who's a little on edge when he or she gets to deal? Who's plying you with drinks a little too aggressively? That person you've identified, friend, is the cheater in your crowd. Have you noticed that someone you play with always wins? Does he or she win only when another person joins them? Again, this is your cheater.

The reality is that because poker is a psychological game at heart, there's no formula for identifying the cheater. The cheater will come up with a method that works best for his or her own particular quirks and run with it. The only way to tell if you've got a cheat in your crowd is if you think someone is winning too easily or if the pots they're raking in are unusually large. The most important thing is to act quickly once you find the cheater and eject him or her from your game. Or casino. There's no fun in knowing you're going to lose, and that's what the cheater's presence guarantees. Gambling is all about the possibility of winning. Without that, you're throwing a weekly money disposal party. With Doritos.

❧ *Would I Lie?* ❧

1

One common way of cheating at poker is to punch a tiny hole in each card in a different location, depending on which card it is. This was originally the preferred method of crooked gamblers, before people started to catch on. When a tiny hole is punched from the face side of the card, it is barely visible on the back of the card. With this method, the dealer can usually determine the card he is holding by touch, and some players can figure out their opponents' cards by looking very carefully.

2

James Butler Hickok (1837–1876) became known as "Wild Bill" because of his reputation as a gunslinger in the Wild West. He claimed to have killed over one hundred men, although historians think that number is an exaggeration. Besides being responsible for the first real Wild West gunfight, Hickok was also well known for his poker playing, in which he often won large sums of money from his opponents and was suspected of cheating. On August 2, 1876, Hickok was playing poker at a saloon in Deadwood, South Dakota, when his poker opponent of the day before, Jack McCall, came in

(continued)

and shot him in the back of the head. Hickok's hand when he died included a pair of aces and a pair of eights, a combination that is now known as a "dead man's hand."

.... **3** ....

The first illustrations of card cheats can be seen in oil paintings from the 1600s by Georges de La Tour and Michelangelo Merisis da Caravaggio. In de La Tour's *The Card Players,* a woman gazes suspiciously at one of her opponents and gestures for her servant to investigate what he's up to. *The Cardsharps* by Caravaggio depicts two young boys playing cards; one boy has extra cards tucked into the back of his belt, where his opponent cannot see them. There is also a shady character signaling to the boy while looking at the other boy's cards. Similar paintings by de La Tour and Caravaggio, as well as other artists' paintings of card cheats, appeared over the next century as the once private courtly games became a focus of public view. In 1910 C. M. Coolidge painted one of the most famous depictions of a poker game to this day, titled *Looks Like Four of a Kind.* Most people, however, just refer to it as *Dogs Playing Poker.*

FALSIFYING INSURANCE CLAIMS

MAKING ILLNESS AND MISFORTUNE WORK FOR YOU

Insurance fraud is defined as the act of filing a claim with an insurance company with the intent of receiving funds, but basing that claim on false information or pretenses. In other words, insurance fraud is lying for money. It's a classic cheat. Insurance fraud is so common and so socially accepted that nearly 10 percent of all Americans try to do it each year, and 30 percent wouldn't even bother reporting it if they knew someone else was doing it.

Why do people care so little about insurance fraud? What is it about this particular cheat that makes it such a nonissue for so many people? Why is it that lying, cheating, and (let's face it) stealing in this manner are so acceptable? For the most part, it's because people don't like being cheated, and if they think they are, they'll happily strike back. In this case, most Americans feel that insurance companies charge absurd amounts of money for very little coverage and care. This is particularly true of medical insurance. Where we once had relationships with family doctors who would visit our homes when we became ill, we now have to put up with clinics with impersonal care and pay through the nose for it. And it's all because of the insurance companies and the way in which they reimburse medical practices. It seems reasonable that we would want to strike back at the entities that took away our Norman Rockwell–style medical care.

Thanks to the ire of the general public, insurance fraud costs insurance companies and federal agencies billions of dollars each year. The logic of insurance scammers seems to be that the money they feel they shouldn't have to pay for bloated premiums and high copayments will be made up by their false claims. That money adds up when 25 percent of the country says that they see no problem with defrauding insurers. That's a lot of people, a lot of claims, and a lot of money. It's also a major act of rebellion that insurance companies don't seem to be able to recognize. And so the struggle continues.

People continue to defraud insurers of every stripe. Medical insurance fraud is very common, but so are car and property insurance. The Insurance Research Council found that one-third of all claims of physical injury in car accidents involve fraud. In an effort to make up for the loss, insurers add to the premiums, increasing them by multiple billions of dollars. Same thing with property insurance. The same researchers found that the number of people willing to torch their own homes and businesses to collect the insurance accounts for around one-quarter of all fires that take place each year. Several states have had enough of this rampant fraud, and bills are being introduced into state senates trying to beef up the penalties for insurance fraud. More fraud cases would be prosecuted, and heavier sentences/fines would be incurred. No fun for the arsonists in your crowd, but it will certainly help to keep premiums down.

If you are affected by all this insurance insanity and wish you could get an answer to how to secure a better deal, you've got two options. You could just dole out your insurance yearly, deal with the premiums, shop around to find the best insurance company you can, and allow for the amount of coverage the companies allow. Or you could decide how much you feel you're entitled to and make the appropriate claim or fake the appropriate accident to get the money you're looking for.

THE UPSIDE

The good news about insurance fraud, as evidenced by the billions of dollars that are successfully collected on fraudulent claims each year, is that you can get away with it. There are simply too many cases for insurers to investigate each year. There's no way that any insurance company can get the resources to look at everyone's bad behavior. They have to limit themselves to the really egregious cases. Additionally, the case load would be too enormous for any district attorney's office to prosecute, so you've got a pretty good chance of flying right under the radar.

Another great feature of insurance fraud is that it's a "victimless" crime. While it is difficult for most people to do harm to an individual who can really be devastated by someone else's wrongdoing, that's not the case when you're messing with a huge company. You're not doing any physical harm to anybody else, and you don't see anyone suffer. To make it even more palatable, the insurance companies are making too much off our backs anyway, so if they're harmed, it's a good thing.

Finally, the obvious upside of this cheat is the money you get from doing it and what that money brings: Burn down your house—get a new one. Crash the car or report it missing—get a new one. Claim you had a terrible disease—you're going to Disneyland! The payoff is just too good to ignore.

THE DRAWBACK

As great as the upsides are, the drawbacks to doing this cheat are no picnic. Let's not forget that insurance fraud is a punishable offense that should not be taken lightly. If you are faint of heart and without a good attorney in your arsenal, think twice about this cheat. Now that you've thought twice, here's what you could be up against:

It's jail time, ol' man. Not fun. Also not good, considering that you'll probably use up all the money you scammed from your insurer in order to pay for your lawyer. You'll also get hit with some fines should you get caught. This is, clearly, less horrifying than jail time. It is doubly horrifying, however, if you get both a fine *and* jail time.

Despite the fact that it's hard to identify and prosecute all the insurance cheaters in the U.S., the FBI is trying to do it. It has organized more task forces in the last few years to find all you little cheaters intent on bilking insurance companies and bring you down. The bureau probably can't make a huge dent in the problem, but you don't want to be one of the few bozos caught in its web.

Another drawback to cheating insurers is that they can (and do) retaliate by raising their premiums. Government agencies that provide health care do the same, which results in higher taxes. Essentially, ripping these guys off will possibly lead to you paying the same amounts anyway. Do the math and see what works for you. Finally, and this is really the biggest drawback, a badly planned accident that you've staged to collect on auto or property insurance can lead to death or serious injury. Unless you really know what you're doing when you stage your fake accident, you could wind up in deep trouble. Having a real injury isn't worth the risk.

TOOLS OF THE TRADE

Now that you're ready to do this cheat, you'll need a few weapons in your arsenal to get you though. Here are the essentials:

1. Thorough knowledge of the characteristics of the claim you're faking
2. Good acting skills
3. Good storytelling skills
4. Ability to handle paperwork/filing claims
5. Medical information

WAYS AND MEANS: HOW TO PULL IT OFF

There are two major groups that try to pull off insurance fraud. If you're planning this cheat, you're probably either a regular insured average joe, or you're a doctor. Depending on which group you fall into, there are different methods you'll follow to successfully execute this cheat. Feel free to improvise, but here are the best ways:

1. EXAGGERATE THE CLAIM—Instead of completely inventing a false ailment or accident, just use whatever has actually happened to you as a springboard to earning more cash. Let your claim be based in reality; it will be harder to argue against.

2. HAVE A WELL-THOUGHT-OUT PLAN—If you haven't thoroughly considered what you're doing from the start, you'll get in trouble halfway through. Know your plan from A through Z in case you run into any static along the way.

3. COURAGE OF YOUR CONVICTIONS—Don't second-guess yourself. If you punk out at any point during your scam, you'll reveal yourself as the cheater you are. Your insurer may drop you. Once you've started, stay committed.

4. TRUST NO ONE—You don't want too many people in on your plan, as it opens the door for mistakes and infighting over the payoff. Keep it simple and don't rely on others to vouch for you. At the end of the day, everyone will try to save themselves and leave you in the lurch.

5. PREEXISTING CONDITION—If you need insurance and worry that you can't get it because you're already ill, have no fear. One type of insurance scam is to find a way to conceal your condition until you're covered. Having a doctor to collude with you is a good idea.

6. COLLUSION—Having a doctor in your pocket to back up any false medical claims is helpful. You may need to split your earnings with him or her.

7. DOCTOR WHO?—If you can't find a doctor to help you out, invent one! Research which medical forms need to be filled out by your physician and falsify your heart out.

8. I DIDN'T DO IT—If you're a doctor, you can bill the insurer for services and procedures you never performed. Invent a few patients and particularly lucrative conditions, and you're ready to collect.

9. NAME THAT DISEASE—If you're faking an ailment, have a good working knowledge of what it is and what the symptoms are. Don't blow it by displaying symptoms that don't make sense.

10. MURDER BY DEATH—If you're ready to enter the world of film noir, you can always take advantage of your insurer with some macabre activities. Fake a death or murder someone you hold a policy for. Double indemnity, anyone?

11. DRIVER'S ED—If you're too good a driver to have an accident that you can embellish, go ahead and fake a car accident. Drive into a tree, jump the median, whatever works for you. Try not to kill yourself or get seriously injured in the process. Use a car you don't care about.

12. FLAME ON—If you're a firebug, try torching your house or business. Arson is one of the most popular forms of insurance fraud, as it's hard to pin it on the insured. If you're nervous about doing the deed yourself, hire your neighborhood arsonist.

13. CLEANING HOUSE—If you're tired of your stuff and want to go on a shopping spree, fake a robbery of your house. Get someone to come in and clear out your belongings, and don't forget to simulate forced entry. Store your old stuff, hawk it on eBay, take it to the town dump. Time to start fresh!

MOST LIKELY TO SUCCEED

Who's likely to do this cheat and succeed? Anyone who feels entitled to more than they've got will try to bilk their insurance company. You'll get away with it if you keep a low profile and don't look for a huge payout all at once. You'll also fare well if you don't scam the same insurer over and over. Finally, if you can stay mum and not brag to the neighbors, you've got a better chance than not at staying in the clear.

CATCHING INSURANCE CHEATS
AT THEIR OWN GAME

There are a few ways to catch an insurance cheat, should the insurance company or the FBI decide the cheat is serious enough to be worth catching. If you are trying to target an insurance cheater, here are the easiest ways to do it.

First, you have to look for the likely cheats. These are people who have multiple insurance claims yearly or are looking for improbably high payouts. You can also look for any claims that seem odd. Is someone trying to collect a claim because a car crashed into their house or because an exotic animal mauled them? You've probably got a cheater on your hands. Then you can organize a sting operation. Pretend to be a patient of a crooked doctor, or offer to help a frequent offender pull off a cheat. Find a way to get the cheater to do what they do best right under your nose, and bust them without further ado. You can also try to find property-damage or theft claimants who have storage facilities in their names. It's possible that the facility is filled with the "lost" belongings they're collecting on. Finally, if nothing is obvious or jumping out at you, but you have an inkling that they're up to no good, hire a private investigator. If your private dick sees that the claimant who's supposedly broken every bone in his or her body is really on a skiing trip, you've got your cheater nailed.

~ *Would I Lie?* ~

.... **1** ....

A Florida man was arrested in 2004 for having filed a false insurance claim pertaining to his house having burned down in December 2003. Investigators determined that the fire at his home was caused by arson but could not prove who had set the fire. Contractors boarded up his house and charged him $3,200 for it. The man, John Carstea, submitted an altered receipt to his insurance company on which he claimed the cost had been $7,008. He was charged with insurance fraud, grand theft, and uttering a forged instrument. He was later acquitted of any wrongdoing, making Mr. Carstea a possible hero to insurance cheaters the world over.

.... **2** ....

A California man was arrested in 2006 for filing false insurance claims and other charges. He preyed on the elderly by trying to sell them fake insurance policies. If they agreed, he'd pocket their money and disappear, but if the person turned him down, he would assume their identity and open policies anyway. He used fictitious information to create the policies so that the insurance company would then send him commission checks.

.... **3** ....

A former bar owner from Columbus, Ohio, was indicted by the grand jury in 2005 for insurance fraud and other charges.

(continued)

Martin J. McNamee, who owned the bars Pockets, Shooters, and the Out-R-Inn, was charged with money laundering, conspiracy, and mail and tax fraud, partially because of an insurance claim filed in 2001. McNamee intentionally flooded his home and filed a claim for the damages. He received the money but did not use it properly and was later charged with three separate counts of money laundering regarding the claim.

...............................⟨4⟩...............................

In 2004 Kerri Dunn, a California psychology professor at Claremont McKenna College, was charged with insurance fraud and filing a false police report for claiming that her car had been vandalized and that she had had $1,700 worth of property stolen from inside the vehicle. Professor Dunn claimed that she had found her car covered in anti-Semitic, racist, and sexist graffiti, and that her windows were broken and tires slashed. She filed a police report, the FBI became involved, and the college held a huge peace rally, with media swarming the campus. Soon after, two witnesses stepped forward and told investigators that they had seen Professor Dunn drive into the parking lot with the graffiti already on her car. They also saw her smash her own windows.

GETTING AWAY WITH PERJURY

I PROMISE TO TELL THE WHOLE TRUTH AND NOTHING BUT THE TRUTH SO HELP ME GOD

If you watch any of the prime-time dramas on TV, you're bound to wind up seeing tons of courtroom action. From *Law & Order* to *CSI* to ol' *Matlock,* there are plenty of legal high jinks to go around. If you are a devotee of these or similar shows, or can't get enough of movies like *A Few Good Men* ("You can't handle the truth!"), the concept of perjury is definitely old hat to you. For those who are less familiar with Hollywood's offerings and didn't suffer through law school, here's a quick overview from Legal Process 101. Perjury is the act of making false statements under oath in judicial or government hearings. In other words, it's lying in court or a quasilegal event, though you swore you wouldn't. Perjury is not, however, making a false statement unknowingly. Then it's just a boneheaded statement, and you can't get penalized for being a bonehead. No matter how tempting it may be.

If you do manage to lie in court, with full knowledge that what you're spewing is a bunch of claptrap, and with full intent to do so, then you are guilty of perjury. If you're successfully prosecuted for being a liar liar pants on fire, then you're in the slammer for fifteen to twenty-one months. If that comes to pass, it's a good thing that you're no stranger to lying. Be sure to tell your fellow inmates (assuming you're not sunning yourself in Club Fed) that you're in the clink for arson, murder, or anything tougher than fibbing.

But why is perjury such a big deal? Why is it such a bad thing to do? Simple. As a culture, we frown on lying. We also frown on negative actions that can hurt far more people than the one acting out in the first place. Perjury is a big deal because it's a lie that affects lots of people, and it's done publicly. By perjuring yourself, you can affect everyone who is part of a court proceeding. If you get away with it, it's tantamount to a community agreeing to your lie. That's no good.

If it's such a terrible thing, why do people do it? What's the allure of perjury? Essentially, it's that no one wants to admit to embarrassing information about themselves or others that can land them in hot water. Considering our current culture of entitlement, with so many high-profile people displaying a self-involved attitude, it shouldn't be surprising that perjury has been in the news a lot lately.

Accusations of this particular crime have been lobbed at politicians, journalists, athletes, and entertainers. And why shouldn't they try it? Why tell the truth if they can get away with not embarrassing themselves in public? It seems reasonable to take a shot at avoiding jail time if the penalty for perjury is jail time anyway. Either you're off scot-free or you're where you were going to end up anyway.

So, you could tell the truth and take your lumps—or lie. Perjury is a hard accusation to make stick. Just concoct a story that sounds plausible and practice saying it with a straight face. Leave the rest to your lawyer.

THE UPSIDE

In ancient Greece, oaths were sworn to the gods, who acted as both witnesses and guardians of the oath. If you committed perjury, you were guilty of the offense of connecting your lie with the god's name you invoked in the first place. The gods were supposed to punish perjurers for using their names in vain.

One of the upsides of committing perjury in the modern age is that you are totally avoiding the wrath of the gods, not to mention the Judeo-Christian god. You might incur the wrath of an attorney or a judicial body, but you're dodging fire and brimstone. That's a major improvement for which to thank over two thousand years of progress.

Another upside of perjury is that if you get away with it, you can avoid saying anything really embarrassing about yourself. You can also avoid revealing anything incriminating about anyone else. Which is, on occasion, a real investment in your own health and safety. If you're trying to decide if you should rat out that mafioso and his consigliere, the good bet is on perjuring yourself.

Perjury is the good bet because, frankly, it's a hard crime to prosecute. A successful prosecution requires proof that you knowingly lied about the information you revealed in court. This is a really difficult burden of proof, as it's nearly impossible to tell what someone else was thinking at any particular time. And since it's the prosecutor's job to make a perjury claim stick, you're not faced with having to preempt his or her case and prove what your state of mind was or was not.

THE DRAWBACK

The drawbacks to this cheat are well known to most people. If a district attorney sinks his or her claws into you and actually proves their perjury case against you, you're on your way to jail. Just make sure that your attorney works like the devil to get you in a minimum-security penitentiary. It's much better to make potholders in arts and crafts for a year or two than run in circles hoping no one will catch you in a maximum-security pen.

Public censure isn't any fun either, and you'll get loads of it. No one likes a liar, so if you find yourself being successfully fingered for perjury (which is distinctly different from being successfully fingered in jail), don't expect anyone to come to your rescue. After a little time goes by, you'll probably have a few true-blue pals come out of the woodwork. In the short term, it'll feel like everyone on earth lost your number.

And then there's the press. They won't be kind. If you're a public figure, you're going to get skewered. Think back for a moment to Bill, Monica, and a cigar—now let's move on. If you're a private citizen, you'll just get a healthy dose of the *eewww* factor. Everyone will know what you said and why you said it, and will enjoy thinking how gross you are and that they're better than you. This wouldn't happen without our journalist friends. Learn to say nothing to them. This will be hard for you, considering it's your big mouth that got you in trouble in the first place.

TOOLS OF THE TRADE

There are no bells and whistles to perjury. It's you, a courtroom, and a lawyer. Being a successful perjurer is all about having decent composure, so the tools you'll need come from within you (for the most part). With that in mind, you'll need:

1. A good lawyer
2. A good poker face
3. The ability to believe your own lie
4. The ability to remain calm under pressure (stress-relieving techniques)

WAYS AND MEANS: HOW TO PULL IT OFF

Much like the tools required for this cheat, the methodology is relatively simple. Just keep in mind that you need to sound honest, believable, and, most of all, realistic. Wild stories and denials in the face of overwhelming evidence will turn out to be fruitless and will just make you look lame. Here's what you need to do to walk away from a perjury charge (and anything else you're on trial for) like you're dipped in Teflon:

1. A GOOD LAWYER—As we've all learned after watching innumerable celebrity trials over the years, the key to walking away from any legal proceeding without a care in the world is having a good lawyer. If you have a major shark on your side, or a whole dream team, you can get away with murder. In your case, all you're trying to do is tell a few fibs on the stand. Considering the burden of proof that's on the prosecutor, any lawyer worth his or her salt can take care of an accusation of perjury. But if you're telling a whopper or just want an insurance policy, keep an ace up your sleeve by having a great lawyer on your side.

2. REHEARSAL—Ask any actor or actress, and they'll confirm that you rarely turn in a perfect performance the first time. It's essential to practice delivering your winning testimony to make it sound sincere and impenetrably true. Don't wing it. If your lawyer is really going for the win, he or she might even run lines with you until you've got it down.

3. IGNORANCE IS BLISS—If you're going to perjure yourself and then use the "I just didn't know" or "It was an honest mistake" defense, it's a good idea to generally present yourself as a moron. If you can't handle looking really stupid, just feign ignorance about a lot of other facts that you should have a handle on so that your perjury-related ignorance blends in.

4. "I DIDN'T KNOW HE HAD IT IN HIM!"—If you're a pillar of the community, no one will believe that you did anything scummy. They won't want to, and it will require overwhelming evidence to get them to buy that you're a liar. Considering that public opinion counts so much these days, what your neighbors think of you will matter. So buy Girl Scout Cookies, participate in local events, and consider it an investment if you ever get in hot water.

5. HERO WORSHIP—If you're a public figure, keep your nose extra-clean. If you're a great guy or gal who's always doing charity work for kids and accepts role model status, public opinion will be on your side. If, however, you act like a tool, you're on your way down. There's nothing more entertaining than watching the mighty fall.

6. EQUIVOCATE—Meet your new friends, vagueness and ambiguity. If you keep all your answers mushy and indistinct, no one can say you're guilty of perjury. Why is this? Because you didn't say anything in the first place. Keeping your answers so indistinct as to not even be answers is an art form. Practice, and watch tapes of celebrity trials. Every gem that falls from the lips of the people involved in those cases should be studied and used.

7. KEY PHRASES—If you need a little help understanding how to answer questions equivocally, there are a few key phrases that will serve you in good stead. Use them wisely, and you'll be safe and sound. Try peppering your speech with: "To the best of my recollection . . ." "I am under the impression . . ." "My understanding is . . ."

MOST LIKELY TO SUCCEED

If you're the type who can tell tall tales, you'll do well. Inventing information on the spot is a component to doing well with this cheat. You're also in good shape if you can remain cool under pressure. If you can remember to count to ten before you answer questions and don't easily crumble in front of authority figures, you're also golden. Finally, believing your own lies always helps, as it can get you to respond to allegations of perjury with righteous indignation, which can really sway public opinion.

CATCHING PERJURERS AT THEIR OWN GAME

If you're trying to catch someone in the act of perjuring himself or herself, you're probably a lawyer, and you don't need tips on how to catch the liar. If, however, you're just out of law school or you're a juror (or simply following a trial on Court TV from the safety of your own home), here are a few ways to catch this cheater in the act.

First, a careful deposition in which you rake the potential perjurer over the coals is a good idea. Anything they say in the deposition can be brought up at trial and used to contradict what's said on the stand. Unless the cheater has been really well prepped, there's a decent chance that they'll forget exactly what they said in the deposition. That's your opening.

Ask the cheater clearly worded questions, as you don't want to add opportunities for ambiguity, and check all answers for precision. Never let your witness get away with wishy-washy answers. You should hold your witness to the standard of a "reasonable person." In other words, whatever the cheater says shouldn't prompt a courtroom response of "Oh, come on!"

Finally, look for a motive to lie. Where there's smoke, there's fire.

❧ Would I Lie? ❧

.... **1** ....

In 2005 rapper Lil' Kim was convicted of perjury for trying to protect friends of hers who were involved in a shooting outside of the New York hip-hop radio station Hot 97 in 2001. Kimberly Jones (the rapper's real name) was with her entourage, which included manager Damion Butler and friend Suif "Gutta" Jackson, outside of the station when they ran into rival group Capone-N-Noreaga, and a shootout ensued. Jones testified that she didn't notice the two men at the scene of the crime, but surveillance photos show Butler opening the door for her. Even more incriminating was the fact that in separate trials, Butler and Jackson pleaded guilty to gun charges. Lil' Kim's assistant was also charged with perjury.

Dr. Cecil Jacobson was an infertility specialist who operated a reproductive clinic in Virginia until 1989. He was convicted of fifty-three counts of fraud and perjury for artificially inseminating at least seven women with his own sperm instead of sperm from different donors. He told his patients that sperm at the clinic came from carefully screened donors, but it was actually all his own. It is believed that he may have fathered seventy-five children through his scheme, but only seven women agreed to have paternity tests performed.

Public official Alger Hiss was convicted of perjury in 1950 after testifying about the nature of his relationship with Whittaker Chambers, an American journalist turned Russian spy. In 1942 Chambers was questioned about his past Communist contacts, and he named his "close friend" Alger Hiss. Hiss claimed to have never met Chambers and denied any association with the Communist Party. Over the next few years, more and more evidence proving that Hiss and Chambers had indeed been friends and associates came out, including secret State Department documents that Hiss allegedly gave to Chambers (the documents were typed using the same typewriter that Hiss had in his home). Hiss was sentenced to five years in prison on two counts of perjury but ended up serving only three years and eight months.

FALSIFYING YOUR RESUME

WELCOME TO THE WORKING WEEK

When it comes to looking for a job, one rule always holds true: The more desirable the position, the heavier the competition will be to win it. Everyone is vying for the same workplace rewards of fame, power, and fortune. But only a few ever get their fair share of even one of these elements, and sometimes smarts and hard work just aren't enough.

Hollywood is a perfect example of this truism. For every bit part in a grade Z film, there are one hundred wannabe starlets who have just gotten off the Greyhound bus from Middletown, USA. Despite their best efforts and intentions, just how many of these girls will end up with a starring role and how many will wind up taking orders at the Waffle House? The odds aren't good.

The odds are just the same in the business world. If you went to a top school, graduated magna cum laude, spent all of your holidays doing something to save the world or its inhabitants, and have amazing family connections, you might have it made. Your resume might land at the top of the heap in HR headquarters, and perhaps you'll be able to climb your way up the ladder from there.

If, however, you're pretty much an average Joe (mind you, there's no shame in that), and you're not a Rhodes scholar and your father didn't prep with the Kennedys, nor are you particularly well rounded or gifted, sorry to say, but luck is not on your side. You're going to need a leg up to make it in the work world, and there are a couple of ways to make that happen.

You could take the time to reinvent yourself, to reassess your life, your goals, and your dreams. You could develop new skills and really show the world what a bright self-starter you are.

Or you could just reinvent your resume.

THE UPSIDE

There is only one upside to falsifying your resume, and it's a big one. It works. If you do it right, you can land the job of your dreams without having to spend all the time and effort necessary to actually make all the statements you make on your resume hold up under scrutiny. Furthermore, another point in favor of falsification is that it's arguably a victimless crime. Who really gets hurt, after all, provided you do a good job once you've got it? Statistics show that as many as 1 in 3 people have invented a portion of their resume in some way, and, clearly, 33 percent of the working population hasn't been fired for this offense. So there's proof positive that it works.

With that said, be sure not to do anything outrageously creative such as claiming to have a medical or law degree. Chances are, you won't pick up the skills you need once you're on the job.

THE DRAWBACK
You may get caught.

Companies these days are prone to a lot more due diligence than they have been in the past. This can be attributed to all sorts of reasons, many of them falling under some vague umbrella concept of "security." If you're caught, you'll probably get fired, which will, of course, likely jeopardize your chances of getting another job any time soon. Needless to say, this is a regrettable situation that should be avoided if possible. The good news to be found in that scenario is that lying on your resume is not illegal (again, provided you're not claiming you're a licensed professional), so chances are that the worst that will happen is a rapid and harsh dismissal and the usual effects caused by joblessness.

TOOLS OF THE TRADE
A simple, inexpensive list of tools is necessary to pull off falsifying your resume. Be sure to assemble all tools prior to commencement of the falsification, so you don't have to rework your resume multiple times. You will need:

1. Imagination
2. Friends
3. Office supplies

WAYS AND MEANS: HOW TO PULL IT OFF
Now that you've got your tools lined up, here's the methodology to follow to make the cheat come together:

1. SCHOOL QUALIFICATIONS—Do not lie about the school you attended or the degree you earned, as that is very easy to check. If you're a recent graduate, a new employer will definitely look at this section of your resume first and will most likely verify it.

If a background check isn't deterrent enough, keep in mind that nothing is as embarrassing as saying you went to such-and-such school, only to have your prospective employer say "Oh, my daughter went there, and she was in your class; let's see what you looked like in the yearbook."

2. JOB EXPERIENCE—The more you can massage the truth without lying outright, the better off you will be. Your goal is to create a credible profile that is not outrageously far off from who you really are and to keep from sending up any red flags. Each job listed on your resume must be believable enough that whoever is interviewing you won't feel compelled to delve into your past. Don't claim to have been a NASA employee unless you're ready to field unexpected questions about the space shuttle in interviews. Try to avoid awkward situations like this at all costs.

A great way to enhance your job experience is to insert a few fictitious tidbits that can't be traced. For instance, there's no problem saying you managed a large budget, even if you've never laid eyes on a spreadsheet. Just be sure to save the specifics for the interview; nobody is likely to call your former employer and ask them to confirm a resume padder like this (unless you're applying to be a chief financial officer, in which case it's probably a bad precedent to lie about fiscal matters).

3. PRESENTATION—Make sure that your resume looks absolutely perfect: Remember, it's literally you—or the "you" you want them to think you are—on paper. Never forget the importance of high-quality paper and envelopes. Choose something with an attractive watermark

and high rag content. Keep an eye out for spelling mistakes or anything else that would make someone think twice about you. Pay attention to looking the part when you walk in the door: neat, tidy, on time— certainly nothing that would give the interviewer a reason to look too far beyond what you've written down.

4. BACKGROUND CHECK—You're going to need to supply work and personal references. Your friends can step in to fill both of these roles. If you have a friend who has a business of some kind, say you worked there and make up a decent title for yourself. Then, over drinks (you're buying), you and your friend must come up with an airtight story about what you did and how much you contributed.

If your friend is squeamish about bringing his own company into your scheme, there's another route for you. If you were a staffer at a particular job, but want to claim to have been a manager (of course, you'll also have to say the company folded since then), you can have your buddy say that he was the director you reported to. He'll have to be ready to turn in an Oscar-worthy performance when he sings your praises. Don't forget to rehearse.

Get a few friends to do this with you, and you've got a whole re-sume full of fabulous jobs and titles.

5. SALARY—Ironically, this is probably the easiest one to finesse. How much money you earned at your last job is very easy to lie about; in fact, if money's all you're after, then save the cheating for this, and this alone.

Due to privacy issues, about the only thing your previous employer is likely to be able to confirm is that you did indeed work there, and perhaps the duration of your job and your title. If asked what your sal-ary was, they may provide a ballpark figure, but if you're ever called on this, you can always say that number didn't include your bonus, which no company will ever verify.

6. THE INTERVIEW—This is where you can really clinch it. Most interviews are really about the interviewer making sure that you have the right kind of personal presentation and delivery for the job. It's all about the interviewer getting the right vibe from you.

Be extremely confident and do not hesitate. You must be able to back up and elaborate on everything you've written down. It's a great opportunity to exaggerate with even more impunity. The interviewer may be taking notes, but it's unlikely that he or she would ever call a former employer to confirm information that came up in the course of a conversation.

MOST LIKELY TO SUCCEED

In large measure, the extent to which your bluff will be believed depends on the industry. It would be very difficult—nearly impossible—to lie your way into a job that involves very specific—indeed, measurable—skills for which you may even be tested as part of the application process. Don't even think about bluffing about medicine, engineering, accounting, chemistry, or law. Anything that requires a graduate education that you don't have should be avoided unless you're looking for a high-drama situation down the road.

On the other hand, more "service"-oriented jobs—advertising, marketing, communications, customer relations (especially customer relations)—call for a wide and oftentimes less defined range of "people skills" that are much easier to pretend you have. A lot of it comes down to common sense and confidence, and, in fact, if you've made it to the interview, you probably have some modicum of both the skills—and the chutzpah—necessary to succeed.

CATCHING RESUME CHEATS
AT THEIR OWN GAME

For those of us who would never consider falsifying a resume or lying, cheating, or stealing their way into a job, how do you spot a resume cheater and keep them at bay? Simple. Be a good listener, a good reader, and follow up on everything the job applicant has written.

Start with the educational credentials, and check them. Does the applicant seem too young, or too early in the career trajectory to realistically have had the kind of responsibilities he/she claims? Check all references—and pay attention. Are all the referees' phone numbers cell phone numbers? Does the referee answer the phone with a company name or just "hello"? This will give you a clue as to whether the referee is a plant.

At the interview—if the candidate makes it that far—observe body language: Does he/she seem more nervous than is normal for an interview? Don't start at the top or bottom of the CV, as the candidate may have rehearsed answers in some kind of order; pick a spot somewhere in the middle and talk about this. Does he or she look you in the eye, and have quick and comprehensive answers to all of your questions?

The best thing you can do to protect yourself is to write something into your company's human resources policy that indicates that if ever it is determined that the person whom you hired lied on their resume, you have a right to terminate their employment.

~ *Would I Lie?* ~

.... ① ....

In December 2001 George O'Leary, who had just been hired as head coach of the University of Notre Dame football team, was forced to resign when the school found out that he had lied about his background. "According to New York University," ESPN.com reported, "O'Leary never earned a master of science degree in education from the school, as claimed in this year's Georgia Tech football media guide. An assistant registrar at NYU as well as a clerk said that O'Leary attended the school of education for two semesters from September 1970 to June 1971, taking one course each semester, but never completed his degree."

.... ② ....

In February 2006 RadioShack CEO David Edmondson admitted to lying about his academic record on his resume. He resigned shortly after. He claimed that he had received degrees in theology and psychology from Pacific Coast Baptist College in San Diego. The college had no record of his graduation, however, and did not even offer psychology degrees. Edmondson subsequently revealed that the only degree he received was a ThG diploma, which is awarded for completing three years of study in theology. He blamed his resume falsehood on an oversight—apparently he thought he had earned a bachelor of science.

(continued)

3

In 2002 Ronald Zarrella, CEO of Bausch & Lomb, was lucky not to lose his job when his resume's educational information was discovered to be a lie. He claimed to have earned an MBA from NYU, but the school confirmed that he had not. Past employers, including General Motors, had not checked into this lie either. Zarrella was allowed to keep his job, but he had to forfeit a $1.1 million bonus that he was due.

CHEATING ON YOUR SIGNIFICANT OTHER— CYBERSEX

WWW.INFIDELITY.ORG(ASM)

While it has its rewards, having an affair can be a messy and sometimes troublesome undertaking. As most people know (and as we have already covered in this book), there is a huge amount of preparation required, not to mention subterfuge and organization, in order to set up a successful affair and keep it going for more than a few days. Frankly, it often winds up being more trouble than it's worth. So what's a prospective philanderer to do if he or she is short on time or strategy and long on desire?

Thanks to the enormous technological leaps forward that have taken place over the last ten years, there's a whole new outlet available for those who are ready to dip their toes in the perfidy pool. It's cybersex, and it's the ultimate in no-muss-no-fuss action on the side.

The fun part of cybersex is that it comes in so many different flavors. You can find a multitude of adults-only websites that feature lovely ladies (and gents) who are more than willing to tell you a bedtime story with the happiest of endings. The only drawback there is that your burgeoning love affair will cost you approximately ninety-nine cents per minute, more if you opt for the video version. You can find cyber love of the unpaid variety if you seek out like-minded people in chat rooms, blogs, or online fantasy role-play games. Once you find your paramour, you can keep the chat flowing using instant messaging, email, or chat rooms (complete with webcam if you choose).

Now that you're all set up with an anonymous hookup who's most certainly not even in the same state as you, you will most likely ask yourself, Am I really cheating or just playing around on the computer? Join the club. The best part about cybersex is that there is still a raging debate about whether or not it's a sexual outlet that can even be classified as "cheating" or infidelity. How marvelous that you can get it on with someone outside of your relationship and still be able to rationalize that it's not even really sex, and, therefore, not cheating. Genius! Cybersex may really be one of the best forms of faithlessness around because of this built-in ambiguity and wiggle room for the cheater. Kudos to the intrepid adulterers who have blazed the way for the rest of us by keeping the term *cyber* as the prefix to this particular type of sex! What happens on the internet stays on the internet. Right? Let's see.

THE UPSIDE

The primary upside to cybersex is all the gray area that's inherent in the act. For anyone who's doing something they know they shouldn't, having an argument at the ready to counter anything the injured party might say is a fabulous insurance policy. You can create doubt, defend yourself loudly and frequently, and even print articles you've found online that support your views and actions (happily, there's no shortage of these editorials). Your beloved might shred these missives and throw them at you, but it's the American way to let societal norms rule the day, and the jury's still out on this particular situation.

The secondary upsides are no less fabulous for the cheater on the prowl. One of these is that the only virus you're likely to get is of the bits and bytes variety. There's no risk of getting an STD when the only human contact you're having is with yourself. Your lover on the other end of the fiber-optic cable might be typing salacious tidbits for you, but you're on your own for the big finish. Additionally, everyone out there in cyberspace is pretty open minded and ready for a good time. It's remarkably easy to find someone willing to role-play your favorite fantasy, no matter how bizarre or unprecedented. Want to get it on with a guy in a raccoon suit? No problem. Feel like getting whacked with sashimi-grade tuna while reciting the Declaration of Independence? You got it. Whatever gets you through the night. Or day. Or whenever you decide to sit down at the keyboard.

THE DRAWBACK

The drawbacks are particularly interesting with this type of deception, as your actions could land you in some legal hot water. But first, the obvious drawback: losing your significant other. Sure, you can double-talk and argue that sex is an intimate physical act and that what you're doing doesn't even involve two people in the same room. Sure, you can argue that all you're doing is masturbation (this might lead to some hard feelings anyway, but that's a relationship hurdle of a different stripe), but if your S.O. has more than a few brain cells rattling around, he or she won't swallow your story. As long as there's someone else involved, virtually or otherwise, there's a good counterargument for infidelity.

The legal difficulties that you might encounter are twofold. First, cybersex is rapidly becoming grounds for divorce in several states across our fair and increasingly techno-savvy land. All it takes to lose your spouse and a good portion of your personal belongings is getting caught in front of the monitor with one hand on the keyboard and the other down your pants. Not a dignified way to end things. Your friends, however, will thank you for a story they can dine out on for months.

You could also run into major (and far more embarrassing) legal problems when you find out that the hottie you've been IM-ing is not a busty babe draped in chiffon who's letting her fingers do the walking, but an eleven-year-old named Buster. Those pesky kids and their computers! While this may not be the most likely of scenarios, it's a cautionary tale. Remember, there's no way to know who's really on the other end of your chat.

Finally, you run the risk of developing internet-related agoraphobia. Should your cybersex relationship become too central in your life, you may be staring down the barrel of shut-in status as you spend increasing numbers of hours each day planted in front of the monitor in a full-on self-pleasuring meltdown. A few months of this behavior, and your bloated, pasty, creepy self will wane in actual desirability and become merely virtually desirable. In person will no longer be your best side. This level of commitment to cybersex should be avoided.

TOOLS OF THE TRADE

There's very little equipment required to make this particular cheat work for you. The ease with which anyone can indulge in extracurricular cybernookie is exactly what makes it so popular. Here's what you need to get started; their uses need no elucidation:

1. Computer
2. Rich fantasy life
3. Hands

WAYS AND MEANS: HOW TO PULL IT OFF

Now that you've got your tools lined up, here's the methodology to follow to make the cheat really come together:

1. IF YOU LIVE ALONE—If you live alone, this is a fairly easy cheat to pull off. You know the drill: Turn on the computer, settle into a comfy chair (Aerons are recommended, but try a few to find your favorite), crack your knuckles, and get to work. Other than that, keep tabs on when your significant other normally comes over to your pad, as well as when he or she requires your undivided attention on the phone. As long as you know you can get down and dirty with H0tLvr219 (or whomever you pick up online) without any interruptions, you're home free. Or at least at a low price if you go the ninety-nine-cent route. Do, however, create a separate, private account for your online dalliances in case you have a jealous partner. Suspicious or jealous girlfriends and boyfriends just *love* logging on to check your email or IM history when you're in the shower. This is a fact. Don't question it, just act accordingly. It's also a bad idea to IM with your loved one while you're IM-ing with your "special friend." It's pretty much guaranteed that you'll accidentally respond to your girlfriend's question about dinner reservations

with "just put it in your mouth, you dirty girl." This will be hard to explain.

2. IF YOU COHABIT—Needless to say, whenever you share space with someone, it's harder to pull off nefarious deeds. Don't let this deter you. Just because it's a little tricky doesn't mean it can't be done. As when you live alone, secrecy is key. But you'll have to step it up a bit more than your friends who fly solo. Definitely get private email and IM accounts and memorize your partner's routine. You'll also have to come up with a spate of excuses for alone time with your computer. Some of the classics are: doing work, preparing taxes (or some other ungodly task that no one in their right mind would want to join), noodling on eBay, or playing a video game. These are good, but all of that could feasibly be done out in the open on a shared computer. If you're really wise, you'll get a laptop and make your living space a wireless environment. What could be better than settling into the privacy of the bathroom with a laptop perched on your knees (or the sink or tub, depending on the layout of your loo) and having a ball with St33lR0d behind a locked door? A door that any reasonable person with nothing to hide would lock? Nothing! The point here is that you've got to carve out a space that's yours and yours alone. Otherwise you will get busted. Note to the wise: Do not think of your office as an "alone space." Your internet history will be checked, and you will get fired. No severance.

MOST LIKELY TO SUCCEED
If you're already a computer nerd, this cheat is made for you. You're already known to come home and immediately set up in front of the computer with your snacks and settle in for the evening. No need to create a cover, you've already got it. Additionally, anyone who's a little naturally antisocial, needs to work at home at odd hours (attention telemarketers, this could be a real perk for you!), or who's

happiest keeping relationships at a safe distance will take to this cheat like a duck to water. As always, an ability to keep illicit information on the down-low is key.

CATCHING CYBERSEX CHEATERS AT THEIR OWN GAME

If you want to avoid falling victim to this cheat in the first place, stay away from dating anyone with a propensity to lose themselves in hours and hours of computer activity. This could be gaming, programming, hacking, emailing/IM-ing friends, whatever. Anyone who is that much more comfortable interacting through a filter like this is going to be really happy engaging in a sex life that's once removed as well. That's not to say that all computer geeks are cybersex cheaters, it's just that the likelihood is higher. Think of this activity as a gateway drug.

Anyone with a serious proclivity for porn also falls into this category. It's a short step from online ogling to reaching out and virtually touching someone. Once the world of enticing possibilities dancing around on your monitor becomes one's primary environment, why not jump in whole hog? Keep an eye on porn stashes and porn caches that your sweetie thinks he or she is keeping from you. Again, a gateway drug.

As far as detecting and confronting goes, the usual mine sweeping for alternate email and IM accounts, browser history, and credit card bills featuring chat site or other suspicious online purchases is the way to go. As with all situations that involve infidelity, vigilance is key. New and strangely secretive behavior always has something behind it.

······························ **1** ······························

John and Diane Goydan—In January 1996, John Goydan filed for divorce from his wife, Diane, after discovering that she was carrying on an internet affair with a man who called himself "the Weasel." He discovered dozens of emails and messages between Diane and the also-married man (identified in court papers only as Ray from North Carolina) in which the two wrote about wanting to be together. He also found evidence that they planned a real-life romantic weekend at a New Hampshire bed-and-breakfast.

······························ **2** ······························

John Allen Angeles—In 2003 in Nightcliff, Australia, John Allen Angeles was arrested for murdering his wife and stepdaughter because of a suspected internet affair that his wife was having. She allegedly met a man over the internet and then began a real-life affair. Angeles threw her and her daughter out of the house after discovering the affair, and several months later he beat them to death.

······························ **3** ······························

Ji and Gven—In China, a married couple, Ji and Gven, managed to find each other on the internet and have a cybersex affair for a month without knowing that they were communicating with each other! Despite being happily married for twelve years, Ji felt that there was something missing in the relationship. She posted a message of "I want you" on a personals site and received hundreds of responses. Her husband happened to see the posting, and he responded. For the next month, the couple carried on an internet affair, staying late at work and making excuses to each other, until finally they arranged to meet. When they saw each other, each one thought that the other had been spying on them, and it wasn't until they were taken to a police station for physically fighting that they realized the truth.

·· 4 ··

Marion Walton—In 1996 an Arkansas man, Marion Walton, was having a cybersex affair with a Canadian woman, and his wife discovered his adulterous emails. In order to stop his virtual affair, she deleted his entire email program. He then proceeded to beat her on two separate occasions in retaliation.

FAKING BEAUTY

EYE OF THE BEHOLDER

Let's face it. It's easier to be good looking than it is to be unique or even downright ugly. Whether we like it or not, we live in a world that is obsessed with looks. It always has been and probably always will be. Sure, there are a few people who get away with being a bit left of center in the looks department. For these lucky few, the French in their inimitable way have even come up with the phrase *jolie laide* to categorize and legitimize this odd type of sex appeal. The direct translation is "pretty-ugly," or as one might say to describe someone like Oscar winner Adrien Brody, "he's so ugly he's gorgeous." If you're pretty-ugly, you probably know it. You have a certain *je ne sais quoi* (to borrow another perfectly expressive French phrase) that has admirers following you in droves. If you're not sure if you've got it, you don't. You're just plain "ugly-ugly."

What does this world hold for you if your looks are lame? Sadly, it's not a pretty picture. In small and subtle ways, you are discriminated against. Sure it's hard to get a date, but the shunning you'll endure goes far deeper than dating woes. You could miss out on getting the job you'd like, you could have problems making friends, and, worst of all, it's been shown that even on a grade school level, teachers favor good-looking children over plain ones. What can be done if you're less than perfect? Is all hope lost if you're a downright dog? Are you to be relegated to the dust heap of snaggletoothed wallflowers never to get a date or a job?

Absolutely not. With modern science on your side, there's quite a lot that can be done to make yourself far more attractive than you are naturally. Thanks to the ancient Egyptians, who pioneered rhinoplasty in 3000 BC, we now have a wide array of procedures that can rescue anyone from dreary drabness and make him or her a truly sexy beast. Asymmetrical features can be made perfectly regular, skin can be resurfaced, and fat can be sucked out of you by the gallon. Does it matter why you want to do this? Does it make a difference if you're doing it to impress others, bolster your failing confidence, or simply give yourself the tightened-up neck of your dreams? As long as you've got the will and the cash, there's a way. Dream big.

Sure, you could spend all of your grooming budget on therapy so you can accept yourself as you are. You could learn to live with a nose that travels east to west on your face instead of north to south. You could wear your imperfections as a point of pride and find the mate who will love you as you are. But why waste the energy? A handful of perfectly executed beauty cheats, and you'll be on your way to getting whatever you want. Save the soul searching for another day.

THE UPSIDE

Being a beauty cheater can yield surprising rewards if you do it right. It is important to note that standards of beauty can range wildly from country to country, not to mention state to state. It's important that you get a handle on the look you want to create before you begin your transformation process.

It is exactly this kind of Dr. Frankenstein approach to beauty, cobbling together a look based on your own taste as well as cultural norms, that's so appealing. If you treat your appearance as a totally blank slate, you can really make yourself over into anything you want to be. You can let go of the constraints of your own face and body to completely transform yourself. Your can commit to making your outer self match your inner self to a T. It doesn't matter if your outer self starts out as a short, chubby brunette with an acne problem. With a little gumption and a lot of energy, you can become a busty blond babe of at least average height. Similarly, a ninety-eight-pound weakling with a sunken chest can make himself into the envy of muscle beach. No one needs to know that those muscles are really silicone implants.

The direct benefits of all this are obvious. You'll have more dates, your partners will be better looking, and if you're a woman, they'll probably have more money. Job interviews will go more smoothly, and people will seem to magically see things your way more easily. Life will be less of a struggle. If you've already got a mate, they'll get an instant upgrade thanks to being seen around town with a far hotter property than before. The fallout of your good fortune will benefit them too. Pretty is more fun, and they'll thank you for it.

THE DRAWBACK

There is a flip side of having a partner or spouse who hooked up with the plain version of you, only to find themselves with the more desirable version down the road. It can be very intimidating to deal with a beautiful person and all the social confidence that comes with beauty if you're not used to it. It's not uncommon for the recipient of a major makeover to dump his or her spouse once they experience the favorable attention they receive post-overhaul. If you like the person you're with, consider the drawback of losing them over the new you.

Most beauty treatments can go horribly wrong if you have the wrong person working on you. A dye job can leave you bald, a peel can scar you, and plastic surgery could even leave you, well, dead. Most procedures that drastically change the way you look can be just as damaging as they can be beautifying. Properly researching whoever's in charge of your body work can really mean the difference between life and death. You don't want to be known as the person who checked out early over a butt lift.

TOOLS OF THE TRADE

Beauty is a full-time job, as evidenced by the number of tools and professionals needed to achieve full-on gorgeousness. Sure, you can forgo a few of the items listed below, but if you're really going to get glammed up, there's no point to half stepping. You will need:

1. Hairstylist
2. Waxer
3. Tanning booth
4. Dentist
5. Plastic surgeon
6. Personal trainer

7. Aesthetician
8. Makeup
9. Hair products
10. Cleansers
11. Shopping consultant

WAYS AND MEANS: HOW TO PULL IT OFF

The numbers have it. The ranks of people seeking physical perfection are constantly on the rise. More than seven million people are getting cosmetic procedures done yearly in the United States. Are you ready to join them? Here's how.

1. HAIR—Hate your hair? Is it thinning, too curly, too limp, won't grow, or is it just plain old gross? Have no fear! There's no shortage of ways to give yourself a glorious mane that Fabio or Jennifer Aniston would envy. If your crop is thin, you can find yourself a can of spray-on hair (if you go for the shoe-polish look) or get a weave to bulk yourself up. A weave is also great if your short hair won't grow, and you absolutely must have hair you can swing around to be the envy of others. If your hair is too curly or frizzy, and walking out of the house in the rain is out of the question, get a Japanese straightening treatment for perfect, silky locks. Just remember, synthetic hair looks and feels tacky. Never let this be attached to your head under any circumstances. If you are so follicularly challenged as to require a wig, opt for human hair and don't let your wig tape show.

2. NAILS—Nail biting is gross. Those horrible little pillows of skin you get at your fingertips if your nails are too short are completely gag-tastic. If you can't keep your hands out of your mouth, or you must have dragon-lady talons, fake nails are for you. Go to one of the nail salons that contribute to a $6.4 billion industry and get yourself some linen,

gel, silk, or acrylic nails. Anything other than silk looks thick, sort of like you've got Fritos for fingernails. Anything is better than a press-on nail. Don't even think about this option unless you want to leave a trail of little plastic nails in your wake. They fall off at the worst times. Although nails that fall off are better than fungus-ridden nails, which can happen if water gets under your acrylics. Do you *really* want talons?

3. MAKEUP—This is, of course, one of the least invasive ways for women to spruce themselves up. If you don't wear any makeup at all or have a horribly dated look, get thee to the local department store makeup counter for a consultation. Be firm with the makeup artist. Tell him or her that you don't want a full-on drag show look. Subtlety is your guide. Guys can try this too, but if you do, you're probably going for the full-on drag approach. Proceed accordingly.

4. FACE—Scientific studies have proven that facial symmetry is the secret behind great beauty. Even infants, who haven't been exposed to societal norms of beauty, gravitate toward images of people with symmetrical faces. Clearly, those of us who have been exposed to conventional ideas of what is beautiful have to work overtime to buck the system. If you have no interest in deviating from this ideal, there's quite a bit you can do to have the face of your (and everyone else's) dreams. The short list of top facial procedures and treatments are: Botox injections, eyebrow plucking, nose job, eye lift, brow lift, face lift, collagen injections, silicone cheek and chin implants, and chemical peels. You can fill in wrinkles, reshape your face, and resurface your skin to a smooth finish. Overzealousness with any of these treatments should be avoided, or they could result in bus-tire lips or foreheads that hint at rigor mortis.

5. BODY—A youthful, firm body is a sign of good health. Men and women can both benefit from having a taut physique. Maintaining a

healthy diet and going to the gym can prove to be too much for some, however, and plastic surgery goes a long way to helping the dream of the perfect body come true. If you just can't manage, or bother, to put in the work, let the doctor do it for you. You can have liposuction to remove fat, silicone implants in your chest, butt, calves, and boobs, or have your breasts reduced to minimize upper-body bulk. As long as you've got the cash, you can have the body. While you're at it, you can work on your tan. No need to sit in the sun for radiant skin, get your tan sprayed on or rub it on yourself at home with a self-tanner. While you're busy turning yourself into an Oompa Loompa, don't forget to remove excess tanner from your palms. Tan palms are the faker's give-away.

6. TEETH—Ah, what could be more fake than fake teeth? While the days of enormous, shiny, blindingly white capped teeth are behind us, veneers are now the fake teeth of choice. Capped teeth could look weirdly plastic and thick, not unlike cramming a set of wind-up chattering teeth in your mouth; veneers are thinner and much more realistic looking. They are not, however, anywhere near real. To get veneers, you have to have your real teeth filed down, sometimes to creepy little nubs, and then the veneers are glued in place on top of your nubs. If this isn't appealing, you could opt for gangsta grillz instead. These flashy gold (and sometimes bejeweled) caps can be made in a snap-on/snap-off version so you can wear them when you choose. They're like Bedazzlers™ for your mouth, hip-hop style.

7. WARDROBE—Are you an apple or a pear? Do you carry your weight on top or bottom? Even if you get your body worked over by a Beverly Hills plastic surgeon, you've still got to dress yourself properly to hide any remaining flaws. A few basic rules can get you through some of the most serious fashion crises. No one needs to wear horizontal stripes.

Ever. No one needs to wear white shoes. Ever. Even if it's *before* Labor Day, white shoes make your feet look big. A monochromatic outfit makes everybody look thin. Thin heels on your shoes can make your ankles look big. No one looks good in a skirt that cuts across the calves. Guys always look better in a blazer. The jacket, not the car.

MOST LIKELY TO SUCCEED

If you've got the money to remake and remodel the goods you were born with, you can be a first-class beauty faker. Cheating at beauty isn't complex, but it does require time (about an hour every morning, time at the gym or surgeon's office, appointments at the dermatologist, and so on) and effort. Effort like that can be sustained with a healthy sense of determination, but a dollop of self-loathing keeps the flame lit.

CATCHING BEAUTY CHEATS
AT THEIR OWN GAME

This is not hard. Fake boobs don't move, fake teeth are too white and even, and impossibly thin thighs are, duh, impossible. Fake hair grows overnight, and fake lips always make you look like Donald Duck. It's not difficult to spot the faker, you just have to ask yourself if after all that exertion the cheater achieved his or her desired effect. At the end of the day, is a manufactured look really all that attractive?

Would I Lie?

1

In 2004 a new reality show premiered on Fox called *The Swan.* The show's premise was that women who considered themselves to be "ugly ducklings" would be transformed into "beautiful swans" through plastic surgery and other methods, with "the Ultimate Swan" being crowned on the show's season finale. Each contestant was assigned a team to work on her transformation throughout the three-month filming process: a life coach, therapist, physical trainer, cosmetic surgeon, dental surgeon, and stylist. The winner of the Ultimate Swan title lost her husband when the show ended, proving that cheating beauty isn't always the best way to achieve happiness.

2

While some celebrities make themselves look worse with plastic surgery than if they aged naturally, many would argue that Cher is the exception. She has openly referred to herself as "the plastic surgery poster girl." Her first procedure was a rhinoplasty because she couldn't stand her nose when she saw herself on film for the first time. After pregnancy, when her swollen breasts shrank down to their normal size, she had breast implants put in. While she has her critics, the actress-singer-superstar looks better at sixty than some women look at thirty, and she's never tried to hide how she does it.

.... **3** ....

Jessica Simpson's stylist Ken Pavés created a line of synthetic hair extensions that he sells on the Home Shopping Network, called "Hairdo Clip-in Hair." The extensions are designed to look and feel like real hair and come in eleven different "multitonal" shades. The clip-on hair comes as one piece and pins onto your natural hair to add length or body. An $87.50 price tag doesn't seem to faze those women who are entranced by the idea of having beautiful, flowing hair. Pavés created the product based on styles he does for Jessica, and supposedly she personally tests each of them.

.... **4** ....

Jocelyn Wildenstein, New York socialite and ex-wife of the billionaire Alec Wildenstein, took her husband's love of wild cats a little too far when she had her face surgically transformed into a catlike mask in an effort to keep him from leaving her. Her eyes are slanted upward, she has cheek implants, and her lips are so full of collagen that they look like they may explode if a fork takes a wrong turn. She is often referred to as "the Bride of Wildenstein," and is infamous around Manhattan for scaring the living daylights out of anyone who accidentally comes near her.

CALLING IN SICK AT WORK

YOU'RE NOT THE BOSS OF ME

We all know that except for the select few, everybody has to work for a living. That doesn't mean that we have to like it. Let's see what a typical day might entail and determine if this antipathy toward our jobs is reasonable. We get up every day at some horrendous hour (which could be 4:00 a.m. for some, 8:00 a.m. for others), make ourselves look somewhat human, endure an annoying commute, arrive at the office only to be dragged into a meeting about scheduling a meeting, listen to some jackass go on about last night's game at the water cooler, eat a microwaved lunch, stare at a computer for six hours, listen to our bosses go on about a variety of issues about which they know nothing, do the commute in reverse, get home, and squeeze personal stuff into a two- to three-hour window before we go to bed.

Yep, seems pretty unpleasant. Antipathy is, indeed, warranted. Even the lucky individuals who like their jobs eventually get worn down by the routine. Routine is, by definition, mindless and soul crushing. What to do? Whether you get paid sick days or not, sometimes you just have to feign illness to put the brakes on the monotony and claim a little personal space. Most companies are so focused on output and profit, they leave little room for employees to just be honest and take a day off for mental-health reasons. As a result, the faked sick day was born. It is now a well recognized and thriving institution among employees across our great land.

True, you could try to keep grinding away until you actually get sick, but that seems like a level of self-sacrifice that's just unreasonable. You could also take excellent care of yourself and power through until you can use your vacation days, giving your boss plenty of notice. Get real. There's no way anyone can survive 365 days of straight work with one to two weeks off without any room for personal care. Try if you like, but you'll probably go stark, raving mad before you succeed.

So you're back to calling in sick. Remember that pretending you're sick with some semblance of realism is a skill. If you perform well, your boss and colleagues will probably be more than happy to hold up their end of the bargain and look the other way. They're human too and will need to call in their chips when the time is right. Until then, cheat away and have fun at home, or on the golf course, or wherever it is that you most enjoy being deathly ill.

THE UPSIDE

There's no shortage of benefits to staying home from work. We miss out on so many things we could be doing with our lives because we have to show up in our cubicle and do whatever it is we do to earn money. So we can keep the status quo going. So we can keep our standard of living. So we can keep our jobs. It's a vicious cycle that keeps most people on the hamster wheel until it's time to collect the gold watch and call it a day.

We become so accustomed to spinning away on our hamster wheels at our jobs that sometimes we lose track of what could be done with the eight to ten hours a day we're giving up to The Man. Here's a brief list of some things you could be doing instead of showing up to work that would be major life enhancers: catching up on valuable sleep, attending to appointments and errands (could be anything from visiting beloved relatives to getting those posters framed that have been under the bed for years), learning a new hobby (glass blowing, anyone?), joining a community project, spending time with your kids (you learned *what* on the playground?!?), seeing old friends, and, most notably, going on job interviews. And that's just a start.

The larger implication of taking time off for yourself is that once you remember you're an individual who can call your own shots, you can reclaim your sense of free will. You can start to think more creatively about what you *really* want to be doing with your life, and to quote Martha Stewart, that's a good thing. True, unwarranted sick days constitute lowered productivity and decreased profits for the companies who receive these calls. And it may also be true that only 38 percent of all employee illnesses are legitimate. But that's your boss's problem.

THE DRAWBACK

Anyone who calls in sick too much gets labeled a shirker and a wuss. This holds true from grade school through working adulthood. No one wants to deal with a complainer or someone who claims (despite evidence to the contrary) that they're too frail to perform whatever duties they've agreed to do. If you don't call in sick too much but do it in a really predictable and stupid way, you'll get to be known as a liar. Also an unpleasant title to hold.

On a less personal note, if you call in sick or leave work due to supposed illness too frequently, you'll wind up having used all your sick days. Not a good thing when you really do get the bird flu, and you face the dilemma of going into work and possibly dying at your desk or staying at home and not getting paid. This is clearly an inadvisable situation in which to find yourself.

Finally, and most obviously, if you leave your boss and your colleagues hanging too frequently, they'll resent you. Resentment leads to lack of support and sometimes even sabotage. With or without the sabotage, if you don't do what's required of you on the job, and no one wants to go to bat for you, you'll get fired. The point of this cheat is to keep your job but not have to work yourself into the ground, not give up your job entirely. So unless you win the lottery, keep track of your sick days and don't let too many people in on your slacking ways.

TOOLS OF THE TRADE

This is a very low-budget cheat. No investments need to be made, and the tools required to pull it off probably exist in your own home. Should you find yourself without at least one of the required tools at your disposal, you've got bigger problems than being burnt out at your job. You will need:

1. Phone (landline or cellular are both fine)
2. Computer with internet connection
3. Email account
4. Exhaustion and/or aggravation

WAYS AND MEANS: HOW TO PULL IT OFF

It's always best to call in sick for yourself. If you want to try to execute a more complicated move, you could try to have a spouse or roommate call in for you. The success of the assisted sick call really depends on your coconspirator's acting chops. Make your decision accordingly. There are two basic methods to claiming illness to get out of work, and these are the call-in and the email notification. The best ways to use these two methods to claim your unwarranted day off are as follows:

1. THE CALL-IN—There are differing opinions on the call-in. Some cheaters claim that high drama is most convincing. Others claim that playing it cool and giving very little detail is the way to go. The following is a synopsis of some of the most reliable methods, but keep in mind that convincing someone you're legitimately ill is a kind of mind game. You have to know your audience, and you must play directly into their sympathies, fears, and interests.

Make sure that you know what illness you want to simulate before you make the call. A stomach flu (or food poisoning) sounds very different from a cold or flu. Practice your sick voice and get others' opinions. Have them close their eyes while they listen to make sure they aren't projecting anything onto your performance. One very helpful method used to simulate general malaise is to call in before you speak to anyone, drink anything, or brush your teeth. The likelihood that you'll sound pathetic, gross, and Wookie-ish is very high and will probably be accepted on face value as illness of some variety.

So what illness should you elect to have? Everyone uses the excuse of a stomach problem (or diarrhea) to get out of going to work. Why? Because they're counting on their boss's not wanting to know the details. One mention that you're on the can all day pretty much guarantees that no one's going to ask for the specifics—unless they're deeply into scat, and let's hope you don't find this out while you still work with them. While it's true that most people won't want to talk about your bowel problems, it's such an overused fake-out that it could clue your coworkers in to the fact that you're cheating your way out of work. If you don't care, or your team is particularly gullible, go right ahead. If you're a woman and want to fake your way out of work, gynecological problems are a better way to go. This subject is still potentially gross and very disturbing to others, particularly men, and you probably won't get pumped for details.

When you call in with your unbrushed teeth and raspy voice, make sure you psych yourself into how bad you feel and that you're legitimately sick. It doesn't matter that you aren't really ill. This is method acting at its finest. For the ninety seconds or less that you're on the phone, you must believe that you are on death's doorstep. Focus on how wretched you feel and that even raising your head from the pillow is a nightmare of pain. Call your boss. If you're lucky enough to get voice mail, just leave a *very brief* message that you're sick (do not be specific) and that you hope to be in tomorrow. Do not promise to check email or phone in. Congratulations, you now have one day of vacation. If you get an actual human to pick up the phone, do exactly the same thing. If your boss or colleague has the audacity to ask what's wrong with you, answer with utmost brevity. Whatever you do, don't cave and give details. The details will haunt you the next day when everyone is standing around your desk shooting the breeze, and you have to report on how sick you were and what you did all day. Avoid allowing your lies to multiply.

2. THE EMAIL—This is a great move if you feel you can get away with it. The email notification requires no acting and offers no chance of ac-

cidental elaboration. Just title the email something like "Out of Office Today Due to Illness" and in five lines or less explain that you are ill and will not be at your desk. If necessary, say that you'll check email *if you can* (always give yourself the out) and hit Send. Turn off the computer, end of story. This technique is available only to the very lucky few.

3. A BRIEF PRIMER ON COMMON MISTAKES AND WHAT *NOT* TO DO—It would be impossible to list everything you should or could do to successfully pull off this cheat. The possibilities are endless and really depend on whom you work for, what your relationship is, and your level of value to the company. What can be provided is a basic guide of what you should absolutely *never* do, and allow creative and determined cheaters to go from there. With no further ado, avoid the following mistakes: too many dead relatives, claiming injuries that take more than one day to heal, calling in on a Monday or Friday, calling in on either end of a holiday break, hanging out anywhere near the office, using an excuse that's too unique (examples of this are: sudden elopement, pet repeatedly hit the snooze button, someone slipped you a Mickey the night before, had to check a friend into rehab, and so on), claiming a terminal illness (it'll get old when everyone keeps asking how you feel), having kids who are constantly ill (are you poisoning them?), and, finally, the ultimate bush league mistake, calling in with a hangover.

MOST LIKELY TO SUCCEED

It's best if you have a boss who can acknowledge that you're a human being. Some managers out there are such drones that they actually hassle people when they're legitimately ill, forget faking it. Things also tend to go your way when your colleagues are willing to take up the slack for you. As we all know, we get by with a little help from our friends. Finally, your success rate is highest if you know how to count. Too many sick days add up to a lying employee. Keep track of what you're doing, lie with a shred of authenticity, and you'll get the rest you so badly need and deserve.

CATCHING SICK DAY CHEATS AT THEIR OWN GAME

Detecting who's sick and who isn't is pretty easy. Considering that 62 percent of the sick-day calls made in the U.S. are fake, chances are good that if you receive such a call, it's not on the up-and-up. The real question is whether or not the faker has been taking advantage of your better nature and company policy. The easiest way to determine this is to invest in one of the readily available software programs that can track employee sick days. These programs will keep count for you and track patterns in fakers' sick calls. Once the program sends up the red flag, it's up to you to give the faker the boot or call their bluff.

⇜ *Would I Lie?* ⇝

1

If you're calling in sick to work just because you really need a day off, it's important to not get caught. Don't go out anywhere near your office, even if you live close by. Another important thing to remember is that nowadays everyone has a camera phone, and if you live in a city, there are probably video cameras posted on every other corner. Imagine coming into work the next day and having your boss show you a picture of yourself that someone took with their phone. It's also

(continued)

---

dangerous for you to attend a parade or big sports event on your day off (especially if you're all dressed up for the occasion), because your boss may just end up seeing you on the nightly news!

2

Thanks to the InterActivist Network website, we have the all-time best excuse ever for missing work: "I'm too fat to get into my work pants."

3

If you work in the food service industry, you have a built-in excuse to call in sick when you don't feel like working. It's actually illegal for someone who works in food service to go to work while they have diarrhea. So next time you're sick of waiting tables or working in the kitchen, just tell your boss that you have a terrible case of the runs, and you'll be off the hook!

4

Here are a few of the more harebrained excuses collected by hiring managers, thanks to a report on CareerBuilder.com:

- I couldn't find my shoes.
- A hit man was looking for me.
- I had to ship my grandmother's bones to India.
- My cat unplugged my alarm clock.
- I forgot what day of the week it was.
- Someone slipped drugs in my drink last night.
- I hurt myself bowling.
- My curlers burned my hair, and I had to go to the hairdresser.
- My monkey died.

FAKING SICK
TO AVOID SCHOOL

"MOM! I NEED YOU TO
WRITE ME A NOTE!"

Little Peggy Anne McKay didn't want to go to school today, and frankly neither do most kids. Going to school every single day of the school year is a drag. Routine of any kind is a drag, but having to show up day in, day out to a building that smells like hundreds or even thousands of adolescents is not fun. It's also not fun to have adults tell you what you should or shouldn't be doing every second of every day. Provided that your parents aren't of the rotten variety, it's easier to swallow whatever they have planned for you because you know they have your best interest in mind. Any kid worth his or her salt knows that 90 percent of the faculty at their school is just as focused on getting through the day as they are, and what you're told to do is more for their convenience than yours.

Most school skipping is based on avoidance. It could be that you're avoiding a bully who shakes you down for lunch money or, worse, just takes pleasure in pounding the stuffing out of you. It might be that you're avoiding the indignities of climbing a rope in gym class. You might be avoiding a test that you didn't study for. Whatever it is you're dodging, most kids opt out of going to school when something particularly onerous is looming before them. This is not unreasonable. Sometimes, no matter how much you want to step up and tough it out, you just can't muster the strength. Adults feel exactly the same way about work, so it's amazingly disingenuous when they force their kids to go to school without fail. Even so, that's how it goes.

On the rare occasion, a kid doesn't want to go to school because there's a test or assignment coming up that needs extra preparation, and they have to stay home to do it. If you're this kid or are the parent of this kid, attendance is probably not that big a deal. That work ethic probably has you choosing which Ivy you want to attend, and you're not sweating if the gym teacher is going to be pissed that you missed the presidential physical fitness test day.

Whatever the reason, it is occasionally necessary to get out of school. You can get your parents to call you in sick, pretend you're sick once you get to school, or play hooky and insist you were sick the next day. All of these approaches can work, provided that you know how to feign illness convincingly. How sick you have to pretend to be depends on how lenient your parents are, how gullible the school nurse is, and how many times you've pretended to be sick so far in the school year. Whichever course of action you choose, turn in an award-winning performance and enjoy your day off.

THE UPSIDE

Mental-health days can work wonders. Despite what parents and other assorted adults tell you when you're a kid, childhood can be an incredible bummer. Staying home to regroup and hang out with your stuff, your dog, or just to stare at the wall without the usual hubbub around you is an important thing. Kids are so overscheduled with playdates and after-school activities, taking a day off every now and then should actually be mandatory. If you play hooky, all the better. You can run amok a little and blow off some steam. If you've got a car or live in a city with decent public transportation, the world is your oyster. As long as your parents don't know you're missing (this will result in major heart failure for them and punishment for you), playing hooky is the gold standard of faking illness and skipping school.

There are also definite advantages to feigning illness if you do it once you get to school and then hang out in the nurse's office. Obviously, you'll get to avoid whatever it is you're dodging in the first place. You'll also get to see who else is pretending to be sick and can find out why, as well as have a front row seat to the drama of the legitimately sick kids. This is an excellent place to stock up on gossip and rumor for the next week or so. If you're a cafeteria schmoozer or just need dirt on someone, the nurse's office is a great place to get your information.

THE DRAWBACK

There's a lot of opportunity for negative repercussions because of the total lack of autonomy you have over your life as a kid. The goal of your parents (or guardians) and the school administration is to keep you going to class and getting you through graduation. If you do anything to foul up their plans (not to mention fouling up your own future), they'll come down hard on you.

If cutting out of school is a onetime thing for you, you'll probably just get detention. If it's a habit you just can't break, you're looking at something more serious, possibly suspension or enforced after-school activities. Your parents will go nuts and punish you, but the severity and style of punishment will vary from household to household. Know your audience. Parents who ground for excessive periods of time or do anything truly over the top just shouldn't be provoked.

If you skipped school to avoid a test or some other assignment that you weren't ready for, you may have a major disappointment waiting for you when you get back to school. If your teacher is really on the ball and actually cares about properly educating you, there will be a replacement exam scheduled for your return. Nice try, but no payoff.

TOOLS OF THE TRADE

The tools you need will be used to simulate illness or create it temporarily. Don't go too far and make yourself so sick that you can't enjoy your day off. Be careful not to underplay it, though, or you'll be sent packing. Your flu, stomach virus, or general malaise can be faked using:

1. Lamp
2. Coins
3. Stocked medicine chest
4. Microwave
5. Milk

WAYS AND MEANS: HOW TO PULL IT OFF

Now that you've got your tools lined up, here's the methodology to follow to make the cheat really come together:

1. ACT DEPRESSED—Are your parents on Prozac? Do they worry about your mental health? Have they been scared by a lifetime of after-school specials and Lifetime movies into thinking that all kids are only one step away from peril or a mental breakdown? If so, you can orchestrate getting out of school pretty easily. Mope around the house and act listless. Talk about "not being able to take it anymore." Cry. Then beg for a day off just to collect yourself so you can go back into the jungle that is school. Yes, it's manipulative and a little mean, but you have your needs.

2. HOT LIQUIDS—If you do need to fake actual physical illness to get out of going to school, a fever is easily faked. Depending on how your morning routine goes, you could go to the kitchen and boil some water for this purpose. If that won't work, run the hot water from the tap until it's scalding and put it in a cup under your bed. Moan and cry a little, and then take your temperature to show your mom or dad. If they're controlling or you're young enough, they'll do it for you. Just make sure that right before the thermometer goes in, you've had the chance to hold the hot liquid in your mouth for a while. You may want to practice this so that you don't accidentally get rushed to the hospital with a fever of 107 degrees.

3. WARM COINS IN YOUR MOUTH—Yes, this is gross, but it's another way to get the thermometer to read a feverish temperature. If you've got a backgammon piece, that can work too, and you'll avoid the horrific taste of the coin. Heat it up with hot water or a lamp, but don't burn yourself. A legitimate visit to the emergency room with a blistered

tongue is no fun, and the pain will last for days. You'll also get teased for looking like you've got herpes. You don't want *that* going around the lunchroom.

4. HOT WASHCLOTH IN MICROWAVE— This technique is useful if your mom or dad takes your temperature by feeling your forehead. Take a page from your local Japanese restaurant and heat up a damp washcloth in the microwave. Apply it to your forehead before you start moaning that you're sick. When the thermometer appears on the scene, stick it in the hot washcloth to raise the temperature when no one's looking. Note: Do not let it rise above 102 degrees.

5. VOMIT TECHNIQUE I— If you can't get out of school by having a fever, vomiting is your next option. While a hard-core parent might send a slightly feverish kid to school with a few Tylenol, a vomiting child is a little more pathetic. If your family keeps ipecac (or any other kind of emetic) in the medicine cabinet in case someone poisons themselves, let it work for you. Take a swig and let the barfing begin.

6. VOMIT TECHNIQUE II— You can get the same effect as the emetic by gagging yourself by sticking a finger or some other long object down your throat. If you have a basic fear of choking or gagging, this is not a technique for you. If you do choose this route, it's best to eat a bunch of crackers, bread, or cereal and drink a glass or two of milk first. It creates more realistic vomit, and the milk makes it less acidic.

7. DROWSY-FORMULA BENADRYL OR NYQUIL— Unless you're an accomplished method actor, simulating early symptoms of the flu is easier if you've got a little help. Acting drowsy, listless, unfocused, and generally out of it is much easier if you actually are all those things. Get your hands on a few Benadryl or some NyQuil and take the recommended dose (don't take more; there's no need to poison yourself). Pretty soon you'll look like a real basket case who has no business sitting through class.

MOST LIKELY TO SUCCEED

Most of these techniques require that your parents don't hover over you all the time. You need a little time and space to prepare this subterfuge. If you don't have more relaxed parents, or you live in close quarters, you'll succeed only if you make your preparations before anyone wakes up in the morning.

You'll also have an easier time pulling off this cheat if your parents are already nervous about your well-being and are even a little germ phobic. Having overprotective parents can be a real drag, so make it work for you once in a while.

If you're interested in playing hooky, you stand a chance only if both your parents work, or if you're in a single-parent household and that parent works. Playing hooky is really the domain of the latchkey kid and should not be attempted by anyone whose parents keep tabs on them.

CATCHING JUNIOR SICK DAY CHEATS AT THEIR OWN GAME

Depending on whether you're the parent, the school nurse, or the school administration, there are different ways to catch kids who are trying to get out of going to school. Whatever method you choose, remember that kids get embarrassed easily and will buckle quickly under the strain of humiliation. They also respond poorly to boredom and will change their ways if they're forced to do nothing.

If you're a parent, you can take all the fun stuff out of a kid's room if you think they're prone to faking illness. It's no fun to stay in bed and stare at the wall if you're not sick. Taking away video games, the TV, the phone, or anything else your kid enjoys should flush out the little faker quickly. You can also take the drastic step of talking to your child to see if there's anything going on at school they're trying to avoid. Reports of bullies, tests, or boredom will all point to the reason why your kid wants to stay home. If you're a school nurse, embarrassing the faker with intimate questions or attempts to examine him or her in front of other kids will expose suspected fakers. So will reporting intimate details about the faker in the nurse's office in front of other students.

~ Would I Lie? ~

1

If you are a student with an assignment due at the end of the week and you know that you will have to stay home from school to be able to finish it, you should begin faking symptoms of illness earlier in the week. This way it won't surprise your parents when you wake up one of the next mornings and say you're sick; they'll probably tell you that you should stay home because you haven't looked well all week.

2

One good trick is to apply some makeup to your face the night before you plan on faking sickness so that you will look either pale or flushed when you wake up. It is important not to overdo the makeup, though, or else it will look like makeup, and you'll be caught in a lie.

3

Most parents won't let their kids go to school if they're vomiting, so here's something you can try if nothing else works. If you know how to use a blender, and your parents can't catch you in the act, you can mix up some fake vomit by blending food together with syrup. The best bet is to use some leftovers from dinner the night before, because if you ate carrot soup last night and pretend to throw up creamed spinach, it might raise some flags. The morning you want to stay home from school, pour the fake vomit in the toilet and sit in front of the pot doubled over in pain while hollering for Mommy.

4

If you want to fake a nice general symptom that can help out your cause, clammy hands are a good way to go. While faking a stomach cramp in front of your parents, double over in pain and moan, and then discreetly lick your palms. Your hands will feel clammy, and in combination with that stomach ache you've been complaining about, you should be allowed to stay home. Clammy hands are a symptom of conditions such as mercury poisoning, emotional shock, anxiety, hyperventilation/panic attack, and alcohol withdrawal. If you want to go with one of those, make sure it's mercury poisoning, because alcohol withdrawal probably wouldn't go over too well!

CHEATING ON A DRUG TEST

ONE TOKE OVER THE LINE

Ah, the pleasures of illicit drugs. Despite Nancy Reagan and her brilliant "Just Say No" antidrug campaign, illegal drugs are still a major problem running rampant in America. Even the cuddly and strangely ominous image of Nancy teetering precariously on Mr. T's knees did little to convince our nation's youngsters that making a bong in ceramics class and learning how to use it is a bad idea.

Unfortunately, wacky tobacky has given way to much scarier drugs since the halcyon days of flower children running around the Haight (and Mr. T's days on *The A-Team*). Methamphetamine labs are cropping up around the heartland, and cocaine is back in vogue with yuppies and hipsters alike. The average age of first-time drug use has dropped, and general vigilance among parents, school officials, and employers is on the rise.

If you happen to be one of the many Americans who prefer living in an altered state, not only do you face the personal problems that accompany drug use (forgetting to do your homework, nodding out in meetings, getting incinerated in a meth lab explosion), but you could face some pretty serious administrative problems as well. The primary way to find yourself in this kind of a pickle is via a drug test.

If you've got a shred of a sound mind left, chances are you want to avoid some of the usual results of failing a drug test, such as a stay in the clink, expulsion from school, or getting fired from your job. True, you could stay clean and "just say no" (thanks, Nancy) when someone brings out their goody bag. Then again, there's very little fun in that. So if you want to avoid getting nabbed for tripping the light fantastic, there are a few methods you can use to trick the system and cheat your way out of the drug test. Just be sure that you're making the best choice for you. Remember that the Betty Ford Center is there for a reason.

THE UPSIDE

One of the central characteristics of taking drugs is that it's a secret. No one walks into his or her office waving a coke vial and spoon (or pen cap or set of keys) in the air shouting, "Look at me, people! I'm doing drugs and I love it! Woo-hoo!" True, if you were working at *Rolling Stone* in the seventies, popular lore dictates that indeed you might have, but these days it's not such a good move. A lot of people mistake the secrecy of drug taking as a kind of shame from which anyone would be relieved to be delivered. This is a wrong assumption. Until you're a full-blown addict, shame has nothing to do with it. The secrecy attached to drug use gives it a clubby feel, a sort of "cool kids against the stiffs" vibe. It is precisely that feeling that anyone who knows what "E-Z Wider," "Zig-Zag," "K-hole" (not to be confused with K-Fed, although it's similar), and "rolling on E" means is not willing to sacrifice by letting nonusers in on what they're doing. No one wants to kill the buzz with a lot of nay-saying. No test, no proof, no buzz kill. Sweet.

So, in brief, the major upside of not taking a drug test is simply that you're not busting up the party. If you don't take the test, no one will know that you've been waking and baking before class every day. Nor will they know that your lengthy stays in the lavatory at work have less to do with irritable bowel syndrome and more to do with "I have to put more cocaine in my nose" syndrome.

Another advantage of cheating on a drug test is avoiding worrying your loved ones. Thanks to the unrelenting antidrug campaigns on television, scare-tactic programming on every TV and radio show imaginable, and community outreach/alarmism, anyone who's remotely sentient is aware of the potential evils of drugs. If you know you've got it under control, why worry anyone? The less they know, the less anxious they have to be, and the less you have to hear about it.

Finally, refusing a drug test will serve you well if you want to stay on your sports team, in your school, or on the job. True, your ability to keep the wolves at bay may not last forever. Even so, if you can hold them off just long enough to get the drugs out of your system, you can eventually take the test, prove you're clean, and pick your habits back up where you left them. No harm, no foul, right?

THE DRAWBACK

The only thing worse than getting caught doing drugs is getting caught cheating on a drug test. Let us not forget the many Olympians whose human frailties would have been forgivable had they not lied to their country (and the judges and their fellow sportsmen). As much as we love our winners, we seem to love vilifying our losers (and cheaters) just as much.

Cheating on a drug test essentially reveals the cheater as having delivered a double whammy of lying. Not only is the cheater telling the falsehood that he or she didn't take drugs, but when it's revealed that he or she did, that person will then be known as a drug taker. For better or worse, drugs carry a social stigma that is (in a word) bad. If you're a recreational drug user, you'll be seen as a decadent wastrel who doesn't have full control over his or her appetites. If you're a school athlete who's taken drugs to enhance performance, you're seen as someone who couldn't excel in the sport without help or didn't have the confidence to do so. None of this adds up to an appealing profile.

If you get caught cheating, the results are always pretty severe. You'll get removed from your team or your job and get branded as a bit of a loser, at least for a while. Employers are particularly concerned about drug use by their employees, as safety becomes a legitimate concern when you've got someone who's supposed to be operating a forklift who's stoned and has the reflexes of a marmoset. Those drug-related accidents can cause an increase in workman's comp claims, higher insurance premiums, and cost of employee replacement. Definitely not a situation to shoot for if you're on the legal side of the spliff debate.

Another seriously un-fun part of getting caught smoking, sniffing, or shooting up is the possibility that you'll end up in a drug rehab program, whether you really belong in one or not. There's little tolerance for recreational drugs in the U.S. these days, so if you're going to imbibe, get ready for the shunning and reprimands that may come with getting caught. If this doesn't appeal to you, you can always just book a flight to Amsterdam to get it out of (and into) your system.

Drug testing has become an incredibly prevalent practice in schools and workplaces, and frequently leaves students and employees feeling like their privacy has been invaded. There are those intrepid souls who flat-out refuse to take drug tests, but they could very easily find themselves off their school team or out of a job. In the event that a drug test being administered by the police is refused (yes, roadside alcohol level testing is considered a drug test), the refusenik could even find him- or herself in a nice, cozy holding tank.

TOOLS OF THE TRADE

Now that you've made a serious commitment to your existence on an alternate plane, your choice will have to remain undetected for the reasons stated above. How to do this? Certainly you can do your damnedest to hide what you're doing in the first place. Don't leave paraphernalia around, don't go to class or work and try to do anything terribly complex while you're stoned, and don't make promises to be responsible for anything at all. You'll definitely fail and tip your hand. As an extra precaution, you may want to watch *Permanent Midnight* a few times as a training video for what not to do.

Once the inevitable happens, and you're faced with a drug test, your tactics will have to change. Make sure you have the following:

1. Time
2. Gym equipment
3. Water
4. Credit card

WAYS AND MEANS: HOW TO PULL IT OFF

The most common types of blood test are chemical analyses of five substances: saliva, breath, blood, hair, and urine. Urine is by far the favorite for standard drug testing, while breath tests are the number-one choice for pissed-off cops who can't believe anyone would get on the road with a blood-alcohol level of 0.2.

Urine tests work to find traces of drugs, called metabolites, that can last in your body long after the buzz has died. The trick to successfully cheating your way out of a drug test is to make sure that these metabolites aren't lurking around in some back alley of your bloodstream or to mask their presence. Thankfully, there are a few ways to address this problem.

1. IT'S GOT SCRUBBING BUBBLES!—Amazingly, there is a booming industry in at-home kits that will clean all traces of drugs out of your system. While no formal studies have been done to verify their efficacy, these kits have an avid following and can be found within a click or two online. Professing to rid your system (at least temporarily) of drug traces and effectively tricking urine, blood, hair, saliva, and breath tests, if these really do work, they're God's gift to users. If they don't work, they're God's gift to motivated entrepreneurs. The terrifying thought that goes along with these kits, however, is what your innards look like when the test is through with you. Non-FDA-approved "personal cleansing tablets" sound scary, but then again, if you don't have a problem with speedballing, this is probably the least of your worries.

2. IT'S IN THE BAG—If cleansers that can scour your system in minutes flat leave you a bit worried, this may be the answer for you. For a decent price, you can buy (usually online) what is essentially a colostomy bag. This catheterized plastic bag gets filled up before you scamper off to a scheduled drug test so that you can deliver the urine of your

choice and get off scot-free. Note: *The urine of your choice in this scenario should be that of a non-drug-taking person.* As that may be hard to find in this day and age, your willing participant may have to be a niece or nephew who is easily bribed and knows the value of silence. Be forewarned: If anyone finds out, you're in a world of trouble. No one likes to have his or her kids involved in narcotics-related subterfuge.

3. TIME IS ON YOUR SIDE—Try to stall. If you can wait long enough, the offending substance will work its way out of your system naturally, and you'll get a clean result. Booze takes up to 48 hours to take a hike, while a single joint can take up to five days. Amphetamines take approximately 96 hours, while cocaine takes about two days. PCP can take 120 hours, but if you're on angel dust, you're likely gibbering in a corner somewhere, and a drug test probably isn't on your agenda anyway.

4. SPLISH SPLASH, I WAS TAKING A BATH (AND DECIDED TO DRINK THE CONTENTS OF THE BATHTUB)—You cannot flush drugs out of your system with water. Period, end of story. What you can do, however, is dilute your urine so severely that you could get your results rejected. This is excellent, and it works hand in hand with the stalling tactic. Do this at your own peril, as water overdose can lead to death. As can overdoses from amphetamines, coke, and a lot of other stuff you're probably playing around with. Just be careful. Plus, you will have to show up again for a redo.

5. POPPY SEEDS AREN'T JUST FOR BREAKFAST ANYMORE— True, you'd need to eat a ridiculous amount of poppy seeds to have a false positive for opiates, no matter what popular sitcoms would have you believe. Nonetheless, if you're willing to scarf down enough of the little buggers, you could get a questionable result that would require a

retest. This works in tandem with the water and stalling methods and is not an assured method, but at least it won't kill you. A recommended alternative to poppy seed bagels (not enough seed delivery per bagel) is the delightful hamantaschen. Purim pastry treat to some, drug test skulduggery to you, yummy goodness all the time.

6. WORKING OUT—Finally, you could give working out a try. Speeding up your metabolism could cause you to process the metabolites out of your body faster. This method could provide a clean result in half the time you would have spent just waiting it out. Then again, you're a drug user who's being asked to go to the gym. Never mind. If you're a speed freak, you might have a heart attack on the elliptical trainer. Bad idea.

MOST LIKELY TO SUCCEED
You'll succeed at this if you're not too stoned to follow instructions and if you're great at double-talk. If you get a positive result, be prepared to loudly contest it and demand a retest. This is a common tactic, but if you can carry it off with aplomb, you're likely to be home free. Believing your own bullshit doesn't hurt either.

CATCHING DRUG-TEST CHEATERS AT THEIR OWN GAME
Dilated pupils? Missing from class or work often? Looks checked out or, conversely, weirdly amped up? Guess what? These people are indeed on drugs! If you're beginning to feel like the teacher Mr. Hand from *Fast Times at Ridgemont High,* and you're lamenting that everyone around you is on dope, just start testing. When you get a weird result, don't wait to retest. Do it on the spot and keep retesting that person for a proscribed period of time that they're not aware of. If you've got a kid who you think is on dope, raid their room.

Come on, no one has privacy until they go away to college. Isn't that why people *go* to college? If it's an employee, offer the choice of getting fired or rehab. Your suspected resident Cheech (or Chong) will fess up soon enough.

❧ *Would I Lie?* ❧

1

Most specimen-collection facilities put the person being tested in a "dry room" and have them put on a hospital gown so that they cannot hide additives or synthetic urine in their pockets. Once taken, the sample is sent to a screening lab where it is tested initially and then confirmed if the first test is positive. An initial test must detect at least 50 ng/ml (nanograms per milliliter) of a drug in order to be considered positive. The positive sample is then retested, and to be confirmed as positive, the levels must be at least 15 ng/ml.

2

One method for cheating on a drug test is basically foolproof, but it can be painful and difficult to pull off. The person taking the test must obtain clean urine from someone they trust, preferably of the same gender and age group. They must then completely empty their bladder as close to the time of taking the test as possible. The key step is to then insert a catheter into their bladder. For men, this is more painful than it is for women, because it requires pushing the tube from the tip of the penis all the way through the urethra to the bladder. At this point, they inject the clean urine into the bladder through the catheter, so that the next time they urinate, it will be the clean urine that comes out.

.... 3 ....

One felon on probation knew that he was going to fail his upcoming drug test, so he taped a balloon to his leg that was filled with his eleven-year-old neighbor's urine. He wasn't counting on the test being supervised, so of course he failed. Another man tested positive for pregnancy—he had used his wife's urine instead of his own. There was one man who worked at a dairy barn who actually thought he could get away with submitting a cow's urine sample as his own. Another method that criminals have tried to fool their parole officers with is drinking vinegar, which induces nausea but doesn't really cleanse the system. The only truly foolproof method is to stop using!

SLEEPING YOUR WAY TO THE TOP

HOW TO SUCCEED IN BUSINESS WITHOUT REALLY TRYING

Everyone wants to find a way to climb the corporate ladder faster and more easily than those around them. You might do it by having a special skill that's invaluable to your company. It could be that you're the boss's kid, and the whole thing is going to get handed to you on your mom's or dad's retirement. You could even land an account or develop a product early in your career that is so revolutionary that you have to be handsomely rewarded in order to keep you at the firm.

If you don't have any of those options open to you, you can always take the cheater's shortcut and sleep your way to the top. No matter what your industry, no matter what job you're trying to land, if you have a boss, you can try to manipulate him or her into promoting you by creating a sexual relationship. If your boss wants to keep the relationship going, he or she will probably do whatever's necessary to do so. That could mean giving you gifts, showering you with attention, or giving you the opportunities and promotions you're angling for on the job. They'll also probably do quite a bit to keep the affair quiet.

The pitfall for a lot of people who try to go this route is that they actually wind up having serious feelings for the supervisor they choose to hook up with. To really manipulate someone effectively, you have to keep your emotions at bay. Falling in love with your target isn't going to make the situation any easier and may in fact short-circuit your plan. If you think you don't have the necessary ruthless demeanor for this cheat, watch out. You could wind up in a fruitless affair without any professional advancement. If you do think you've got the chops, but your boss doesn't want a relationship and only indulged in one-night-only after-hours fun with you, don't despair. You might still be able to get what you want. It will, however, most likely be through bribery or threats of sexual harassment. That's distinctly different from sleeping your way to the top. But you go ahead and work that angle if you dare.

THE UPSIDE

The obvious upside of this cheat is that you might be able to achieve the holy grail of the work world: work less, achieve more. If you can swing this cheat properly, you'll rocket forward in your career in record time without breaking a sweat. You'll get a better title (or titles), more money, more perks, and you won't even have to work to get all the experience and training someone might normally need for the job that's being handed to you.

If you work for a small company, you could find yourself engaging in this cheat without even having to hide it. Most small companies no longer have rules against employee or employee-supervisor fraternization. This leaves the door wide open for you to cozy up to the person who calls the shots. Conversely, it could leave the door open for a company owner to cozy up to you.

You could actually find the man or woman of your dreams this way. Since you both work in the same industry, there's a good chance you have at least a few things in common. What starts out as a ploy might provide you with a great change in your life, and you could become a legendary story of hope for employees everywhere. Not only could your mood lift as a result of your good fortune, but studies say that office romance can improve workplace morale and performance. Your good mood could create a happier workplace for everybody. Hooray for love (or at least sex)!

THE DRAWBACK

As great as the upsides are to this cheat, the drawbacks are pretty foul. As they're all rather serious and could make your work life hell, consider them seriously before you embark on your love campaign.

The first big upset could occur if your office paramour gives you a job for which you're totally unqualified. It's one thing to angle for a job you know you can do but you can't seem to catch a break. It's another if you're in way over your head. All your scheming could land you in a worse position than where you started. No use sleeping your way to the top just to get fired because you can't deliver.

You could also make your big play for the boss and get rebuffed. If your boss isn't into a little after-hours slap and tickle under his or her desk, you could not only get the brush-off but also a reprimand from HR. A disinterested supervisor will want to keep his or her ass covered and give you a wide berth. Not good for future advancement. If you're really aggressive, your boss can even make a sexual harassment claim against you. Also not good for your career.

If your coworkers find out about your dalliance with your supervisor, they can sue you. They can nab you for creating a hostile work environment. If they can prove that any nookie has been going on and that you're receiving special treatment, they'll likely win the suit.

TOOLS OF THE TRADE

The usual tools of seduction will suffice for this cheat. Slap on a little perfume or cologne and use your best flirting techniques. Work in a few special little favors for your boss, like getting him or her coffee when you get yourself some. Essentially, do what you normally do to reel someone in, just do it carefully so that your colleagues don't know what you're up to. Your tools, therefore, are simple. You'll need:

1. You
2. Gifts
3. Notes (email and IM will work)

WAYS AND MEANS: HOW TO PULL IT OFF

Now that you're feeling like you're ready to go out on the prowl, here are the best steps for successfully pulling off this cheat. Remember that you're engaging in a very delicate maneuver. You don't want to tip your hand to anyone but the person you're seducing. And you can't scare him or her off. Tread lightly and follow this methodology:

1. **CHOOSE WISELY**—First determine if your target can actually help you. Find out if he or she is going to get terminated soon, or if they are deeply ensconced in the company. Is your possible lover a player or a dud?

2. **REPEAT PERFORMANCE**—Has your boss done this before? If you're looking for a love interest, it's not great if he or she has. If you're looking only for a step-up, it's great if this is not the first time for your boss. You're working right in the comfort zone. Excellent!

3. **SELLING POINT**—If your company has a ban on supervisor-subordinate relationships, make it work for you. Everything that's illicit is more fun!

4. **MAY/DECEMBER AFFAIR**—If your boss is significantly older than you, you may have an easier time with this cheat. Like everyone else, older people need to have their egos stroked, but it happens much more rarely for them. Make your silver fox feel sexy and special. This is called the "you still got it" move.

5. **KEEP IT QUIET**—Enough said.

6. **SINGLE OR MARRIED?**—If you work in an office that frowns on fraternization, don't add fuel to the fire by choosing a married person as your workplace sugar daddy/mama. You'll only add fuel to the fire for colleague censure.

7. ROAD TRIP—You can bond with your boss if you find a way to give him or her a lift to work, or cadge an offer for a lift yourself. You'll also have ample time to make nice if you can travel for work together. Orchestrate getting assignments for overnight trips that your boss is going on too. Spend time at the hotel bar getting to know each other.

8. TOE THE LINE—Don't forget that your boss is your work supervisor, not just a target for your cheat. One of the best ways to get our boss's attention is to do a great job. Show that you are of value to the company, and therefore of value to him or her. Exhibit enthusiasm for what you do and a good attitude about doing it.

9. NEATNESS COUNTS—Most supervisors have little things that matter to them that will make all the difference when you're sucking up. Could be that you need to be fashionably dressed, or that you never eat at your desk. Whatever it is, do it. You'll have an easier time making nice.

10. BE ON TIME—Making your boss look good is part of your job. Making your boss look good will make him or her feel good. Which will, in turn, make you feel good. Just figure out when your boss arrives in the morning and get there fifteen minutes earlier.

11. IT'S NOT ABOUT YOU—Don't lose sight of the fact that your suck-up strategy (which will, of course, lead to your amorous liaison) is not about making you feel supported and loved. That's what you're giving your boss. All you're getting is the raise, promotion, perks, or whatever else you're angling for. It's not your boss's job to flatter you or shower you with gifts. That's your job.

MOST LIKELY TO SUCCEED

It takes a particular type of person to be able to pull off this cheat successfully. You have to be comfortable enough with your own appeal that you don't feel like a total dork trying to seduce your supervisor. You also have to be ruthless as you climb over colleagues who might be more qualified for the job you're jockeying to get. Another major characteristic that a successful cheater will have is the ability to enter into a romantic liaison without getting emotionally involved. While it's more common for women to try this maneuver, men have the market cornered on that quality. This isn't about love, it's about advancement. Frequently, that nuance is forgotten. It shouldn't be. Other qualities that will help you out are unbridled brazenness and a total disregard for office gossip. It's hard to stay under the radar when you're courting someone in such close quarters. Even if they don't know for sure, your colleagues will have an inkling about what's going on. They'll gossip, and you can't feel bad about it.

You'll also do well if you aren't in a relationship you care about. You have to be pretty cold to sleep your way to the top while carrying on a normal relationship. This isn't unheard of, but it's usually love (or a misguided sense of love) that prompts people to jeopardize an existing relationship. If you are a heartless bastard, give it a try.

CATCHING WORKPLACE SEDUCERS AT THEIR OWN GAME

Figuring out who in your office has got a little supervisor-employee hanky-panky going on is not that hard. People aren't that subtle, no matter how cagey they think they are. Here are the telltale signs that someone is getting a promotion thanks to their extracurricular activities:

- They're making way too much electric eye contact with their boss in meetings;

- the suspect and his or her supervisor work late behind closed doors more than is necessary;
- the two supposed lovebirds are spotted out on the town together;
- the employee is receiving inexplicably high-profile assignments;
- and the coup de grâce, the promotion that should have been anyone else's goes to the boss's pet.

Once you know what's going on, the question about what is to be done remains. You can tattle to HR, or you can keep quiet. If you keep quiet, you could use the information to your advantage. And that's a cheat in its own right.

❧ *Would I Lie?* ❧

In 2005 actress Karrine Steffans published a tell-all book about sleeping her way to the top, called *Confessions of a Video Vixen*. Steffans has been in countless rap videos and earned herself the nickname "Superhead" in the hip-hop world. Her book describes all of the famous men in music and sports she slept with in order to fuel her career. It was only when she almost died of a drug overdose at a trendy L.A. restaurant that she decided to clean herself up and stop her groupie ways.

(continued)

Dorothea Lieven (1785–1857) was a Baltic Russian who was raised in Catherine the Great's court. She had a great deal of interest in politics and power, and in 1800 she married Prince Khristofor Andreyevich Lieven, who would later become the Russian ambassador to Britain. The prince and princess moved to England in 1812, and she carried on affairs with many European politicos in the 1800s. Among her lovers were the Austrian chancellor Prince Metternich, King George IV, and at least half a dozen prime ministers. With each change of leadership in Britain, Lieven changed lovers, thus always making sure to hold a high enough position to have some political influence in Britain.

3

Grace Dalrymple was born in 1758 in Edinburgh, Scotland. By age fifteen, she was considered beautiful and sophisticated, and soon met and married Sir John Elliott, a Scottish doctor who was twenty years her senior. She had affairs with other men and ran off with Lord Valentia in 1774. Elliott divorced her, and Grace found herself sent to a convent in France. She wasn't there for long, however, because another one of her lovers, Lord Cholmondley, brought her back to England. He introduced her to the Prince of Wales (who would become George IV), and they began a relationship that resulted in the birth of a daughter in 1782. She later moved to France to live with another lover, the Duke of Orleans. Dalrymple continued her dalliances until her death in 1823. For fifty years, she enjoyed the life of a princess by having affairs with rich, powerful men.

GETTING AWAY WITH TAX FRAUD—PERSONAL

HOW MANY DEDUCTIONS CAN I TAKE?

The incomparable Judge Learned Hand once said, "There is nothing sinister in so arranging one's affairs as to keep taxes as low as possible. Everybody does so, rich and poor; and all do right, for nobody owes any public duty to pay more than the law demands."

Hand was not alone in his sentiments. In fact, those words reflect the way that almost every American approaches paying taxes. There are, however, a few who go beyond Hand's philosophy and explore a more thorough way of keeping the tax man's hand out of their pockets.

Taxes are a necessary evil. While the government takes an inordinate amount of our dollars earned away from us, it does use the money to fund public-interest programs and build the country's infrastructure. Well, theoretically that happens. That money also goes to fight wars that not everyone is necessarily on board with, or gets earmarked for pet projects that are surprisingly close in nature to figuring out how many licks it takes to get to the center of a Tootsie Pop.

If our tax dollars were used in ways that were less misguided or bizarre, perhaps people would be more inclined to part with 33 percent of their income. As it stands, they're not. They're far more inclined to pay the 17 percent or so that big corporations do, but that's a little hard to do as an individual. Instead the individual taxpayer finds little ways to creatively hold back their earnings as best they can.

This is a good time to make the distinction between tax avoidance and tax evasion. What we are really talking about when we say that our accountant did a good job for us is that we avoided paying too much tax. In other words, we legally used the tax regime to find ways to pay as little as possible. On the other hand, tax evasion is the practice of not paying your full taxes owed by illegal means. That translates to: The tax code did not anticipate the actions you took to evade paying your 33 percent.

We'll review some methods both legal and illegal on our journey to cheating our way out of paying taxes. Just remember, everyone has to report their earnings in one way or another. Surprisingly, the government even expects the criminal element to file their tax returns.

Just like the rest of us, gamblers and other nefarious types have to report earnings, whether they're legal or not. Can you imagine working at the IRS and getting *that* return? What is the real likelihood of someone declaring $4 million of earnings from the sale of several pounds of sticky Panama Red, or a little Panamanian Boom-Boom Powder? Let's say . . . *slim*. Divulging that kind of information is tantamount to walking directly to the federal pen and locking yourself in. Not going to happen. So how should this tax situation be dealt with? You could get rid of 33 percent of your income, or you can find the loopholes and run with them. If you decide to go for the full-on evasion route, please don't waltz into H&R Block with all your receipts and a plan that will require it to report you to the IRS. Know your audience.

THE UPSIDE

If you're a true patriot and wouldn't dream of doing anything to disrupt the message of our founding fathers, this is absolutely the cheat for you! Don't forget your grade school history lessons at a time like this. Remember the Boston Tea Party? Remember those brave guys who dressed up like Native Americans and threw tea over the side of the boat it was stored on? That, my friends, was a protest against unfair taxation. In that case, it was taxation without representation. Whatever your particular beef is with the tax code, you can exercise your right to protest it by (figuratively) dumping your tea into Boston Harbor. Cheating on your taxes as a form of protest is your legacy as an American. The upside to this cheat is that you're exercising and exhibiting behavior that could happen only in America.

Probably in no small part due to acts of rebellion like the Boston Tea Party, political resistance is part of our cultural landscape. It's also seen as being totally acceptable if what's being resisted is paying taxes. Unlike a lot of other illegal activities you might indulge in but not want to talk about at a cocktail party ("Hey, did you see that prostitute I picked up over on Beacon? Not a looker, but, boy, *howdy*!"), there's no problem chatting about getting out of paying taxes. In fact, you'll be applauded. A lack of public censure is a real upside.

Finally, and most importantly, you're not likely to get audited. There simply isn't enough manpower at the Internal Revenue Service available to address every questionable return. All that the beleaguered IRS employees can do is to look for major cheats. Drug dealers and other people who obviously get paid tons of money off the record are real targets. The IRS guys want to look for a modern-day Al Capone, not a pharmacist who saved an extra five grand. So unless you get crazy greedy, you'll probably fly under the radar.

THE DRAWBACK

If you do get caught, the IRS will have a field day with you, so be prepared. Get your lawyer and accountant ready to enter the fray with you. No matter what, don't go it alone. That's a surefire way to go down. You'll pay everything you owe and then some. While you're sitting in the hot seat, here are a few fates you might consider:

1. The feds could hit you with fines for having tried to defraud the government, not to mention interest for every day the taxes were not paid properly and on time. You've now possibly doubled what you owed. If that isn't bad enough, you could have a forfeiture carried out against you. In other words, the feds will come and take your stuff. That's a bad feeling. If you want to know how that whole scenario goes, Martin Scorsese gives you a little snapshot in a few of his films. Still haven't had enough punishment? How about having your wages garnished? In this delight-

ful scenario, your employer is directed to give a portion of your earnings to the IRS directly. You don't ever see that money. Creepy, right?

2. If you feel like you just need to get away from it all, you can always opt for a stay behind the walls of your cheerful neighborhood penitentiary. Yes, that's right, if you owe a large enough amount, and you can't pay it back, you could go to the pokey. You might go there anyway if the manner in which you withheld your tax dollars was egregious enough. Interestingly, one of the ways that people most commonly find themselves experiencing this particular drawback is when a disgruntled spouse turns them in. You heard it here, people. Be nice to your husband or wife— you have no idea what they're up to.

TOOLS OF THE TRADE

Unless you're a brilliant financial planner or accountant, you'll need help to do this cheat. Clearly, that means that your accountant will need to be in cahoots with you. If you can't get that to happen, you can always ask an accountant how to prepare your tax return the way you want to and then do it yourself. Now you've got the info, and the honest accountant isn't roped into doing anything shady. Here's what you need to cheat your way out of paying your taxes:

1. A good accountant, preferably one who will get involved in preparing your forms for you. A creative accountant is one in a million.
2. Discretion. Don't tell the neighbors! They'll turn you in if you piss them off by doing something like encroach on their property.
3. False social security number (fake second identity).
4. Two sets of financial records.

WAYS AND MEANS: HOW TO PULL IT OFF

Now that you know the principles behind successfully cheating on your taxes, and you've got your tools at the ready, here are a few well chosen methods to help you pull it off:

1. DECLARE LESS INCOME—This method is truly the domain of employees paid in cash. Waiters and waitresses are famous for this, as are illegal immigrants and criminals. No need to declare your tips, folks. Also, no need to declare the million dollars you score selling combat rifles.

2. OVERSTATE DEDUCTIONS—It's time to show your charitable side. Make the biggest donations you can to the Salvation Army or similar organizations. Whatever you give them, overestimate the value. Of course those old boots are worth three hundred dollars!

3. DON'T BE A KNOW-IT-ALL—If you think you found a tax loophole on your own (and you're not an accountant), you didn't. Don't think that you can suddenly find your true calling as a shady accountant. If you're going to cook your books, get someone who knows what he or she is doing.

4. ALTER EGO—Ever feel like being someone else? Now's the time! How about declaring no income, living off the grid, and making all kinds of money as your alter ego? Then kill off your doppelgänger and move to the Maldives! Sweet scam!

5. TAX SHELTER—If you can't commit to reinventing yourself completely and living anonymously in some other country, let your money do it for you. You can let your cash live the high life by sending it to live in an offshore account. You can also establish offshore credit, debit, and

charge accounts to dump income into and keep it free from the grubby hands of the IRS.

6. OFFSHORE RESIDENCE—Ever wanted to live somewhere else a few months a year? Well, you should. That way you can keep the IRS out of your life. By not being a full-time U.S. resident, you don't have to pay full-time U.S. resident taxes.

7. FAKE DEPENDENTS—It helps to be able to declare dependents on your tax return. A few kids really takes the edge off what you've got to pay. But why stop there? Why not declare a few relatives you may or may not have? What about Fluffy and Rex? They'll feel so left out. Just make sure you don't go too crazy and claim you live in a studio apartment with fifty other people.

8. MY BUSINESS IS MY LIFE—Create a shell business and attribute everything you normally do or spend in your private life as being done for the business. Dinners with friends become client events, home repair becomes building an office, your phone bill is a business expense— you get the picture.

MOST LIKELY TO SUCCEED

No one wants to pay taxes, but a few of us are really set up to succeed at squirming out of it. If you don't feel any shame or concern about not doing what the government tells you to (baby-boomer hippies are particularly good about this), or you're self-employed, you'll do well.

You'll also do well if you're illegally employed, since you're getting paid under the table anyway. Creative types who love to spin a good yarn do well, as do those who make enough money to set up offshore identities. Basically, if you work a nine-to-five job, it's a little difficult for you. For everyone else, all that's required is imagination and a total disregard for paying for our "infrastructure."

CATCHING TAX CHEATS AT THEIR OWN GAME

The IRS is very skilled at catching tax cheaters. The problem for them is that they simply don't have the manpower to catch every little cheater on the block. They have to focus on cheaters who don't pay large amounts, as well as repeat offenders. Even so, they could come looking for you. Here's what they look for to nab you:

The IRS looks for "badges of fraud." These are common types of tax fraud, and can be everything from doctored checks to manufactured receipts. They'll also look for underreported income. Don't forget that the IRS gets your W-2 and 1099 forms. They know how much you officially made. Anyone who tries to say otherwise is instantly known to be a cheater. Finally, if you've got a big, luxurious lifestyle, but you claim you make minimum wage, you're a tax cheater. You're also probably a gangster, but that's for the guys over at the Bureau of Alcohol, Tobacco, and Firearms to deal with.

∾ *Would I Lie?* ∾

··· **1** ···

In 1990 country star Willie Nelson owed the IRS $16 million in taxes that he couldn't pay, so he got creative. The IRS sold his ranch and held an auction for his belongings, and many of his fans bought his things and gave them back to him. To raise the rest of the money, he offered the IRS a deal to give them royalties from his next album, which they ac-

---

cepted. *Who'll Buy My Memories? The IRS Tapes* was released in 1992, and the IRS earned $3.6 million from its sales. Nelson also agreed to pay $9 million over the next five years, and the IRS was happy.

.... 2 ....

Dr. Martin Luther King Jr. was charged with tax evasion in February 1960 after moving his Montgomery, Alabama, church to Atlanta, Georgia. The governor of Alabama, John Patterson, tried to thwart Dr. King's civil rights activism by claiming that he had allegedly taken money raised by the church as his own income without reporting it on his tax return. In May presidential candidate John F. Kennedy supported King to help him to be acquitted of all charges.

.... 3 ....

One of the most legendary gangsters of all time, Al Capone, was arrested numerous times but always managed to evade jail. Just when it started to look like the U.S. government would never be able to keep him in prison, they mounted an investigation into his accounts and found that he had committed tax evasion. Capone pled guilty to tax evasion charges in 1931 and was sentenced to eleven years in a federal penitentiary, along with having to pay the government $7,692 for court costs and $215,000 plus interest for all of the back taxes he had never paid. Out of all of the crimes that Al Capone committed in his lifetime, it was the U.S. Treasury Department that finally put him away.

(continued)

4

Billionaire hotelier and real-estate magnate Leona Helmsley earned the moniker the "Queen of Mean" in the eighties by being condescending and awful to everyone she came in contact with. It was no tragedy, then, when she was convicted of tax evasion in 1989 and sentenced to two years in prison in 1990. She was also fined $7 million to be paid back to the federal government, which must have pained her greatly considering the fact that she has been quoted as saying that "only the little people pay taxes."

GETTING AWAY WITH PLAGIARISM

RECYCLED WRITING

Plagiarism has been a hot issue in the media world for the last couple of years, even showing up as the subject of movies and in major networks' TV lineups. But what is it, and how can you use it to better your own circumstances?

At its core, plagiarism is a cheat. It's not a method of writing or researching that can be bastardized into a tool for cheaters. Plagiarism is the act of taking other writers' work and re-creating it word for word in your own work, claiming it as your own. Footnotes and credit are not given to the original writer, and the plagiarist's goal is to appear to have had an original thought or done original research without the help of others.

Plagiarism is particularly common in a few venues: the worlds of academia, journalism, and book publishing. These are all areas in which it is necessary to produce original thought, be it for a grade or a publishing contract. The pressure to produce is enormous, and sometimes it just seems impossible to add anything new to the canon or to have the time to do research, internalize it, and then regurgitate it with your own unique spin. When time, intellect, or inspiration is not on your side, plagiarism can seem like the only answer. And sometimes it is! The trick, of course, is not getting caught.

In the old days, turning in a term paper at school was unbelievably arduous. You'd have to find a ton of resources at the library, photocopy or handwrite your desired quotes, write down all the material about the source you used, and then write it all over again in your paper. By the time you did all that work, it was more than likely that you'd actually learned something about your topic and could provide the necessary unique regurgitation. Nowadays, that's not the case. Thanks to the internet, myriad browsers, and no end of decently researched sites, finding source material can take a fraction of the time it used to. Not only that, but the magic of cut and paste can put all the material you need into a fresh new document at the click of a button. So with a few hours and a few mouse clicks, you can have a fully completed term paper. One problem remains: The entire paper has been plagiarized.

Don't fret. It can be avoided. But before you read ahead to find out how, a few more interesting tidbits about scamming someone else's intellectual property.

The question comes up, why would you want to avoid being caught for plagiarism? The answer is simple. Creative output, particularly when it's original, is a kind of currency. Ideas have power, and people who are original thinkers identify themselves with the power of their own words. Doors can be opened in innumerable ways by original thought, and the creator of that thought reaps the benefits of having influenced the people around them. Original thinkers who write are also protective of the people who came before them, their mentors and influences. So if you're ripping off someone's words and ideas and not acknowledging where they came from, you've stolen someone else's currency. Not cool. It *is* cool, however, if no one knows.

Students are notorious plagiarists. Estimates of how many students plagiarize on any given written assignment and get caught run at approximately 17 percent. That's pretty high. Of course, these kids claim that they had no intention of plagiarizing; they did it unintentionally by forgetting to include quotes or to use the accepted formats for footnoting. Whatever the case may be, if you're going to steal, don't be one of the 17 percent.

Even weirder and lamer is the act of self-plagiarism. This is so pathetic, it barely merits discussion. Self-plagiarism happens when you rip off yourself and reuse formerly written material in a new work. By doing this, you violate the copyright of your original material. Duh!

Journalists, in their frenzy to hit deadlines, are constantly in the hot seat for plagiarism. Plagiarism violates journalistic ethics (see above for all the reasons it's considered bad to use someone else's original "currency") and can result in some seriously embarrassing moments. Journalists have no problem sending their brethren to the lions for this one. You'll know that a journalist plagiarized, because all the other journos will be so freaked out that their stuff is next to get ripped off (or that they'll be the next one caught) that they love to make an example of their peers. So much for solidarity.

THE UPSIDE

The primary upside of plagiarism is, essentially, the reason you'd want to do it in the first place. Plagiarism allows you to create the written work that's expected of you with very little effort. You can look smart and cool, or even get paid for your work, and not have to really lift a finger. So the upside is, less work equals more accolades.

The ease with which anything can be plagiarized is another terrific upside to plagiary. All you need to create a reasonable term paper or article is two hours, an internet connection, and a word-processing program that allows you to cut and paste information from the web browser to a new document. Compared to what it would have taken to do the same thing ten years ago, it's like magic.

Unlike so many other cheats this book explores, you can't go to jail for being a plagiarist. Sure, you'll take your lumps, but you're not going to jail. No orange jumpsuits, and no opportunity to teach a Making Shivs 101 at the Learning Annex once you've been sprung. Even better, no jailhouse memoir will be expected of you.

As much as people freak out when they detect a plagiarist, it's actually pretty hard to find one. It's like a bird-watcher stumbling on that rare Hermit Warbler—you know they're out there, but it takes a lot of work and a bit of luck to see it. In order to find the plagiarist, you have to intimately know the sources they used, or you have to happen across a written work that ripped off something *you* wrote! The good news is that people don't really have to time to second-guess you. They have to get smacked in the face with what you did.

Finally, if you're a really lazy student, you can just buy a term paper. This is the most blatant show of plagiarism, as there aren't even any original words submitted by the writer at all. Except, perhaps, his name at the top of the page. Buying a paper written by someone else and simply putting your name on the top to claim it as your own is the most thorough and blatant plagiary there is. The upside of this method is that there is absolutely no work required.

THE DRAWBACK

The drawbacks to being a plagiarist aren't life threatening, but they can be kind of embarrassing. Essentially, if you get caught plagiarizing, you look like a bit of a boob. It's definitely a survivable situation, but not fun.

If you're a student who plagiarizes, you will have the full weight of your college or university's academic censure come crashing down on you. That means that public opinion won't be with you. Fellow students will be annoyed, because they worked hard, and you tried to get away without toiling. You'll definitely receive a failing grade for the paper, if not the course. If you're really in a pickle, you can get expelled. You might even get considered for expulsion if your plagiarism had nothing to do with material written for the school, as happened to the much-maligned Kaavya Viswanathan of Harvard University (see sidebar). To add insult to injury, you may screw up badly enough to have academic degrees you've already earned taken away.

Journalists who dip their pens in poisoned ink are just as likely to get a major spanking for their troubles. Journalists are always skewered by other journalists for cheating, so the bad press you'll get will be phenomenal. You could get suspended or fired from your job; if your publisher is feeling really generous, you might be able to get away with a printed apology. Whatever is done to punish you, your credibility will be shattered for a while, and it will feel like you've got to start from the bottom all over again.

TOOLS OF THE TRADE

We've already covered the basic requirements, such as a computer for word processing and research. There are a few more specific examples that will set your feet firmly on the plagiarist's path. These are invaluable, and you should never lose sight of them. They are:

1. Internet connection
2. Good research skills
3. Browser
4. Nexis
5. Knowing your audience
6. Good reputation

WAYS AND MEANS: HOW TO PULL IT OFF

OK, you crafty little writers-to-be. Here's how to plagiarize with the best of them. As with all cheats, you will probably develop your own style that works for your particular circumstances. Even so, here are the tried-and-true methods to keep you writing, plagiarizing, and undetected.

1. CUT AND PASTE—When doing your research, remember that you must keep a Word document open on your screen at all times. As you find usable tidbits or even passages with language you just admire, copy it and paste the material into the open document. You'll be pleasantly surprised how it seems like the document just writes itself.

2. PROMISES, PROMISES—If anyone does detect your cheating ways, you can always pull the "Stephen Ambrose" and say that you were not aware that you hadn't properly credited your sources but promise to give credit in future editions. Being contrite can smooth so many un- necessarily ruffled feathers.

3. OPEN LETTER—If you're a journalist who may have been identified as a plagiarist, you can always admit loudly to your guilt (protesting that you didn't mean to do it, of course) and be so self-flagellating as to

print an apology in the paper. Your mea culpa will be so thorough that it will take the fun out of flogging you.

4. MANUFACTURE QUOTES—If you lift blocks of text directly into your work, you can obscure it a bit and throw off anyone who's looking for a direct cut-and-paste job by inserting quotes in and around the text. Make it seem as though someone else has been interviewed and is weighing in on the subject. The quotes will work to break up the text and make it, technically, not a direct quotation. They'll also make it seem like you did some original work.

5. FICTION, SCHMICTION—Another way to sidestep plagiarism is to insert copy from a nonfiction text into your work of fiction. A court ruling involving Dan Brown of *The Da Vinci Code* fame declared that this is not plagiarism. Weird but wonderful.

6. COMMON KNOWLEDGE—One of the best ways to sidestep claims of plagiarism is to claim that the material you wrote about was common knowledge. Anyone in the field would know that information, and it couldn't be deemed proprietary. Furthermore, any similar wording is merely coincidental.

7. PARAPHRASE—Since plagiarism revolves around the direct use of specific language created by another person, paraphrasing is the plagiarist's best friend. If you don't have the time to do a lick of work, just take your research and reword it. This requires very little effort in the grand scheme of things and is a perfect insurance policy against claims of lifting text.

8. USE PURCHASED ESSAYS WITH CAUTION—This is barely worth mentioning, but considering how stupid people can be, perhaps it *is* worth mentioning. If you bought a paper to turn in at school, you

might want to check if your professor has already been given that paper. Similarly, journalists should know what their editors read; turning in plagiarized work that they may have even edited themselves is a ridiculous mistake to make.

MOST LIKELY TO SUCCEED

You'll succeed at this cheat if you're careful, but you've got to be looking over your shoulder most of the time. You can't think that there aren't other plagiarists out there trying the same game. There's a limited amount of material to rip off, and you've got to be canny. You'll do well if the person reading your material is clueless. That means either you used really obscure material, or they're not familiar enough with the subject matter you're writing about to know what others have written.

Finally, if you have a little extra time on your hands, you'll do great. That means you have time to paraphrase. Paraphrasing is the golden ticket. Use it, and you'll enjoy the best of both worlds.

CATCHING PLAGIARISTS AT THEIR OWN GAME

Thankfully for professors, editors, and publishers, there are a few telltale signs of plagiarism. Here's a five-point test to apply to all material you review. Even one of these points can be an indication that you have a cheater in your midst.

1. When you receive a paper with citations, it has *ibid* (denoting "in the same place") repeated six times or more in reference to a block quote. That's a lifted quote masquerading behind some flabby citing.
2. On the other side of that coin, there could be a complete failure to cite sources in what is known to be a researched document.
3. Next, if you know the writer's style, but the paper seems to be

written in someone else's voice, guess what? It has! Check for voice and tone to catch a cheater.

4. Next, know which search engines your students and writers use, in addition to a few extra ones that you know really cover certain subject matters. By typing in the key words in the paper you're reviewing, you'll find the original sources pretty quickly.

5. Finally, you simply need to know your subject matter. If you're up on your field, you'll know who's been writing what, and you'll also know all the original source material. You'll be hard to dupe.

Would I Lie?

1

In 2006 Harvard University undergraduate student Kaavya Viswanathan published her first novel, *How Opal Mehta Got Kissed, Got Wild, and Got a Life*. The nineteen-year-old made headlines for the two-book publishing contract she signed with Little, Brown and Company. Shortly after its publication, however, allegations were raised that the book was plagiarized from two novels by author Megan McCafferty. Viswanathan admitted that she had borrowed ideas from McCafferty's novels but insisted that any plagiarism was unintentional, as she had probably internalized the works. The publisher canceled her contract and recalled about fifty thousand copies of the book. A few months later it was found that Viswanathan had also taken passages from the novels *The Princess Diaries* by Meg Cabot and *Can You Keep a Secret?* by Sophie Kinsella. *(continued)*

Jayson Blair was a *New York Times* reporter for four years, but he resigned in 2003 after plagiarizing and fabricating close to forty articles (that the *Times* staff is aware of). Investigations into his articles and behavior revealed that he frequently lied about his location, claiming he was reporting from different parts of the country when he had actually never left New York. He also fabricated conversations, used photographs to describe scenes that he had never been near, and lifted material and details from other news services, often going so far as to lie about emotionally charged interactions and events.

··· **3** ···

Former University of Colorado ethnic-studies professor Ward Churchill, whose racist and controversial views have earned him the nickname "the 9/11 Prof," was charged with plagiarism, falsification, fabrication, and other related charges after an investigation by the university's Standing Committee on Research Misconduct. In his published academic writings, Churchill made such absurd statements as referring to the 9/11 victims as "little Eichmanns" and allegedly plagiarized from several sources while twisting information to suit his agenda. Churchill also made questionable claims that he has Native American ancestry, and he allegedly threatened one of the professors whom he plagiarized when she confronted him, calling her late at night to yell "I'll get you for this!" The university could not oust him for his behavior alone because he had tenure, so it investigated his published works and found the evidence of plagiarism needed to fire him.

CHEATING WITH AN OFFICE BOYFRIEND OR GIRLFRIEND

TAKE THIS JOB AND LOVE IT

Infidelity comes in so many shapes and sizes it can boggle the mind. One of the fastest growing ways to meet your extrarelationship love interest is at the office. And why not? We work longer hours than ever before and have little time or energy after work to join clubs, go to bars, play on intramural teams, or whatever anyone might normally do to meet new people. So what's the busy office worker to do when he or she gets the itch? Scan the expanse of cubicles stretching out to the horizon and start choosing.

Apparently this method of selecting a special friend is so popular that one study has reported that 70 percent of single employees will become romantically linked with someone at their office during the course of their career. Another study reports that up to 60 percent of married people indulge in affairs, and that the office is the number one place to meet a willing partner. If you didn't know it before, now is the time to recognize that your office is less workplace and more roiling dating pool. Huzzah! Let the games begin.

To make matters even more entertaining, it seems that so many people are actively enthusiastic that church socials and singles bars are fading into the background in favor of high times in the boardroom. About one-third of office managers polled in a national survey admitted that they had dated a coworker, and 67 percent said they approved of dating in the workplace. The only cloud in the sky regarding workplace dating is when superiors date their subordinates. While 96 percent of those polled had no problem with peer relationships, only 24 percent were OK with bosses dating their employees. This may be sobering news for upper management, but chances are that employee censure isn't going to get in the way of a determined canoodler.

Another intriguing aspect of dating on the job is that there are two different levels of workplace romance in which the rogue lover can indulge. One variety is the tried-and-true full-on office romance, complete with fumblings in supply closets, accidental butt xeroxing, coded messages that everyone else can decode in a nanosecond, and drunken Christmas party promises. The second variety is the "emotional affair." This in-between type of affair has all the longing, clandestine intense discussions, and passion of the classic office affair but never makes it to physical consummation. The emotional affair is an insidious little beast, as it can carry the same intense wallop as the full-blown affair and can still herald the demise of the primary relationship, but without the climactic payoff. People fall into this one because they *think* they're still being faithful and are trying to be well behaved. But they're not. Once the horse is out of the barn, it's awfully hard to get him back in.

Once again, if you're not into cheating, go ahead and find your office sweetie and dump your significant other before you let things progress behind cubicle walls. For those of us who like to hedge our bets, there's the "office boyfriend/girlfriend."

THE UPSIDE

When it's going well, there's nothing more exciting and entertaining than a hot, furtive office affair. We all know that the daily grind can be exhausting and demoralizing. Whether you're working for The Man or you *are* The Man, getting up every day to face your everyday routine and minidramas of office politics can eventually leave you feeling like a dried-out husk. Now imagine that every time you show up at the office, you get to act like a giggling high-school kid with his or her first crush. And that crush is into you too. Awesome! Every activity is filled with new meaning and even the smallest tasks can become an opportunity for a thrilling tête-à-tête. Get coffee downstairs? I'd love to!

Every day takes on a sparkly quality. If there's one thing more entertaining than having something fun going on in your life, it's trying to keep it secret. What was once a humdrum existence is now filled with love and drama. Move over Bogart and Bacall, there's a new mysterious couple in town. Office lunches become midafternoon dates, and you can sneak off to empty areas of the office to snog each other silly. Now you have someone to confide all your workplace woes to, a person *who really understands,* unlike your spouse or partner at home—who's never met the players in these dramas and can't possibly understand the politics involved. If you work together, your sizzling energy will infuse your projects, and your work product could dazzle all who enter your love orbit.

For those who aren't getting it on physically but are emotionally enmeshed with an office love, this is the ultimate outlet for all your pent-up feelings. Can't tolerate your home life? Your enthralled audience will want to listen. Despise your coworkers? Office lover wants to know. Craving a connection with someone who lives the same day-in, day-out issues that you do? Are you desperate to find someone who can look you in the eye and say "I really, really get you"? Chances are, your emotional-affair partner is the one to provide all this and more.

Generally, creating an alternate love universe at the office can have some surprising benefits. The shock to the system of feeling like you're coming back to life in the dreariest of environments can remind you that there's no need to live in a rut if you don't want to. You might also find a new partner who's well suited to you, as you probably work in the same industry thanks to shared interests and goals. Not terrible reasons to philander if you have to. It's still cheating, but all the upsides make the rationalizing so much easier.

THE DRAWBACK

Oh dear. The downsides to this variety of infidelity are rather severe. Everything's been rosy up until now, so gird your loins in order to keep reading. Anyone who's willing to stray with someone from their workplace must consider the following: When you cheat under normal circumstances, the stakes are pretty high. You can lose your significant other and a lot of your assets, not to mention custody of your kids. When you play around at the office, you have even more to lose, and the stakes increase enormously. Instead of standing to lose *most* of your life as you know it, you can lose *all* of it. Not for you will there be the cold comfort of snuggling up to the knowledge that "at least I have my work." No, friends, along with your domestic life, you may very well lose your employment as well.

It's not uncommon for an employer or management-level employee to lose his or her job when a lower-level lover claims sexual harassment. Even if sexual harassment isn't thrown on the table, a lot of companies have a no-nookie policy for all employees, and any breach is grounds for getting the ax.

Here are a few other choice concerns for anyone thinking about dipping their pen in the corporate inkwell. Or, for that matter, *being* the corporate inkwell: being the subject of vicious office gossip, being accused of getting special treatment for special favors, having to work together if/when the relationship ends, having your ex–office lover spreading your opinions and secrets to coworkers, corporate espionage by a revenge-seeking ex-lover, just to name a smattering of difficulties you might face. The point is that your job is your livelihood, and if things go poorly in the relationship (or someone else is offended by it), you're opening yourself up as a target to have the security of your job yanked out from under you.

TOOLS OF THE TRADE

Make this very technical. Like an experiment. Get as detailed as possible so that it seems really specific and a little officious. Set it up like a lab if you can. Make sure to list the tools (as shown below) and give descriptions and specifics as need be.

1. Cute coworker
2. Office with locking door
3. Conference room with locking door
4. Private email and IM

WAYS AND MEANS: HOW TO PULL IT OFF

Thanks to the fact that you spend at least eight hours of the day together anyway, the office romance isn't that difficult to pull off, at least at first. Later on, when you want to spend every waking minute with your undercover lover, it presents all the usual problems of an affair. Nonetheless, here's how to go from the boardroom to the bedroom in record time:

1. LATE NIGHTS—What's more romantic than two brilliant and witty people bending their heads together over a puzzling spreadsheet and takeout? This is the stuff of Meg Ryan movies and feel-good fluff the world over. Even if you can't find a way to get assigned to a project with the object of your affection, hang around late at night and make sure he or she knows it. If you've been sending each other sparks while standing on line at the microwave with your Tupperware, chances are good he or she will take the hint. Make sure to consummate your passion in some way at this stage of the game. If not, you're through, or you'll fall directly into emotional affair territory. If you score, you're about to get on board the roller coaster of the interoffice affair.

2. BUSINESS TRAVEL—This should be obvious. You've been assigned by your company to leave town, with a corporate charge card, for at least one night. Do whatever you can to get your honey to come with you. The bigger the company, the easier this is to do (see below for more details). The best part of legitimate business travel with your office boyfriend or girlfriend is just that—its legitimacy. No need to concoct elaborate stories for your spouse or partner; you really are going on a business trip. Who you're going with, however, doesn't need to be discussed. If questioned, the undeniable truth is "just some colleagues, dear." Once you're at the conference, training course, or sales call, resist the temptation to upgrade your room or order oysters and champagne

from room service. These are the telltale signs of hanky-panky and will give the office gossips far more fodder than you want to give them. Tongues will start wagging when your expense report hits accounting. If you are going to do it, pony up the money yourself.

3. SHARED PROJECT—This is just a lovely built-in excuse to spend even more time as a couple. You and your office squeeze have to steal every moment together that you can, and you can wring every moment out of the day if you work on the same project or account. If one of you has seniority or is the other's boss, just take care of securing the assignment yourselves. If you need a little outside help, a simple recommendation to an ally who has the right pull can land the two of you right where you want to be. Be subtle. Overselling your cohort's value can be a tip-off, and discretion remains a key ingredient to the success of your fling.

4. TIMING—This tip applies to all affairs. Studies show that most affairs are successfully embarked on in the summertime. Thanks to good weather and elevated spirits, significant others on the receiving end of this particular type of duplicity tend to be distracted with activities or travel. This is a great time to take advantage of your significant other's lapse in attention to do as you please. They won't know what you're up to until fall rolls around, and those three months can be all you need to get in and out of your affair, or to determine if you want to give it a real go with your workplace partner. Fun in the sun, indeed!

5. REMAIN SILENT—No matter who appears to know what's going on, no matter how sympathetic they may seem, say nothing. Do not breathe a word to anyone about what you've been up to. If you stay quiet, it's possible that even if things go terribly wrong and there's a messy breakup, you can emerge unscathed. It's harder to get fired based

on rumor and innuendo than fact. Remember that no one at the office is truly your closest of friends. Everyone's out for himself or herself and is interested in his or her own advancement, no matter how much they may want it to appear to be to the contrary. Rest assured that when someone's got the goods on you, that information will get used. It may not be immediately, but eventually the time will be right.

MOST LIKELY TO SUCCEED

Anyone who can remain silent and remember not to leave a paper trail should do all right. It also helps if you don't plan on getting too entrenched at the company, so that if you have to leave, it doesn't mess things up for you too badly. Success rates are higher if you work for a large company, as there's far more opportunity to evade notice. At a huge company, there's too much going on for you to garner much attention unless you're consciously trying to turn the spotlight on yourself. Small companies are a ridiculous challenge and should be avoided for this particular cheat unless you're a dare-devil or a sphinx.

CATCHING OFFICE CHEATERS AT THEIR OWN GAME

While all the usual methods of catching this cheat at his or her own game apply, there's one extra wrinkle. From the first day that your spouse or partner is on the job, make sure you are friends with his or her administrative assistant. Admins are the eyes and ears of every company and are usually treated, if not poorly, then not terribly well. A little kindness and consideration (and the occasional gift) will make your significant other's assistant your ally. If your S.O. doesn't have an assistant, there's someone in their orbit at work who you can target as a willing accomplice—someone who will respond well to your thoughtfulness and consideration. When the time is right, all you need to do to know what's going on is ask. You'll be shocked at how quickly your ally will share his or her suspicions and opinions on what's going on. Act accordingly.

was later found in a park, and the cause of death was ruled a homicide, but the case remains unsolved. Condit was never an official suspect in her murder, but Levy's family and various media publications have raised suspicion that he may have hired her killer.

.... 3 ....

Cecil Parkinson, cabinet minister to Prime Minister Margaret Thatcher, was forced to resign in October 1983, when it was discovered that he had not only had a twelve-year affair with his former secretary, Sara Keays, but that she was pregnant with his child. He had promised to marry her and then reneged. He was able to get an injunction to forbid the media to make any references to their daughter, and he paid for her care growing up; however, he never met her or saw Sara Keays again.

.... 4 ....

Harry Stonecipher had been the chief operating officer of Boeing Co. until he retired in 2001. In late 2003 Boeing recruited Stonecipher out of retirement to appoint him CEO of a company wrought by scandal. In March 2005 he was forced to resign after an investigation revealed that he had a consensual affair with a female employee. Boeing directors received an anonymous tip-off that the affair was taking place, and they confronted Mr. Stonecipher directly about it. He confirmed its truth and tendered his resignation, as the aerospace giant's code of conduct prohibits behavior that could embarrass the company.

CHEATING ON A POLYGRAPH TEST

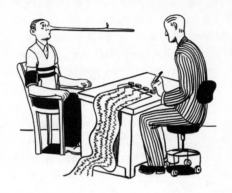

FUN WITH ELECTRODES

Polygraph tests—or lie detector tests, as they are commonly known—are creepy. You get hooked up to a bunch of electrodes, and someone grills you about stuff that you supposedly lied about. No matter how you slice it, taking a polygraph test is not fun, nor is it intended to be. Richard Nixon said it best when he admitted, "I don't know anything about lie detectors other than they scare the hell out of people." He was right.

But what is a polygraph, exactly? It's a device that you get strapped into with a heart monitor and electrodes that records variations in your physical state while you're being asked a group of questions. The machine monitors your heartbeat, blood pressure, respiration rate, and electrical resistance, also known as galvanic skin response. Basically, it all adds up to whether or not you're having a panic attack while being asked certain questions. The theory is that if you panic, you're lying.

Considering who is probably administering the polygraph test, it's a miracle if you're *not* having heart failure during the process. Polygraphs are frequently used by government agencies (such as the FBI and the CIA), police, and employers. Your defense attorney might have you strapped into one too should you find yourself on trial for some heinous crime. None of that adds up to a relaxing experience.

In addition to physiological changes, the test administrator will probably examine the type of lie you tell and why you might be telling it. The four basic types of lies that we tell are: prosocial lies, self-enhancement lies, selfish lies, and antisocial lies. Prosocial lies help other people out, self-enhancers make you look good without harming others, selfish lies help you and hurt others, and antisocial lies are told to deliberately hurt other people. In other words, if you're going to be a liar, it's best to be in the first two categories.

In the event that you find yourself on the wrong side of the electrodes, is there any way to save yourself? Will you immediately be revealed as a liar? What if you didn't lie, but you're so scared you come off as untrustworthy and odd? Well, you could tell the truth. Tell the truth, take your lumps, and get over it. If that doesn't sound so appealing, all is not lost. Considering that a polygraph test doesn't tell if you're lying, it just monitors your physical response, you can trick the test. Control your body, and you can control the test.

THE UPSIDE

The best news of all is that polygraph machines are known have an inaccuracy rate of 30 percent. Those are bad odds for the people administering the test. That 30 percent affords you a lot of wiggle room to argue against the results and demand alternate types of testing or to forgo a test altogether.

Another happy thought to keep in mind when you're getting strapped in and hooked up is that polygraph test evidence is not admissible in most courts. Judges have wisely acknowledged that the 30 percent margin of error is too great and don't want to allow evidence into the record that's so questionable. Let's hear it for the legal system!

Finally, it's important to note that under certain circumstances, it's considered an infringement of your civil rights to be forced to take a polygraph test. Of course, that rarely applies to the government, but if your employer is trying to make you take one of these tests, you can refuse. You might also want to find a new job that is significantly less fascist than your current employer.

THE DRAWBACK

The major downside to polygraph tests is that they're scary. A good test administrator knows this and will use it to his or her advantage. What that means is that the tester will use your anxiety to coax an admission out of you. Despite your best efforts, you might get so freaked out about the whole process (with or without the swinging overhead light and the screaming interrogator that crop up so frequently in movies) that you blurt out whatever it is the tester wants you to say. That can be used as an admission in a criminal proceeding, and then you've got a serious problem.

If you live in New Mexico, you've got a unique problem with

polygraphs. New Mexico is the only state in the U.S. that allows polygraph results as evidence in court. If you live in New Mexico and plan on doing anything shady, think about it twice. Or move.

Finally, if you work for a company that wants to give you a lie detector test, and you refuse it, you may still be out of luck. It's your right to refuse the test, but it's the company's right to infer whatever it wants from your refusal. If it decides to can you for sticking up for yourself and your civil liberties, you've got no recourse.

TOOLS OF THE TRADE

Beating a lie detector test is all about controlling your physiological response to anxiety. If you panic, you're interpreted as a liar. If you can keep all the usual signs of panic at bay, you're golden. That means that you have to keep your heartbeat slow and your breathing steady, and you can't sweat. You also have to give answers that don't give anything away. Ambiguity is great. Here are a few tools that will help you achieve the required Zen state:

1. Belief in your own story
2. Lamaze classes
3. Yoga classes
4. Antiperspirant (applied on your body and fingertips)
5. Body powder

WAYS AND MEANS: HOW TO PULL IT OFF

Controlling your body sounds like a good plan, but unless you're a Hindu mystic, it's probably not likely that you have totally mastered your physical responses and bodily functions. Here are a few methods that will help you lie with ease.

1. THE TESTER IS NOT YOUR FRIEND— To get you relaxed and ready to spill your guts, the test administrator may try to act like he or

she is your buddy. This is not true. The tester is never on your side and will try to be chummy only to elicit more information from you. Don't be duped. You have enough friends already. And even if you don't, this is not the person to try to pal around with.

2. WHAT'S THE STORY?—If you know what subject matter the polygraph tester is fishing around for, you'll be more equipped to resist the urge to talk. You'll also know specifically what to stay silent about. You'll have a lot of different questions thrown at you, but only a few are relevant. Know what they are and don't be surprised when they come up.

3. KEEP IT BRIEF—Keep your answers limited to "yes" and "no" responses if you can. As with any lie or cover-up, the more you talk, the deeper the hole you're digging for yourself. Don't elaborate, as any details you provide can and will be used against you.

4. INHALE, EXHALE—Don't forget to breathe. The easiest way to get control over your body is to breathe deeply, taking long steady breaths in and out. As you do this, you'll notice that your heart rate slows. You'll also notice that the more you concentrate on your breathing, the less you'll concentrate on the things that are freaking you out. You can also mess with the baseline readings of the polygraph test to work in your favor. The polygraph test measures your responses to innocuous questions and takes that as your baseline. If you raise your baseline a little (more to follow) and then lower your response during difficult questions, your test will be inconclusive. In other words, play with your own heart rate and keep 'em guessing.

5. NO PAIN, NO GAIN—A way to raise your baseline reading is by causing yourself pain. You can do this in a multitude of ways. Bite down hard on the inside of your cheek, sneak something sharp into the test-

ing room and jab yourself with it, dig your nails into your hand—you could even pick at a scab. Whatever it is, do it when irrelevant questions are being asked, so any anxiety caused by relevant questions will be undetectable.

6. SMOOTH MOVE, EX-LAX—Another way to create more tension in your body is to make sure you're constipated before the test. While most of us spend a lot of time and energy trying to make sure that we're *not* blocked up, this is one time that it can work for you. The strain and discomfort of constipation can be detected by the polygraph and will raise your baseline higher than it should be, thereby skewing the test results.

7. CATCH A COLD—Illness can read as stress on the machine too. While contracting a serious illness isn't advisable under any circumstances, it's likely that you can handle having a cold. If you see someone at work or in your family sneezing, stand next to them. If it's not socially inappropriate, go ahead and kiss them. Suffer a little in the name of exercising your civil rights.

8. DRY AS A BONE—Antiperspirant applied to your body and fingertips will keep you dry. So will perspiration-absorbing body powder. Sweating, which is a usual sign of anxiety, can be detected by the polygraph. Staying dry will stymie it and keep you in the clear.

9. DRUGSTORE COWBOY—If you can swing it, take a little something to calm you down. If you think you'll get drug tested along with the polygraph, taking any kind of narcotics would be a bad idea. What you can do is take an over-the-counter supplement such as SAM-e (S-adenosyl-methionine) or any supplement containing ingredients that are supposed to make you feel calm, cozy, and a little sleepy, like

chamomile. You'll be less perturbed by the weird situation you're in if you're under the influence.

MOST LIKELY TO SUCCEED

Anyone who isn't intimidated by authority figures will do OK. It also helps if you've been prepared by a lawyer or advocate who has been through the same scenario with other clients. You're also in very good shape if you've been through any kind of legal or quasilegal proceeding before where you've been asked questions under pressure. That could mean a deposition, a police interrogation, or serving as a witness in a trial. As long as you can remember that your word is credible and the only person who can give you away is you, you should succeed at this cheat.

CATCHING POLYGRAPH CHEATS
AT THEIR OWN GAME

If you're administering a polygraph test, or have arranged to have one administered, you probably know that the test isn't definitive. There are many ways to take advantage of the 30 percent margin of error inherent in the test, and if you're the least bit savvy, you should assume that the person being tested might try to take advantage of it.

There are, thankfully, several ways to catch a liar in the act even if the polygraph can't. Watch the polygraph test recipient carefully, and see if he or she does any of the following during the test: cross their arms, shift in the chair, look up and to the right while answering questions, rub their eyes, play with their hair, touch their face, jiggle a foot in the air or touch their earlobe. If any combination of these gestures takes place, you've got a liar.

Once you know you've got a liar on your hands, don't worry about the polygraph picking up whether or not they're telling the truth. Just use the scary, unfamiliar circumstances in your favor. Badger your target until a confession pops up and call it a day.

Would I Lie?

1

The first person to create a "lie detector" device that measured blood pressure in relation to truthfulness (which eventually led to the development of today's polygraph) was also the creator of the popular comic book *Wonder Woman*. William Marston was a psychologist and teacher who invented the protopolygraph machine in 1915. He was fascinated by bondage and actually lived with two women (one his wife, the other a former student) in a ménage à trois for many years. He debuted the DC Comics comic book *Wonder Woman*, a combination of feminism and sexual fantasy, in 1941. It thrived all through the forties and still enjoys a cult-like following today.

2

Oregon's Green River killings were committed by serial killer Gary Leon Ridgway, who confessed in 2001 to committing forty-eight murders in the eighties and nineties. He had been a suspect in the killings in 1984 and was given a polygraph test, which he passed. He was then released and able to continue murdering. In 1982 another suspect in the killings, Melvin Foster, failed a polygraph test thanks to a nervous tic and had his home searched and belongings taken by the police. It wasn't until DNA evidence was found and Ridgway confessed that Foster's name was officially cleared as a suspect.

Chinese-American nuclear scientist Wen Ho Lee was suspected of selling nuclear secrets to the Chinese in 1998. The U.S. Department of Energy administered a polygraph test, and three different polygraphers determined he had passed. The FBI wanted to look at the results, however, so the DOE sent them to Washington. The FBI claimed that Lee had actually failed the polygraph. Its people performed their own polygraph on Lee and also considered him to have failed, although, strangely, they did not inform him of this or interrogate him. Lee was put in prison and then released because the FBI essentially had nothing on him, resulting in the federal government being forced to award Lee $1.65 million in damages. American Polygraph Association chairman Richard Keifer looked at the same original polygraph results from the DOE and agreed that Lee had passed his initial test, thus exposing the FBI in its search for a scapegoat to blame. Funny how in this case it was the FBI, not its suspect, cheating on the polygraph test!

CHEATING AT ONLINE DATING

ALL THAT GLITTERS SURE AIN'T GOLD

So you need a date. Your local bars are turning up the usual losers, and the most attractive person at your office—well, you've already slept with him or her. The cupboard's bare, and you're jonesing for a little companionship. What to do? The easiest way to hook up in our technocentric world is to boot up the computer and take a stroll through the scores of dating websites available at a moment's notice. Once deemed the domain of the desperate, dating sites are now one of the most popular ways to find companionship, whether you're looking for a quick hookup or the spouse of your dreams. So get online, friends, and start thinking about how to make yourself look datable, which is to say taller, thinner, and richer than you really are.

The thing about dating sites is that they take initial chemistry out of the equation and instead allow people to describe themselves, their interests, and their dreams as a means to finding like-minded people—and possible matches. Online dating is all about (at least at first) an intellectual connection with a prospective date. This is not unlike browsing through a furniture catalog. Anything can look desirable in a styled photograph, but it's all about how that sofa looks once you get it home. Similarly, someone who looks great in his or her dating profile can be a total horror show once you meet face to face. The reality is that no matter how great someone looks on paper, chemistry is what really counts.

But in order to find out if you've got chemistry, you've got to get your foot in the door. Sadly, people are pretty superficial, and what gets you noticed online is not necessarily the same set of attributes that will seal the deal later on. You may love that the person you've selected happens to have a mint-condition *Star Wars* collection, or that they can sing every show tune ever written by Rodgers and Hart, but what reels people in initially are always the same things. Men and women alike want to know what their prospective date looks like, how tall they are, how fit or active they are, how old they are, how much money they make, what they do for a living, where they live, what their marital status is (or was), if they smoke, and so on and so on and so on.

The key to successful internet dating is figuring out just how much to lie about yourself. What can you get away with? How far can you bend the truth without having your date turn on his or her heel and walk out the second you enter the room? Careful misrepresentation can open dating doors you never would have been able to walk through before, while blatant lying will make you the pariah of the digital daters. The key to this cheat is subtlety. Bend the truth just far enough to get the date, or languish in Lonely Town with all the others who are just too honest to give themselves a fighting chance.

THE UPSIDE

The upside to this cheat is that you'll get a date. No more sitting at home brushing the cats, no more playing video games all night by yourself, no more lying in bed staring at the ceiling wondering if you're doomed to solitude. The first step to companionship of any kind is making an effort and taking the first step. If you have to stretch the truth to get someone to notice you, so be it.

The other major upside is that you can also have fun being Hunky McStudderson or Stacky Curverstein in the virtual world, even if you can't pull it off in real life. Getting a positive response to who you are is always a great feeling, even if who you are online isn't exactly who you are out on the street.

Finally, a nice rationalization that goes along with this cheat is that even though you're lying about yourself to cut through the initial superficialities of dating, you're doing your potential date a favor. There's a finite number of possible matches out there, and by making yourself appear more desirable than you are, you're just increasing the chances for everybody to find a mate, right?

THE DRAWBACK

The drawback to this cheat is best described in the following vignette: You get someone's interest on your dating site of choice, you flirt and chat and possibly even talk on the phone. Things are going great. Your ego is inflated, and you're feeling like nothing's going to get in the way of you connecting with this great person you've found. The two of you select a mutually agreeable meeting place and time. You show up, look around, and are able to locate your date from his or her picture. You're also able to identify your date because his or her mouth is hanging open and a look of stunned disbelief has turned his or her face into a mask of horror.

Conversely, your date doesn't find you hideous and totally lacking in sex appeal, and decides to stick around. Unfortunately, the second you slip up and reveal that you are not, say, a social worker specializing in elder care but are in fact unemployed and living with your parents, he or she rushes for the door. You've been revealed not only as a loser, but also a liar.

If you don't do this right and handle your subterfuge with delicacy, you're bound to suffer a seriously bruised ego. You'll also likely be turned off to dating for a while and have to start over at square one. Even worse, people in your area who use internet dating sites will start to know you and tip one another off about you. This is not a good situation at all. If you ever hope to date again, you'll be forced to move. Or make apologies. This scenario is too embarrassing for words and must be steered clear of at all costs.

TOOLS OF THE TRADE

Let's review. Lying about some of your most basic traits will get you a date from any one of the dating sites out there, from the most sex-centric to the religiously based. You just have to know what people are looking for and feed it to them. Here's what you need to get the show on the road:

1. Computer
2. Email account

3. IM account
4. Camera
5. Friend
6. Professional photographer

WAYS AND MEANS: HOW TO PULL IT OFF

OK, so now you're emotionally geared up to find the love of your life, or at least someone to fool around with. Time to release the hounds: The hunt is on!

1. SAY CHEESE—If your dating profile doesn't have a photo attached, you have absolutely no chance of getting a date. Anyone whose profile is photo free clearly has something to hide; could be garden-variety hideousness, could be a Discovery Channel—worthy disfiguration, who knows? One thing's for sure: No one will want to find out. So you have to have a photo. In all likelihood, you don't have a photo handy that's date-site worthy (the snap of you wearing the giant cheese wedge on your head at the last Wisconsin game is not the best way to go), so you'll have to have a picture taken specifically for this purpose. Make sure that you're shot from the best angle possible (being photographed from above works for most people and avoids the quadruple-chin issue) and use soft lighting. You'll look absolutely dreamy and five years younger. Think *Barbara Walters Special:* gauzy filters, dim lighting. Essentially, we all look better when no one can really see us. If you have a stellar photo of yourself from a few years ago, don't be shy, go ahead and use it. It's still you, right?

If you just can't take a decent photo, consider if any family members look remotely like you. Does cousin Vito look terrific in every family photo? Does your sister knock 'em dead when class photo time rolls around? Ask them for a photo to contribute to your cause. You're from the same gene pool, so there's bound to be some resemblance. Just have a good cover story for why you've changed so dramatically since the photo was taken. Perhaps you were in a fiery car wreck where you managed to save your whole family from the inferno as well as the family dog? Your great story and heroism will certainly keep the date rolling, at least for a while.

2. WHAT'S IN A NAME—Almost every dating website requires the user to create an onscreen name by which other daters can identify and address them. No one wants to put his or her real name out there, in an effort to prevent stalkers or other crazies from making attempts to find them in the real world. All of this is good advice. Keep in mind that the message you send out with your name is indicative of the type of response you'll get. So, in the spirit of misrepresentation (and this really applies to men), choose a sensitive, caring screen name to reel them in, and then go ahead and be your usual Cro-Magnon self once you've got the lady at your lair. Keep in mind that a lot of people try to come up with a clever online handle and wind up falling alarmingly short of the mark. Men should be warned that any reference to penis size in a screen name (such as hotrod6) is as huge a turnoff to women as it is a turn-on to your own ego. If, however, you are cruising around on one of the many popular gay sites, you'll soon find that that rule not only doesn't apply, but that success lies in a screen name akin to bigboi8u.

For the ladies, remember that the rules are the same online as offline. No one will respond to a screen name like NeedHusband268 or Im2Good4U. These are unappealing. Go the sexy route (HotKitty69) and, much like your male counterparts, reveal your real marital intentions once you've got him in your clutches.

3. VITAL STATISTICS—Every dating website requires or encourages you to include your age, height, weight, hair color, and eye color in your personal profile. Do not be inhibited by reality as you fill this in.

No one can fill out this form without embellishing at least a little bit. Enhancement of these traits is so prevalent as to be expected. If you're a five-foot, two-inch man, feel free to put on your tallest heels and poof your hair up as much as you can. If your new measurement is five foot six, then that's what you write down. The same applies to weight ("Well, I was once one hundred eighty pounds, even if I'm two-twenty now"), or whatever physical traits happen to bedevil you. Have faith that if you manage to email, IM, or even talk on the phone before you meet them in person, you stand a pretty strong chance of your personality carrying you through. True, your potential mate will notice that you lied ("She doesn't have an athletic build at all, and she's at least forty-five!"), but they may be able to look past that and focus on your sparkling wit and extensive knowledge of Biedermeier furniture.

4. LIVIN' LA VIDA LOCA—Questions about lifestyle have become just as prevalent as questions about physical traits. People want to know if you're a drinker, a smoker, or a midnight toker, and you'd be ill-advised to ignore those parts of your sign-up form. Nonetheless, who wants to date a recovering meth addict? How honest can you be in this section without risking blowing the whole endeavor? Social drinking is considered almost universally acceptable, but everything else, from smoking to recreational drugs to full-blown addictions (this includes addictions to sex, drugs, alcohol, shopping, *Desperate Housewives;* whatever your poison happens to be), is a crapshoot. Figure out who you want your audience to be and just answer accordingly. Are you a sinner hoping to find a saint in the virtual dating world? Try not to share that you're lost without your pipe and teeny, tiny spoon. Are you a vegan nonsmoker who's dying for a rock-and-roll boyfriend? Better not reveal that you hate cigarettes and anyone who smokes them. Remember, you'll show your true colors soon enough, but creating this fictitious

version of yourself will open the door to enough dates that one of them just might surprise you and yield something good.

MOST LIKELY TO SUCCEED

Who is most likely to succeed at the cheat and why? What are the examples of cheaters who will do well? Are they distinguished as a group in some way? Do they share traits? What techniques will ensure a lack of detection? Do they know how to ID their patsies in some way?

If you've got gumption, little shame, and are desperately lonely, this cheat's for you. You've got to want it bad to make it work in the internet dating world to begin with (so many freaks, so little time), so opening yourself up to a wider segment of the wacko parade is not for everyone. The real trick is to be desirous enough to do this cheat, but not to have the normal human reaction of depression and horror when it doesn't work out. This is a numbers game, the idea being that if you put out your vibe to enough people, someone will eventually respond. Someone, that is, who doesn't make you want to run in the other direction. So if your ego is particularly strong, but you just can't get a date (and you're willing to deal with some nutbars along the way), go this route. You'll be happy you did.

CATCHING ONLINE DATING
CHEATS AT THEIR OWN GAME

In a word, ask. Once you're in contact with someone, and you've had more than one conversation, you are completely within your bounds if you simply ask if your potential date's stats are true. You might as well quiz them on the age of the photo while you're at it. Most people, no matter how bold they are when they're lying in writing to a nameless, faceless mass, will fold when asked the hard questions point-blank. A recommended method is as follows: Advise your possible date that if they are lying to you, you will walk out on the date immediately, making the whole thing a waste of time, money, and effort. They may think you're a bit hard-line, but a cheerful explanation that you've been burned before (even if you haven't) will separate the wheat from the chaff. If your date doesn't have anything to hide, he or she will surely show up.

Special note: For the totally socially unacceptable, there are special sites just for you. Trekpassions.com obviously caters to the sci-fi Comic-Con contingent. There are others. Happy hunting!

⤞ *Would I Lie?* ⤝

1

The frequency with which internet daters misrepresent themselves in one way or another has caused a debate regarding criminal background checks for internet dating sites. While no one can be prevented from lying about their looks or their job online, someone with a criminal record would have a significantly harder time getting dates from a website if background checks become a requirement. Unfortunately, even this law would not be foolproof. Name changes, moving, aliases, and many other factors can contribute to incorrect information coming up through a background check, which could then pose serious legal problems for the site. If an innocent user is mistakenly labeled as a felon, he or she can sue the website for libel. If, on the other hand, a user is attacked by someone they meet through the site (after the site has supposedly performed a full background check), that user can also sue the website for misrepresentation.

2

One example of how internet dating can be a real drag: A twenty-four-year-old man answered a very sexy woman's internet personal ad. They exchanged hot and heavy emails and spoke on the phone a few times, and the young construction worker was smitten. When he met the woman at a bar, something about her and her friends didn't seem quite right, even though they were all gorgeous. The next thing he knew, his "dream girl" got up on stage to sing karaoke, and her voice was deep enough to be a man's. It was then that he realized that she and her friends were all drag queens! He ran out of the bar as the "girls" laughed and taunted him.

3

Thirty-three-year-old Jeffrey Marsalis of Philadelphia was accused of nine counts of rape and sexual assault on women he courted on Match.com. Philadelphia police believed that there might be other victims who had not yet come forward. Marsalis was very charming in his communications with the women, telling each one a different story about his background and occupation. He claimed to be in the CIA, a doctor, and an astronaut in training, among others, and he led each woman to believe that she was on her way toward a long-term relationship with him. Marsalis would then take the women to a bar or restaurant and slip a date-rape drug in their drinks.

SLACKING OFF AT WORK

TIME BANDITS

I t's impossible to be on the ball 24-7. Even though we'd all like to be productive and efficient in every aspect of our lives, part of being human is accepting that it's just not going to happen. Slacking off is part of who we are. Whether we do it out of boredom or a need to recharge our batteries, taking time out of our tightly scheduled days is unavoidable.

Wasting time at work is all about declaring a little "me time" in the midst of daily activities that usually aren't under your control. You're pushed and pulled from one task or meeting to another with very little regard for the things you need to accomplish in your personal life. When unrealistic goals are set for the use of your precious time, it's natural to push back and carve out a little time and space for yourself. It's wasting time at work that keeps you from being a total pod person or drone. Wasting time is all about asserting your individuality and identity.

An overloaded schedule isn't the only thing that will push you to steal time back for your own use at the office. Everyone knows that time is money. If you're not making the money you feel you deserve, you can look for valuable items you can take that will bolster your wallet, ego, or lifestyle. Time is one of those things you can steal at the office that will add real value to your life. There's nothing like staking your claim, no matter how small it may be, to lighten the load of feeling underpaid, undervalued, and underappreciated.

Time wasting also comes in handy when your job is so boring that every day feels like a near-death experience. Data entry, repetitive tasks, or anything that requires close attention but very little brain activity can drive you over the deep end. The only way to save yourself is to find a few ways to break the monotony doing things you like to do. This could be anything from doing a crossword puzzle on your lap under the desk to sneaking out to do your banking. Whatever it is you choose to do, it's better to risk getting in trouble than letting your brain rot.

And speaking of brain rot, it would seem safe to assume that older workers would be the ones having a harder time staying focused at the office. It's logical to assume that memory loss and fatigue, two usual complaints of the older set, would lead to a lack of focus and more wasted time while working. Not so! In fact, it's the younger members of the workforce who have major attention deficit disorder, or perhaps simply a better developed sense of entitlement. Workers over fifty-five years old waste only thirty minutes or so per day, while people under thirty-five waste two hours on average. Anyone who's hiring young people to energize their workforce clearly has another think coming.

THE UPSIDE

If you successfully pull off this cheat, your quality of life will improve. This is particularly true of the eight hours that you spend on the job every day. That's saying a lot. Considering that most of our waking adult life is spent at work, it's not crazy to try to do whatever you can to make that time pass as pleasantly as possible.

First off, you can get a lot done to make your personal life run more smoothly. You can take care of purchasing your kids' school wardrobe, you can do your banking (either online or in person), you can even sneak off for doctor's appointments or personal grooming. Why let your life fall apart, or even worse, let yourself get run-down and shabby if you can avoid it? No need!

Another advantage to this cheat is that it can work to remind you that your life is your own, and you are an autonomous being. So much of what we do is for other people, and it's terribly easy to lose sight of your individuality and free will. Just because your boss tells you to sit at your desk for eight hours doesn't mean you have to. Can you still get the job done if you take an extra hour for yourself? If the answer is yes, exercise your ability to think independently and act like the adult you are. You are not your job. You are a unique person, and this is one way to keep that idea fresh in your mind.

This cheat can also provide you with a valuable tool at your job. By exercising your independence, you are communicating silently but effectively to your manager that you deserve respect. Managing up is an important part of anyone's job. It's the ability to communicate successfully with your supervisors about what you need and then being able to get it. By demonstrating through your behavior, rather than long drawn-out conversations, that you can get all your work done, *but* you're going to do it your way, you're effecting positive change in the workplace. If your colleagues see you doing this, you're effectively blazing a trail for all the independent thinkers around you.

THE DRAWBACK

For all the advantages to cultivating an "I'll do it my way" mind-set, there are definitely some downsides. The way to be successful at this cheat is to use your time in a way that suits you, but not to get so behind on your responsibilities at work that you can actually be identified as a slacker. Goofing off or taking care of personal obligations without putting any checks and balances in place for yourself can lead to rough times. Getting behind on your works stinks, particularly if you don't have an assistant to help you. If you're behind because your boss has unreasonably burdened you, you might have a few colleagues who will help you out. If you've got piles of work to take care of because you were busy getting an eyebrow wax, it's unlikely that anyone's going to lend a hand. Anyone who's neglected their work knows that the only way to solve the problem is to stay late and work double time until you're caught up. This is the exact opposite of the goal of this cheat. Beware.

If you really get behind on your work, or set a bad tone for the workplace by loudly proclaiming that you'll do things your way, you may be told to take the highway. In other words, you'll get canned. Again, this is not the goal of the cheat. Enjoying the best of both worlds is your goal; in other words, to have a job but do it comfortably.

If your slacking (or perceived slacking) lets down your team, you might have a coworker act unpredictably. This could mean complaining about you to HR, sabotaging you on the job, or even just becoming aggressive and getting in your face about not holding up your end of things. It's always unfortunate when an inflated sense of entitlement makes someone on your team wig out, instead of teaching them a valuable lesson.

TOOLS OF THE TRADE

The tools required for this cheat really depend on what you do for a living, as well as your preferred method of wasting time. A few of the basic requirements, however, are as follows:

1. Computer
2. Phone
3. Car/transportation
4. IM
5. Office with closing door or secluded cubicle

WAYS AND MEANS: HOW TO PULL IT OFF

Everyone has their own very personal ways they like to waste time. You could be a fashion hound who can't resist checking out the look books from Fashion Week. You might be a sports fan who wants to memorize every statistic about the New York Islanders or see how the Manchester United soccer team is doing. Then again, you could be interested in checking in with your extended network of family and friends. Whatever it is you like to do, stealth is the key to success. Here are a few methods for blowing off steam, finding time for yourself, and getting away with it.

1. SURF THE NET—This is the number one way that most people steal time while at their jobs. Needless to say, the possibilities for what you can do online are almost endless. You can get into real time wasters like quizzes, celebrity gossip, or hunting down blogs on your favorite subject. Stay away from porn if you're smart, as you'll eventually get caught.

This will be embarrassing, particularly if you have an odd fetish. Of course, there's always shopping. You can spend up to half your time at work this way if you're careful about being spotted, and you can take care of tons of personal matters while sitting at your desk.

2. SPACING OUT—Interestingly, this is the second-most reported time-stealing activity. Considering how tired people are these days, thanks to poor sleep habits and crazy schedules, spacing out actually seems like a reasonable thing to do. It's sort of like taking a nap with your eyes open. You'll look like an idiot, but if you keep the drooling to a minimum, you should be OK.

3. OFFICE GOSSIP—What's better than getting the dirt on the people you work with? Some brilliant person once said that offices are just like high school, but with better shoes. Well, the part about the shoes is debatable, but it's absolutely true that our love for nasty information about the people we know and the joy of passing that information on never leaves us. A few trips to the break room can add up to an hour or so of pilfered time per day.

4. TECH SUPPORT—Computer crashes and printer jams cause the majority of legitimately wasted time in the workplace. Blame these when you need to fake some downtime.

5. TWO TIMING—A great way to maximize your time and your earnings is to use your me time at the office to conduct a second job. By stealing a few hours a day, you can quietly conduct any business you have for your other job and make double the money you normally would in the same time.

6. SALES CALL—If you need a way to justify time spent outside the office, and you're a salesperson, you've got it made. Just schedule sales

calls for the times when you've got errands to run or any other personal matters to take care of. You'll preserve the illusion that you're a workhorse while you're taking care of (your) business.

MOST LIKELY TO SUCCEED

You'll do great with this cheat if you don't have a manager to report to at all. It's an uncommon situation, but it does happen. You're also tailor-made for this cheat if you have a really low-profile job, like being an IT guy at a nontech company. No one knows what you do, how you do it, or where you go when you're not fixing their computer.

If your manager cares about being liked and will look the other way when someone is slacking off, you'll succeed splendidly with this cheat. If your manager is into whip cracking, you don't stand a chance of pulling it off.

Finally, if you do an amazing job for your company and pull in scores of clients and untold fortunes, you can do whatever you want. Come and go as you please and act as rude as you like while you do it. Money talks, and if you bring it in, your bad attitude won't be asked to walk.

CATCHING OFFICE SLACKERS
AT THEIR OWN GAME

If you're the manager of a time thief, or you think your colleague is one, it's best to catch them in the act before the accusations fly. Here are some of the ways to catch these cheaters in their tracks:

Have a checklist of deliverables that must be accomplished within prescribed periods of time. Follow up with the suspected slacker regularly. Make your suspect join a daily morning check-in. This will cut down on late arrivals. Check email for an excessive number of personal communications or activity related to another job. Check browser history. Too many sessions spent on Paris Hilton–related websites or dating sites spells trouble. Skulk around during phone calls. Listen in for anything unrelated to the job. Join in on sales meetings without warning and have them scheduled at your office.

If you want to be humane, just allow for more mental-health days or give the employee a more challenging assignment. See if there's a change in behavior. If so, congratulations! You've made positive change, and you actually deserve your management role. You are in the minority.

✎ *Would I Lie?* ✎

.... **1** ....

A 2005 survey revealed that the average worker spends over two hours a day wasting time at the office. Socializing with coworkers, surfing the net, and just spacing out are the primary ways in which workers avoid working daily. Another 2005 survey, the Harris Interactive poll, claimed that employees used the internet for personal business an average of 3.7 hours per *week.* If so many workers are actually slacking for more than two hours each *day,* either some people aren't telling the truth, or they have managed to space out on the other 6.3 hours a week that they're not working at work!

.... **2** ....

With the abundance of people surfing the net while they're supposed to be working, some websites have begun to cater

(continued)

to the slackers. One site that's dedicated to jokes and quizzes even has a "panic button" for when your boss unexpectedly approaches your desk. You click on the link, and it takes you to a search page for "productivity tools." The site also features a disclaimer that it's not the site's fault if someone is caught on it by their boss and loses their job. The disclaimer may be unnecessary, as many companies have given up on heavily policing their employees' internet usage.

······································ 3 ·······································

One of the most famous examples of blowing off your job can be seen in the 1999 film *Office Space*. Peter Gibbons works as a software analyst at a company called Initech. The company boasts a corporate structure complete with motivational speeches, mission statements, and paperwork protocols, all of which just make Peter and his friends more and more disenchanted. Sound familiar? The movie goes on to have Peter rise to success by demonstrating absolutely no interest or concern about his job whatsoever. His attitude is considered fresh and innovative. It's a lesson to office workers everywhere that getting overly invested in the insanity of corporate life is a road to nowhere, whereas following your own vision is the road to happiness.

CHEATING ON A TEST

IS THERE GOING TO BE
AN ESSAY QUESTION?

One of the first times in our lives that we encounter the urge to cheat is in school. It could be at a very tender age that we are faced for the very first time with the knowledge that we have to produce information or complete a task that we are just woefully unprepared to do so. The mind races—what to do? Conveniently, our classmate has not yet mastered the art of shielding his or her test paper from prying eyes, and a tantalizing array of answers is a mere two feet away. Sweet salvation! Time to fill in those blanks and enter the world of cheaters.

This is not to say that cheating on tests is confined to elementary school. Oh no. Any scholastic environment, from first grade straight through graduate school, can be a hotbed of exam falsification. Why stop there? Do you have to pass your driver's test? The same methods used to cheat in Biology 101 will serve you awfully well when you're trying to remember the hand signal for a left turn.

The bottom line is this: No one likes to study, and no one likes to fail. This dazzling combination leads most people down the path of searching for shortcuts and crafty cheating techniques. Why dedicate hours of study, review, writing flash cards, quizzing yourself and your friends, and writing practice essays when you could cheat? You'll save a huge amount of time and possibly wind up with the same score you would have anyway. You might even learn something while you're typing up your crib sheets. True, you won't have the same sense of accomplishment and victory that you might when you legitimately get an A plus, but you will experience the warm glow of having gotten away with your carefully crafted subterfuge.

Cheating at tests is a classic cheat, and the one drawback that goes along with it is that anyone administering a test expects certain people to pull a few tricks to get away without studying. If you're a test cheater, your adversaries are skilled at sniffing you out, so be careful and clever about what you do to get that grade. If you're smart and resourceful enough, you can pull it off. Then again, if you're so smart and resourceful, you could probably score without cheating. Then *again,* that would mean expending all that effort. Forget it. Take out your No. 2 pencil and let the cheating begin.

THE UPSIDE

Getting an A is a glorious thing. Your parents will be thrilled, you'll have the heat off you at school for a while because no one will be riding you to study harder, you won't be forced to have a tutor (unless you want a really hot tutor like in those classic eighties movies), and you'll be in the process of creating a great academic record. Rack up enough good grades, and an Ivy League college, top grad school, or great job can be within easy reach.

More than ever, being a self-made person without the benefit of an education is harder and harder to do. In a world where people fight tooth and nail to get their kids into prestigious kindergartens, it's clear that school is not just meant to educate kids but to provide them with a pedigree that could serve them well their whole lives. But what if you get to Andover, Miss Porter's, or Princeton only to find that you're in way over your head? What do you do when everyone else is effortlessly winging his or her way through differential calculus, and you're still struggling to find the square of the hypotenuse? This is why cheating on tests is your ticket to the big time. Don't blow it and get kicked out of the spawning ground for the masters (and mistresses) of the universe. If you can pull this off and stay at the top of whatever school you managed to get into, your parents will be thrilled, and your teenage/young-adult years could be significantly more hassle free than that of your peers.

So get to work on creating the methods of cheating that work best for you and let 'er rip. When you're leaning back in your comfy leather chair in the corner office, you'll be glad you did.

THE DRAWBACK

Getting caught sucks. It's embarrassing, your parents and teachers will freak out, you'll get put on detention or academic probation, and life will generally be cringe-worthy for a while. If, heaven forbid, your school has an honor code, you're doubly screwed. Not only did you cheat, but you signed an agreement saying you wouldn't cheat and would, in fact, rat anyone out if *you* caught *them* cheating. Ouch.

The next step, of course, is that if you get caught cheating frequently enough, you can get suspended and then expelled. This is not part of the plan. Cheating is meant to give you a leg up, not ruin any chances you might have at advancement. If you find that you're a terrible cheater, don't do it. It takes skill and panache to cheat well. If you ain't got it, don't push it.

If you get caught cheating at any kind of test that's not academically related, the consequences can be equally inconvenient and severe. Cheating at a driving exam could result in your not being able to have a driver's license, at least for a while. Not good if you live in an area lacking in public transportation. If you decide to cheat on something a little weightier, like a civil-service exam, you could find yourself barred from ever getting a government job, not to mention on the wrong side of the law.

TOOLS OF THE TRADE

The necessary tools for this cheat are as varied as the cheaters who do it. Imagination is key here, as the more innovative you are at cheating on your test, the less likely it is that your teachers or test administrators will catch on to your game. New technologies are making cheating easier and detection harder, but sometimes it's the tried-and-true methods that really make the grade. Here's a sampling of some tools that might come in handy:

1. Money
2. Good eyesight or corrective lenses
3. Calculator

4. Older sibling or friend
5. Coconspirators

WAYS AND MEANS: HOW TO PULL IT OFF

There are tons of ways to cheat on tests, and people are coming up with new methods every day, but teachers, professors, and exam administrators make it their job to stay clued in to what the most innovative cheaters are trying. The best way to remain undetected is to keep it simple and not get caught with whatever device or crib sheet you've elected to use. With that in mind, some of the best ways to cheat your way through a test or exam are:

1. GET ADVANCE COPIES OF THE EXAM—Most teachers who have been around for more than a year or two find that totally reinventing their tests is too time consuming and arduous. Therefore, test questions get recycled from year to year, and whole tests might pop up unaltered on a regular basis. Students get wise to this and create minilibraries chockablock with old tests and lists of likely essay questions. If you belong to a fraternity or sorority, chances are your fellow Greeks can get you all the old tests and answers you need. If you're in high school or grad school, an older sibling or entrepreneurial alumnus can most likely provide the same service.

2. BRIBERY—If you can't find someone with a library of old tests, there's a chance that someone in the school's copy center can be convinced to share a test paper with you for a mutually agreed upon sum. Choose your mark carefully. No need to get ratted out before you even take the test.

3. COPYING—The classic. This is a particularly good technique for standardized tests, where bubbles filled in with a No. 2 pencil make an

easily recognized pattern on the page. Instead of having to memorize a sequence of As, Bs, Cs, and occasional Ds, all you have to do is note that your brainy neighbor's page looks remarkably like a picket fence turned on its side. Your test-taking experience will take a magical leap from frustrating to fun as you merrily create a similar fence on your own page. If you aren't taking a standardized test, make sure to sit next to someone who's smart *and* has oversized handwriting. Extra points for finding the braniac who doesn't shield his or her paper with a protective arm.

4. **BRING THE ANSWERS WITH YOU**— Crib sheets are great if you can sneak them in, but horribly incriminating if you get caught. Half the work of creating a good crib sheet is the task of writing every possible fact, formula, or theorem that you think you'll need on the smallest piece of paper imaginable. This includes gum wrappers, tissue packets, and candy wrappers. You can also engrave the answers on the soft wood of a pencil, but this requires a level of skill not dissimilar to a jeweler, and unless you've got your loupe handy, this is not a recommended method. The best way to go with crib sheets is to commit your smuggled information to your own body parts, as these can be concealed easily, and it's the rare professor who will dive down someone's shirt with abandon to retrieve cribbed material. No one wants to get fired for groping a student, be they male or female, so line up your ballpoints and start scribbling. Writing the answers on your desk is OK, so long as you're always in the same seat.

5. **GADGETS AND GIZMOS**— Calculators, PalmPilots, cell phones, and digital watches can all be programmed with information in text format that can help you out on a test when you're drawing a blank. You can even sneak an iPod or Walkman into a test with all the answers prerecorded so that you can listen at your leisure as you take the test.

Although this seems like a great way to secretly get information into the testing facility, fooling around with buttons, contraptions, and headphones is so distracting that you'll most likely get caught. If, however, you can pull this off so that it's hands free (like, start the tape running before you even enter the room), then you've got a fighting chance.

6. CONSPIRACY THEORY—If you've got a friend who's interested in cheating too, you'll quickly learn that as in all things, when it comes to cheating on exams, two heads are better than one. Whatever method you decide to use to cheat, if you split up the work, it requires less time and preparation per person in order to get out of the experience with a decent grade. One of the best ways to collude with a pal is to cheat on a standardized test. Then, all you need to communicate to each other is A, B, C, or D, and you're home free. This can be done through a series of sounds (one tap for A, two for B, and so on), movements (cross your legs for A, your arms for B. . . .), or whatever you can come up with. Just make sure that your coconspirator can keep his or her mouth shut about your plan and is smart enough to remember the answers and your code.

MOST LIKELY TO SUCCEED

The person most likely to succeed at this cheat is, of course, the one who can remain discreet about his or her intentions. A successful exam cheater is also inventive and resourceful, as exam proctors are going to be on the lookout for anyone whose actions look the least bit suspicious. The most successful subversive test taker, however, is the one who knows not to be greedy. It's the B minus student who cheats to get not an A but a B or even a B minus who's going to emerge from this situation triumphant. The victorious cheater also knows to remain inconspicuous and to fade into the background. This applies to both conduct in the classroom and your behavior once the results come in. Craftiness, a subversive mind-set, a total lack of fear, and grace under pressure are the guideposts for successful cheaters of this particular ilk.

CATCHING EXAM CHEATERS
AT THEIR OWN GAME

Keep your eyes open and don't fall for students' usual ploys. They'll try every trick in the book, and it's up to you to maintain some sense of order.

A few choice rules to follow are: Under no circumstances should you answer questions during a test. This is usually a ruse to distract you so that your pupils can indulge in a brief but rampant bout of cheating on the exam. Similarly, keep the test takers spaced far enough apart so there's no way that they can eyeball one another's papers during the course of the exam. Confiscate iPods and all other electronic devices, and under no circumstances should hoods or hats be worn during the test. These can obscure headphones and conceal crib sheets that can be referenced with a quick glance ceiling-ward.

Catching students who cheat on tests all boils down to this golden rule: Hope for the best, expect the worst, keep your eyes open, and expect the unexpected.

❧ *Would I Lie?* ❧

1

Students aren't the only ones who cheat on tests—teachers and principals do it too. In 1998 Stacey Moscowitz, a third-grade teacher at PS 90 in the South Bronx, decided that it was time to come clean. She revealed that under the encouragement of her former principal, she and many other teachers at PS 90 had given their students the answers to their standardized tests in order to boost the school's performance levels. Moscowitz approached the NYC schools' independent investigator, Ed Stancik, and after an investigation that lasted eighteen months, he discovered standardized-test cheating at thirty-two schools in all five boroughs. Fifty-two educators were implicated. Sadly enough, most of the schools where cheating was uncovered were the same ones that had recently received great press for turning around their programs and improving their scores.

·· 2 ··

A 1998 survey conducted by the Josephson Institute of Ethics polled 20,829 middle- and high-school students about cheating. Seventy percent of the high-school students and 54 percent of the middle-school students admitted to having cheated on a test or exam in the last year. The incidence of cheating among high-school students went up 6 percent in just two years. In the "Who's Who Among American High School Students" poll, from the same year, 3,123 high-school students with an A or B average were asked similar questions, and 80 percent of them had cheated. Ninety-five percent had never been caught, and more than half of the students said that they thought cheating was no big deal. Thanks to technology these days, many students have a very easy time cheating on tests. They can use their cell phone cameras to snap pictures of their test paper to send answers to a friend, and a

(continued)

lot of students are so good at text messaging blind that they can text "What's the answer to number seven?" to their friend without the teacher even noticing. One student described a day when their teacher was out, and they had a substitute administering a test. A few students distracted the sub while the others took pictures of the test. Some schools have banned the use of cell phones in school as a way to combat this growing problem, but most of them don't even seem to realize what a big issue it is.

CHEATING AT BLACKJACK

YOU'RE SO MONEY, BABY

Blackjack is a really simple game with a basic premise. Anyone can play, which is why it's so appealing. All you have to be able to do is count to twenty-one and do the simple arithmetic to add up the value of your face cards. If your cards' value is equal to twenty-one, you win. You also win if the value of the cards in your hand is higher than the dealer's, but not over twenty-one. It's in blackjack that you can use cool card player terminology like "double down" (betting that you'll win the hand with only one more card) or "split pairs" (making a hand that's a pair of the same card into two separate hands to play). Looking or feeling cool at the table is a big part of having fun when you play and wanting to play more. Gamblers and first-time players gravitate to blackjack tables because they think they can handle such a simple and entertaining game and possibly walk away from the table with some winnings. Think again.

As with all casino games, the odds of winning at blackjack are not in your favor. If you play fair and simply let the cards that come out of the shoe (the dealer's multicard dealing mechanism), the house will always have at least a 6 percent advantage. That means that if you play consistently, you'll consistently lose at least 6 percent of your money. These lame odds have inspired many people to explore how they can beat the house and cheat their way to big money at the blackjack tables.

There are two different types of people who will find themselves cheating at cards at some point in their gambling careers. The first is the cheater who stumbles into it. This is not someone who plans to defraud their fellow players or the casino. This is the cheater who finds himself or herself presented with an opportunity and then grabs it. This is not a career card cheat, but a regular guy or gal who has a shot at making some decent cash once in a blue moon. This opportunistic cheater isn't a real threat to casinos and probably won't get nabbed. The only way that might happen is if he or she gets cocky and tries to cheat beyond his or her skill level.

The second type of cheater is the real card cheat, who plans the way he or she will get control of the table and takes away a consistently large pot. This card cheater is not a gambler. A gambler is someone who doesn't know what the outcome of the day (or night) at the casino will be. This real tactician knows precisely what he or she is doing and what the take will be.

If you just want to have a fun night out on the town, aren't a good planner, can't keep track of large amounts of information in your head, or don't have a team to back you up, cheating at blackjack is not for you. If you're not up for sucker bets or being a casino's patsy, step right up. Take control of the game and cheat your way to twenty-one.

THE UPSIDE

Going to Vegas, or any casinos for that matter, can be loads of fun. They're loud, colorful, have lots of people around, and serve rivers of free booze. Respectable people have flocked to casinos since they first gained popularity, albeit illegally, in 1888 with Richard A. Canfield's Madison Square Club in New York City. In 1931 Nevada legalized gambling and has been a mecca for gaming and betting ever since.

Cheating at blackjack offers the advantage of making a career out of hanging out at some of the most colorful and exciting venues on earth. Provided that you can keep a low enough profile at your casinos of choice, you can ogle the attractive staff, get lots of free drinks, get comped with free rooms, and possibly avoid having to work a regular nine-to-five job ever again. That's pretty tempting for anyone who thinks they've got it in them to beat the house. For those who don't have a plan worked out ahead of time, it's a major motivation to figure it out.

The other obvious advantage is the money. If you create a strategy that works for you, you can rake in huge amounts of cash. Yes, you'll have to make sure the casinos (who won't be as impressed with your cheating skills as you are) never know who you are, and you'll have to figure out how you'll deal with the IRS. Even so, winning big at the blackjack tables can really provide a fantasy lifestyle. You'll have fun, make a profit, and, with any luck, be able to retire early.

THE DRAWBACK

As much as it can be fun to play blackjack for days on end, pretend you're Danny Ocean, and sip free scotch until you fall off your stool, there are some serious downsides.

First off, gambling is an addiction that can rob people of everything in their lives. If you're not looking at your blackjack cheating as a career but as a compulsion, you've got to stop and get help. Compulsive gambling is no less a disease than alcoholism. If you think you're going down that road, you'll be in a world of trouble.

Similarly, gamblers who hang around casinos too long can find themselves with a sweet little alcohol problem. It can be argued that anyone who has an addiction had an existing predisposition, but even if what you've got is a habit and not an addiction, try to avoid cultivating it. Monster hangovers and waking up with weird stuff like unexplainable rope burns just aren't worth it.

The biggest drawback to cheating at blackjack is what can happen if the casinos find out. Initially, you might just get a warning. If you persist, things might get ugly. It's true that 1950s-style ring-a-ding-ding gangster-type tactics may be a thing of the past, but you never know. Do you really want to get caught defrauding the house? Not only will a dwindling number of casinos let you in the door once you've been identified, but you'll spend a lot of time looking over your shoulder. There's nothing good about meeting guys with names like "Vinnie the Hammer" and "Tony the Gun." They will also not be amused when you notice the lack of irony in their nicknames, as they actually do each carry, respectively, a hammer and a gun.

TOOLS OF THE TRADE

A good memory is essential to cheating at blackjack. Whatever you can do to keep your mind sharp will be invaluable. You should also take the time to practice as much as possible. This is definitely not a situation where you can wing it. Weeks or even months of preparation will be necessary. You'll need:

1. A few card decks
2. Coconspirators
3. Ginkgo biloba

WAYS AND MEANS: HOW TO PULL IT OFF

Cheating at blackjack boils down to one thing: counting cards. There are a few other things you can do to try to beat the house, but counting cards is the number one way to get the edge.

1. SHARPEN YOUR MEMORY—There are a few ways you can keep your mind focused and your memory sharp. Crossword puzzles, high-speed arithmetic, brain teasers, and trivia quizzes will all help. You can also take herbal supplements such as ginkgo biloba to help you along. Whatever your course of action, keep it up and don't get lazy. A mushy mind and faulty memory will insure failure.

2. KNOW THE RULES OF THE GAME—There are a few nuances to playing blackjack, and many ways that people approach the game. There's no shortage of books on the market that provide basic instruction on how to play. Don't be overconfident. Do your research.

3. COUNTING CARDS—This is the primary way that most people cheat at blackjack. Card counting is exactly what it says it is; it's the practice of being able to count, or keep track, of the cards that the dealer is dealing out of the shoe on the table. If you can keep track of all the cards that have been dealt and played while you're at the table, you can predict which ones are left to be dealt and therefore most likely to come

up next. Since high cards can lead to a natural blackjack (twenty-one made up of two cards) more easily than low cards, keeping track of the ratio of high to low cards is an important part of keeping count and helps you to calculate your payoff. While card counting is not illegal, it is considered against the rules by all casinos, without exception. Skilled card counters can keep track of the "running count" (the cards still in the shoe) in their heads, but it isn't unheard of for gamblers to carry calculators or other handheld computing devices for this purpose. That is absolutely against the rules and is illegal. You definitely don't want to get caught doing that, or it's a short trip to the parking lot for a stern talking to and then a stay in jail. If you can hold the count in your head, don't be fazed by casinos that use six decks or more in the dealer's shoe. You simply have to divide the running count by the number of decks being used.

4. CARD MARKING—As with all card games, it helps to know which cards are being dealt. In blackjack, you want to know if the high-value cards are hitting the table, and marking the cards can help. You can do this by scratching the laminate on the cards, marking them (subtly) with ink, pricking them with a pin, or whatever else you can cook up. Unlike poker or other games where players can touch the cards, only the dealer touches the cards in blackjack, so sneaking the marked cards onto the table and into the shoe can be tricky. Your only hope may be slipping an altered deck into the dealer's supply before you start playing.

5. DOUBLE DEALING—If there's just no way you can keep all those numbers straight in your head, you can always see if the dealer wants to get in on your scheme. Since the dealer is the only person who can touch the cards and can possibly see them before they're dealt, he or she is in a perfect position to make sure that the right person gets the right

cards. If you're a lousy player but need to make some money fast, you can cut the dealer in on the take provided that you're given the right cards to win. If you do this, make sure it's not a setup by the casino to find dirty players.

6. TEAM PLAYERS—If you can't find a dealer to cooperate, you can get a few buddies in on the act and work the tables as a team. By distracting the casino employees who are supposed to keep their eyes on specific cheaters, blackjack teams can do a lot of damage at the tables before anyone catches on to them. To create a blackjack team, you need at least two people. The first is the person who sits at the table and places low bets. The size of the bets and the manner in which this first player, or "spotter," plays should remain constant. The spotter is also the card counter. It's up to him to determine when the ratio of high to low cards is in his favor, and the deck is about to yield something good. At that point, he signals the second team member. This team member plays the role of a big spender. He or she comes over to the table acting flamboyantly, to take attention away from the spotter. The big spender's job is to swoop in, make big bets and win big returns, and then get out quickly. The spotter follows on his heels. You can add more people to the team as you see fit, depending on how much distraction is needed in the casino and how thick a smokescreen you need to create.

MOST LIKELY TO SUCCEED

If you're good at math, can store large amounts of information in your head, and aren't easily distracted, this is the cheat for you. Extra points for being able to assemble and manage a team of gamblers, who are all probably going to be self-interested and greedy. You get even more extra points if you've got decent acting chops, so you can avoid the pit boss's attention once you're inside the casino.

CATCHING BLACKJACK CHEATS
AT THEIR OWN GAME

Casinos have many secret ways to detect cheaters when they walk in the door. Hidden cameras loom over the tables, constantly monitoring players and their every move. If, for some unimaginable reason, the usual methods don't expose the blackjack cheater, there are a few tried-and-true ways to deter and detect them. Anyone who wins over three thousand dollars at a table should get a second look; keep shuffling the cards; keep a flow of new cards in the deck and check all decks for tampering; change dealers regularly; throw away a few cards in every deck to throw off the count; and, finally, watch anyone who is overly animated or distracting. Anyone who's too zany is probably there to make sure you're not looking at the very quiet person counting cards in the corner.

∽ *Would I Lie?* ∾

.... **1** ....

Richard Marcus is one of gambling's most famous cheaters. While working at casinos and learning the ins and outs of blackjack and baccarat tables, Marcus was approached by a man named Joe Classon, who asked Marcus to join his casino-hustling team. Marcus agreed, and Classon taught him all the tricks of the trade until he retired. Marcus then formed his own team and continued to cheat casinos for twenty-five years. One of his signature moves was to bet three red chips with a brown chip underneath (the red chips being worth $5 each and the brown being worth $500), so that it looked like only a $15 bet to the dealer. If Marcus won, he showed the dealer the brown chip at the bottom of the stack for a payout of $1,030, but if he lost, he quickly swiped the stack for one of only three red chips.

.... **2** ....

Ken Uston was a famous blackjack player who relied on counting cards to win games. He had an MBA from Harvard, an economics degree from Yale, and an IQ of 169. He was senior vice president of the Pacific Stock Exchange by day, Vegas blackjack hustler by night. Uston won so much money playing blackjack in Vegas that he was soon blacklisted from its casinos. He then moved to Atlantic City and proceeded to win millions of dollars until being blacklisted there as well. Eventually he was not allowed into any casinos in the world, because all had learned of his uncanny ability to take their money. He was found dead in his Paris apartment in 1987. The case was never closed, and investigators suspected murder.

.... **3** ....

In the nineties, a group of students from the Massachusetts Institute of Technology formed an extracurricular blackjack club that evolved into one of the most notable card-counting rings of its time. Using well-known strategy books, the MIT students learned to keep a running tally of each card that was played and ended up winning over $3 million while flying from Boston to Vegas for three years. They perfected the sys-

(continued)

tem by creating a method that divided their team into "spot-ters," "gorillas," and "big players." The spotters made small bets and counted cards, the gorillas used the spotters' signals to bet big but play dumb, while the big players were the fa-miliar faces in the casinos—the meticulous high rollers who always bet large sums of money. Eventually one of their team members betrayed them, and they were expelled from Vegas.

GETTING AWAY WITH TAX FRAUD—CORPORATE

THE RICH GET RICHER . . .

As most of us probably know, the average U.S. citizen spends most of his or her mental energy during March and early April trying to figure out how to avoid paying too much in taxes. Despite this mass effort to keep our money in our own pockets and away from our state and federal governments, it isn't the fault of the individual American that between $3 billion and $4 billion in taxes aren't paid on a yearly basis. No, we have American businesses to thank for the discrepancy.

Corporations should be paying roughly 35 percent of their profit in taxes, but thanks to a variety of questionable accounting and legal maneuvers, they pay around 17 percent instead. That's a stark contrast to the usual 33 percent paid by the private citizen. How can this be? Is there a magic formula that businesses use to decrease their tax payments by half? Is there some sort of corporate alchemy that's performed by a secret cabal of CEOs and their accountants, dressed in pin-striped robes over a bubbling cauldron?

No, of course not. In the corporate world, money begets money, and that's the overarching secret behind corporate tax fraud and evasion. If a company is big enough and has enough money, it can generally buy its way to freedom from the statutory tax rate. By lining the pockets of everyone up the legal and government food chain, from lobbyists to senators, the money saved in taxes still outweighs the payments made to these special-interest stooges.

If a corporation is loath to get caught stuffing funds into the pockets of individuals or groups that are supposed to be unbiased, there are a few other ways to hold on to profits. One of the best ways is to set up a clever tax shelter that looks like a normal business decision from the outside. From the inside, it looks like a brilliant tax evasion scheme and could increase the income of the corporate officers immeasurably. The fun is deciding which tax shelter you'll choose and what perks can come with it. The bottom line here is, if you're a huge business with profits in the billions, you're only going to keep getting richer. You could agree to pay taxes the way you're supposed to and see your income decrease significantly. Or you could do what all the other kids are doing and make sure that you protect the status quo. Play dirty, make payoffs, and constantly invent new accounting practices.

THE UPSIDE

As with all cheats that have to do directly with money, the primary upside to this cheat is—you guessed it, money! It's inconceivable that you'd win the lottery by making it to CEO of a multibillion dollar business and then *not* be able to enjoy an obscene bonus or payout from your stock options. Ludicrous! By avoiding paying your taxes, or at least paying only half, your financial life can change enormously. One Learjet doesn't do anyone any good, but one for each member of the family makes perfect sense!

That brings up another aspect of the joy of the kind of wealth that can be received by corporate officers for companies that pay a fraction of their taxes. The toys you can buy are outrageous. Want an entourage? Done. Does your kid want to release an album? Done. Feel like having multiple homes that correspond to where you like to vacation? Done. Rich or poor, it's still good to be rich.

Another upside beyond being absurdly wealthy is that the chances are you'll be able to hang on to your cash. Why is this? Do you have to keep it in cash, stuffed into random pieces of furniture like they did in *Goodfellas*? No, using your hard-earned dollars as part of your upholstery isn't necessary. You're going to be just fine because the chances that you'll be audited are slim. The IRS, bless its heart, is so overworked and short staffed that it turns its attention only to the biggest problems on its rosters, and that means the criminal cases. So long as you can avoid sliding down the slippery slope from prudent business decision to out-and-out theft, you should be fine.

Corporations are also blessed in that they have the home team rooting for them in Washington. It's no secret that big corporations have lobbyists on the hill barking about their cause to any senators or congressmen who will listen. If the cause is interesting enough (from a political perspective) and the opportunity for financial gain is there, politicians will work to forward your cause. They're like your patron saints of politics, watching over your interests every time you pray and leave a tribute.

THE DRAWBACK

Despite the wealth and all the joy that comes with it, there are a few drawbacks to hanging on to money that the government feels is theirs. Should the government audit your business and find that you have a tax shelter, the first question they'll ask is if the tax shelter serves any business purpose beyond getting your money out of the way so it can't be taxed. If the shelter serves no other purpose, that shelter will be shut down. As if that wasn't bad enough, the company will owe back taxes on the entity that was protected by the shelter. Depending on how long the shelter existed and how much was in it, the company could be looking at a situation that would make the good times come to a screeching halt.

When a private individual is on the stand, he or she can invoke the Fifth Amendment. By doing so, the individual can avoid speaking and therefore saying anything that might incriminate himself or herself. Sadly for corporations, that's not the case. A corporation doesn't have all the same rights extended to it that an individual does under common law, as they are recognized as being separate entities with different interests. So a corporation under investigation can't stay mum on any subject. Let's just hope that whoever goes on the stand is coached very well.

Until recently, the laws in place for corporations vis-à-vis taxes have been very lenient and designed to encourage the growth of businesses and jobs. The tides are changing, in an effort to crack down on tax evasion, as the billions of dollars that are going unpaid are causing cracks to appear in our infrastructure. Oops! Time to do something! Petitions for corporate accountability are cropping up that would require big businesses to file a report with the secretary of the state, providing tax information that was previously private. If it's a publicly traded company, that public tax information, along with shareholder information, would keep companies from blithely skipping down Enron's path.

Speaking of Enron, if you bilk the government (and your shareholders) in a completely over-the-top way, you'll get found out eventually. Someone will get fed up and blow the whistle on you. That's when you pray the next stop is Club Fed. Apparently the chicken divan is great there on Tuesdays. If you're not so lucky, be sure to make friends with the right people fast. But you're probably good at that already. Finally, stress can be a serious problem. Sure, it's fun to be king, but if you're running a company, and you see it's getting out of hand, it's up to you to keep all the balls in the air. That can be stressful under the best of times. Be careful, you're only human. Too much financial madness balanced on your shoulders, and you'll go down. Heart attack or stroke, you're going down.

TOOLS OF THE TRADE

Your attorney and accounting department (or outside firm) are your golden tickets. Do not let them run amok with your company's funds, but don't micromanage them. These people will keep your company doing well. Why? There's a lot in it for them. They'll have their own methodology for keeping your financial behemoth alive, but here are a few things for all CEOs, presidents, CFOs, and COOs to remember to have:

1. Good accountant/accounting firm
2. Good attorney/law firm
3. Two sets of books—good hiding place for real books!

4. Discretion
5. Ability to move offshore (have good reason)
6. Extra cash for bribes

WAYS AND MEANS: HOW TO PULL IT OFF

Now that you've got your tools lined up, here's the methodology to follow to make the cheat really come together:

1. TAX SHELTERS—A tax shelter is a method used to protect funds from being taxable. There are tons of ways to do it, but the trick is to find a way so that you can legitimately squirrel away enough money to make a difference. If you're the head of a big company, one option you can consider is moving your company offshore. You may not want to move the whole operation out of the U.S., for a variety of business and political reasons, but at least part of it can go. Consider Bermuda. Others have gone before you, so there will be golf partners at the ready. You'll also get to wear those cute shorts. Think of it: a tropical island, deals to be done, country clubs. Sounds like paradise!

2. GET IN BED WITH THE RIGHT PEOPLE—If you're going to get in bed with the politicos (and you should, or else you'll never have the juice you need to get anything done for your company's interests), make sure that you snuggle up to a well-respected senator or congressman. You'd do well to avoid the current slew of politicians who have a penchant for chasing interns around the desk, or who make outrageous remarks about people with lifestyles different from their own (only to turn out to be living precisely the lifestyle he or she condemned). Stay away from these excitable types and get yourself a nice, steady, level-headed person. Take a page from Tyco, which hired Bob Dole to defend its tax shelter. Wise move, Tyco. Everybody loves Bob Dole, particularly after his honest sharing about his erectile dysfunction. That man is a hero.

3. DEFEND YOUR TAX SHELTER—If you can't get Bob Dole to defend your tax shelter, find someone else fast. And find someone who knows what they're doing. Try not to use the excuse that Accenture did regarding why it chose Bermuda for corporate offices. The company claimed that its European staff didn't want to be in the U.S., and its U.S. staff didn't want to be in Europe. So they settled for Bermuda. This defense makes it sound like the heads of this major company were college sophomores squabbling about roommating dilemmas. Do we live off campus near Pizza Hut or near the Laundromat? Neither, dudes, we have to be near the bar. Oh, OK, dude.

4. PHONY PROFIT REPORTING—In an interesting little twist of fate, the information a publicly traded company has to give its shareholders is not the same information it must give the IRS. You can, as a result, report billions of dollars in profit to shareholders but claim it as a loss to the IRS. This double reporting means that no taxes are paid on the "loss," because the IRS treats the payout as a tax liability, whereas the shareholders get a big, fat untaxed payday. Does this remind anyone of *The Producers*?

5. OPINION LETTERS—These are an inspired and somewhat hilarious invention. For a mere seventy thousand dollars or so, a law firm will write an opinion letter for a corporate client that acts as a guarantee to that client that its tax shelter is legitimate. The letter can then help if your company is investigated by the IRS, which will view the opinion letter as an indication that it should waive any additional penalties that may have been incurred along with the original tax owed. This is the equivalent of getting a note from your mother that you shouldn't go to gym class. There aren't any real teeth behind the note. It doesn't have any meaning. It's just a mutually agreed upon tool to help the cheating along.

6. MOTIVATED ACCOUNTANT—An accountant who stands to gain a lot is a good person to have around. If you make money, he makes money, and that means he'll be as creative as necessary to keep your company's money safe and snug in its little offshore account. A 1991 change in the accounting rules allowed for accountants to be paid a percentage of the money they saved the client from being taxed. Not hard to do the math on that one.

MOST LIKELY TO SUCCEED

The trick to avoiding getting caught at anything you shouldn't be doing is using a little discretion. If you flaunt your questionable activities, someone will eventually step up and bust you. Here are the qualities that the successful corporate shark holds so dear:

If you keep your company midsized, you will avoid the scrutiny you'd normally get if you were a huge behemoth of a corporation. Big companies are on the radar right now. The IRS is too strapped to go after everybody, and the midsized firm isn't a current target.

If you're a ruthless, unscrupulous type with a very healthy heart, no cardiovascular problems, and are ulcer free, you're in great shape. If you don't suffer from any of these ailments, either your sleazy business choices don't bother you, or you don't think they're sleazy. That's great! Either way, you'll stick around for a long time, reaping the benefits of your work.

If you're a CEO who can get his or her ego out of the way long enough to let your ace attorneys and accountants do their jobs, you'll be in good shape. It's the hubris and greed of corporate officers that tend to push things over the edge. Hang back and let the right people for the job do their thing.

CATCHING CORPORATE TAX CHEATS AT THEIR OWN GAME

1. Check productivity. Does the profit being declared match the company's output? Does it seem like profits are being buried someplace?

2. Bring in the public company accounting oversight board. Like the cavalry in old Westerns, they swoop in and make sure everything's as it should be. In this case, that means that accountants, corporate officers, and the board are all reporting properly and doing the right thing.

3. If you can't figure out exactly what's going on, find a possible whistle-blower on staff. There's always someone high up enough who's disgruntled about their salary or inability to advance. Get this person to spill the beans.

4. If you're a lobbyist, you'll be approached at some point to champion a cause that smells a little fishy. See what's going on and decide if you feel like blowing a whistle today.

❧ *Would I Lie?* ❧

1

One former strip club owner was convicted of tax evasion in October 2006 for failing to report almost $500,000 worth of income. James Andrew Yeager, owner of two clubs in Missouri, used money from his businesses for personal use without recording it in his books. He also kept thousands of

(continued)

dollars in cash that came from lap dances hidden and undeclared, as well as paying some of his employees in cash. Yeager can face up to fifteen years in prison, while the club's manager is also on trial for failing to file a tax return in 1999.

.... 2 ....

Larry Gagosian of the Gagosian Gallery was sued by the U.S. government in 2003 for refusing to pay taxes in 1990 on capital gains of nearly $18 million in art sales. In January 1990 Gagosian and his partner Peter M. Brant incorporated the Contemporary Art Holding Corporation (CAHC) in Texas, and five days later they merged with a company called Lerand by buying all of its shares. The only assets owned by Lerand were sixty-two paintings belonging to Richard Weisman, its founder, so after the tax-free merger, the paintings became the property of CAHC. Less than a month later, CAHC sold fifty-eight of the paintings to Thomas Ammann for $17,984,484, and didn't pay the taxes. Two of the four remaining paintings were transferred to a company called GJK, owned by their former corporate secretary, for $10 as a "dividend in kind." GJK sold both paintings for millions. The best part is that the day Thomas Ammann bought the fifty-eight paintings, Gagosian and Brant sold all of their shares in CAHC to GJK, thus leaving CAHC without enough assets to pay their taxes.

.... 3 ....

L. Dennis Kozlowski, former CEO of Tyco International, was indicted in 2002 for conducting a risky scheme to avoid paying taxes on $13.2 million worth of paintings. Kozlowski, who lived in New York, managed to evade his state taxes by having the artwork he purchased delivered to Tyco's New Hampshire headquarters instead of his home. He even had empty boxes and fake invoices shipped there to cover his tracks. His corporate persona was no better; under his leadership, Tyco moved its headquarters to Bermuda and opened subsidiaries in other tax havens like Barbados and the Cayman Islands, thus reducing its tax rate from 36 percent to 23 percent.

CHEATING YOUR WAY TO A BETTER GRADE

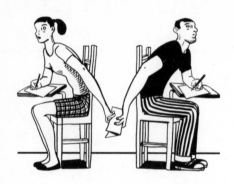

TEACHER'S PET

Sometimes no matter how hard you try, you just can't measure up in the classroom. It's a true but sad fact that no matter what your mother tells you, you're probably not a genius (or all that good looking, but that's a different kettle of fish). We're all on a competitive search for achievement and success from the moment we arrive in our kindergarten classrooms to the day we retire from our jobs, and we learn early on that grades matter. We get graded on how well we color inside the lines, how well we survive in dodgeball, how well we remember multiplication tables, and how well we deliver a thesis on anything from the sexual proclivities of fruit flies to feminist literature in a white male world. Those grades indicate how well we're respected in our schools and if we're going to wind up at Princeton or Podunk U. These, friends, are the facts.

Back to the dilemma at hand. What can you do to compete if you're a moron? What if you're not actually stupid, but just not academically inclined (which is most people, by the way)? The only thing you can do is try your best, make sure you do at least a little studying, and *definitely* pay attention in class and take terrific notes. If you follow those guidelines and still find yourself getting rotten grades, then you have to consider a slightly more imaginative recourse. You'll have to take extra measures to make sure that you can actually get into college—or at least stave off a lifelong career of burger flipping.

Those extra measures could very well be getting a tutor (or a phalanx of them), studying long hours nightly, joining a serious study group, and doing extra credit work to bolster your grades. If all that seems really time consuming and exhausting, you do have one other option. You can cheat your way to a better grade. This involves a variety of techniques, but none of them requires extra academic work, and cheating will leave you with the free time and peace of mind to which you've become accustomed.

A note to the wise: If you are an A-minus student, and you decide to follow these grade-altering suggestions as a means to raising your grade to an A, beware. You are a wiener, no one likes you, and you'll never get laid.

THE UPSIDE
The upside to this cheat is simply that good grades add up to good prospects. Whether it's fair or not, Ivy League schools don't want to

hear from you if you've got a C average. High-level graduate schools won't answer your calls if you didn't go to an Ivy, and white-shoe law firms (and similar job opportunities) are closed to you if your grad school wasn't in the top ten. Cheating to get the grade can't be your only method to make it in life, but it can't hurt to try if you can't make it on your own.

Another advantage stems from the fact that, unfortunately, getting good grades tends to lead to accolades from one's family. If you're getting great marks in school (again, it doesn't matter if you're in grade school or grad school), no one will really get on your case. Of course, your parents always ride you a little, but success in school tends to be the focus of tension and arguments between parents and school-age kids. Avoiding the endless carping from overly concerned parents is like a get-out-of-jail-free card. Life is hard enough without someone constantly on your case for not working hard enough. You'll get enough of that later in life on the job.

Not only will you benefit from the subterfuge, but think of how happy your family will be if you get good grades. Your mom and dad can put one of those obnoxious "My Kid Is on the Honor Roll" bumper stickers on their car. They can brag at family gatherings about you, and, most importantly, it's one less thing for them to worry about. Instead of having a constant heart attack about whether or not you'll succeed in life, they can focus on your sister and what to say about the dime bag they found in her underwear drawer.

THE DRAWBACK

List all the ways that you could get hurt by doing this cheat. What can you lose? What can you get arrested for? What will other people think of you? Will you lose friends? Will you lose family? Is there a religious implication? How long would you suffer as a result of doing this cheat if something bad happened?

If you don't pull this cheat off properly, you'll get known for trying to mess with the school (not to mention your grades), and you'll have to deal with some serious repercussions. These consequences could last a very short time or could haunt you for the duration of your career, so be sure to make your choices wisely.

Should you play your cards wrong, here are a few of the ignominies you could suffer: You might get blacklisted by faculty members and won't be able to contest a grade even if your complaint is totally legitimate. You could also get suspended or expelled, depending on how far you decided to go with your subterfuge. If you did something really out on a limb to help yourself in graduate school, you might get such a bad rap that prospective employers might get notified of what you did. The possibilities are endless and really lie in the hands of the people you messed with. If you challenge a particularly vindictive faculty member and lose, he or she will develop a taste for your blood, and you'll have to contend with a world of pain.

TOOLS OF THE TRADE
The good news is that you only really need one tool for this cheat. But if you ain't got it, forget it. You'll fail, and you'll have only yourself to blame.

1. Hubris*

WAYS AND MEANS: HOW TO PULL IT OFF
OK, got your inflated senses of ambition and desperation all fired up and ready to go? Good. Here's how you enter the grade grubber hall of fame:

* Desperation and a computer help, but only hubris is essential.

1. COURSE SELECTION—Not just any teacher or professor makes a good target for this cheat. You've got to select someone who really cares what his or her students think about them. This makes the professor easier to sway when you complain about your lousy grade. If the professor is worried that he won't be liked or students won't select her course, they'll probably crumble under the pressure. The easiest way to spot this type of teacher is the presence of one or a combination of the following qualities: youth, a proclivity for dating students, and a history of going to the local bars with them. Any professor that desperate to look cool will be putty in your hands.

2. WHINE WITH EVERYTHING—When you just can't tolerate the way that D looks at the top of your test paper, go straight to the school's administration and start complaining. Depending on how rigorous the school's academic program is, how much it relies on students' tuition, and whether or not your teacher has a black mark on his record of any kind, your complaints could very well find a sympathetic audience. If you think the odds aren't in your favor, you could stage a fracas with the professor at the end of the semester. That fabricated bad blood could very well stand up under administrative scrutiny as the basis for a claim of unfair grading.

3. TA-KE THIS GRADE AND SHOVE IT—If your professor doesn't seem like the easily malleable type, turn the bright light of your cheating ways on the teaching assistant. Should you be so lucky as to have a teaching assistant for most of the term (this is common for college survey courses), you can blame the TA for biased grading and have far less to lose than if you go up against a professor. TAs don't have the same sway with the administration as full professors and are really just doing it for the credit anyway. Wearing one of these poor souls down to a nubbin doesn't take much and could yield decent results.

4. GO TEAM GO—Are you an athlete? Do you think you have it in you to become one? In high schools and colleges alike, varsity athletes are groomed to succeed and are frequently rewarded with inflated grades to insure they don't get knocked off the team. Should you really think that you can't cut the mustard academically but are a whiz with a football (or any kind of balls at all), try this method of cheating on for size. Who knows? You might go the distance and get a scholarship to go with the grades.

5. WHAT'S A NICE PROFESSOR LIKE YOU DOING IN A PLACE LIKE THIS?—Threats work. Not all the time, but enough of the time for strong-arm tactics to still be one of the nasty little ways of the world. If you have nothing to lose and really want to go for broke to get a grade, sound the alarm on your teacher or professor. Accusations of nefarious behavior (or at least the threat that you'll make the accusations public) can make a lot of people buckle and choose the path of least resistance. The classic example of this is a female student's claim that a male professor tried to get her into bed, but let your circumstances and creativity be your guide.

6. ERASER HEAD—This method of cheating applies only to multiple-choice tests. If you have no clue as to what the answers are, and you just absolutely cannot fail, try creating ambiguity with multiple erasures and faint circling of answers in pencil. Although not a true grade grub, the indistinctness of your answers could allow you to argue in your favor or at least get a retest.

7. A,B,C EASY AS 1,2,3—Sometimes you just need to change the letter grade written on your test or paper. This cheat is only necessary to employ only if you need to show your parents the grade you earned and simply can't bring home lousy marks. Don't fall into the usual traps of

trying to use Liquid Paper or erase anything. This is beyond amateur-ish, and as long as your parents aren't drunk or semiretarded, they'll know the difference from across the room. Just get a thick marker and change the letter by tracing over it. Ds and Cs can become Bs, but nothing can be changed to an A. If you have to change your grade, you have no business angling for an A anyway.

8. THE RIGHT STUFF—If you've made it to college, and you just can't handle lying (anymore) to get good grades, just opt for a school that won't grade you. Although it seems the stuff of dreams, there are several colleges and universities in the U.S. that allow you to take courses pass-fail. A few of them even forgo the widely accepted requirement of a core curriculum. The amazing part of this collegiate fantasy is that these are some of the best schools in the country, or at least they have really good reputations. So if you con your way well enough through high school, make sure you apply to Brown University, Antioch University, Hampshire College, or Bennington College. It won't matter if you spend four years weaving baskets or studying premed. With apologies to Gertrude Stein, a pass is a pass is a pass.

MOST LIKELY TO SUCCEED

A lack of morality, arrogance, parents who look the other way, and an easily intimidated faculty are the magic combination to succeeding at this cheat. It takes a ton of self-assurance to try this cheat, especially if you're in high school. If you manage to pull this off, you can probably do every cheat in this book and make up an endless list of your own. Just don't go into investment banking or law, because you'll probably wind up in jail.

CATCHING GRADE CHEATS
AT THEIR OWN GAME

The trick to catching people who try to cheat their way to a better grade is to know your students. If you're teaching thirty kids or less in each class, you'll know soon enough what their personalities are like and what they try to get away with. A kid who grade grubs at the end of the year isn't going to start up on the last day of the semester. There'll be indications of it from the first assignment. If you're teaching a survey class, make an announcement at the beginning of the year and before each test that all grades are final. Get the endorsement of the school. Anyone who tries to angle their way into a better grade than what you've handed them is stepping out of line and knows it. This is the definition of a grade grubber.

❧ *Would I Lie?* ❧

1

In a 2005 *Washington Post* editorial by American University journalism professor Alicia Shepard, she describes her first semester teaching and posting her grades on the school's website, only to have two students immediately contact her with complaints about their grades. Because she was new, she questioned her own grading process and decided to look into the complaints. She found that one student's average was a B no matter how you sliced it, so she refused to change it. The other student called, however, and was so persistent on the phone that Shepard decided to bring her B plus up to an A minus, even

(continued)

---

though the student had never spoken in class. Because it was a more subjective grade than an issue of the student's average, Shepard let herself be pushed around by her student.

. . . . 2 . . . .

In 1999 a high-school librarian named Mark Oliver went undercover by pretending to be a student looking for a term paper online. He decided to use a website called High Performance Papers, which promised to tailor the paper exactly to his needs, and as the due date approached, someone from the site informed him that the paper would not be ready on time. The reason was that it was "term paper season," and the site was dealing with about eight hundred requests from high-school and college students per day. His experiment caused Oliver to question whether any students are writing their own papers anymore.

. . . . 3 . . . .

Grade averages among college students have gone up considerably in the last fifty years, and many professors say that it's because of pressure for them to award more As than they used to. Some are reluctant to hand out even Cs anymore. Columbia University Teachers College president Arthur Levine is an expert on grading practices, and he partially blames capitalism for the unjustified rise in marking trends. Most parents pay around $30,000 a year for their child to attend a private university, and they expect them to receive good grades, almost as if the teachers are working for them. They equate a good education with straight As, and when they don't see those results, they go so far as to call professors to complain.

GETTING AWAY WITH OFFICE THEFT

CLEANING UP AFTER HOURS

No matter what your salary, chances are you feel underappreciated and underpaid at your job. If everyone felt great about their job, chances are that Johnny Paycheck's 1977 hit "Take This Job and Shove It" wouldn't have been such a smash. There are lots of ways to console yourself about your career and lousy treatment on the job, and everyone from factory workers to office workers to showgirls does the same kinds of things in an attempt to buck up. They bitch about the boss, go for a few too many drinks after work, or even take the high road and quietly go about trying to find a new gig.

For the less high-minded and decidedly more underhanded group, another avenue to explore is office subterfuge. Knowing that you're taking control of your situation by screwing your manager, the owner of the company, or anyone else who has a higher position than you do can be all you need to feel better. Why not mess with the company that makes every day a misery for you?

The most common type of shady workplace behavior that not only messes with the company but also directly benefits the miscreant is office theft. Stealing everything from Post-its to petty cash can be one of the best ways to remind your boss (and yourself) that benefiting the company is far less of a priority to you than benefiting yourself. Having light fingers at the office is a particularly great cheat if you really are underpaid and need to find ways to bolster your yearly income. Whether you're sneaking a ream of paper here and there or making off with a copy machine, everything around you in an office has value. Claiming that value for your own, and how you do it, is entirely up to you. Sure, you could ask for a raise or apply for a better job in the company. But where's the satisfaction in that?

THE UPSIDE

Getting extra money is great. Having a little windfall when you're least expecting it, or at least saving money here and there, always helps the bottom line. To quote a popular Depression-era joke, "Rich or poor, it's good to have money." So what if you have to get that savings or extra cash in a slightly unorthodox manner?

The upside of sneaking a few extra perks from the office is that almost everyone does it. It's really hard to find someone who is totally faultless, thus making it far less likely that one of your coworkers is going to narc on you. So long as you play your cards right and don't do anything too overt, you can get away with this cheat for a long time without any censure from your colleagues. Half the battle of doing anything off-color is having people look the other way, which is really easy to achieve in a deadened office environment.

In fact, considering how disgruntled most employees are, you're more than likely to be applauded for your efforts. You'll be able to live out your Robin Hood fantasies, albeit on a pretty small (and selfishly motivated) scale.

THE DRAWBACK

It's hard to steal from the place of employment if you don't have a job. If you get too carried away with your office subterfuge, you'll cross the line from monkey business to full-on larceny. The point of this cheat is to enhance your salary and your sense of well-being, not to lose the source of your income. This is an all-too-real possibility for the saboteur who lacks subtlety.

If you do get caught and penalized but not fired, you'll likely see a tightening up in company policy of whatever loophole you tried to slip through. Your coworkers (who were probably doing the exact same thing you were trying to) will not be terribly happy about this development. You'll likely find yourself getting punished by colleagues as well as by your boss. Expect cold shoulders, sudden unhelpfulness, and a lot of lonely lunch hours.

As with most cheats, if you really go way over the line and try something on a large scale, you could even find yourself in legal hot water. No one likes having to face embezzlement charges.

TOOLS OF THE TRADE

Depending on what you've got your sights set on, you'll need different tools to pull this cheat off. Assuming that you're not going to make the mistake of trying to embezzle huge sums of money (requiring offshore bank accounts and shady financial advisors), you'll need just a few items. Having a way to carry your booty home is the most important first step. A car or van is advisable if you have the ability to take a heavy item with you, no need to throw your back out over this.

1. Large car or van
2. Oversized handbag or gym bag
3. Reason to be at work late

WAYS AND MEANS: HOW TO PULL IT OFF

Keeping it small is the name of the game, so here's a good basic list of to do's to pull this cheat off properly. Remain inconspicuous and only improvise on this methodology if your circumstances allow.

1. MAKING COPIES—If you go to your local copy center, a single copy can cost approximately ten cents. Every time you use the company copy machine for something other than work, you can count each copy you make as a savings of ten cents to your personal overhead. Ten copies a day is a dollar a day. Do that every workday for a month, and you've got about $28 saved. Yearly, that adds up to $336, which is the cost of a moderately priced gym membership. Making unauthorized copies is the easiest way to slip an office cheat into your workday. Keep it to ten copies or less, so you're not lugging reams of paper across the office every couple of hours, and you'll evade notice indefinitely.

2. JUST THE FAX—This is the same situation as making copies. Just make sure that you don't have a nosy colleague stationed next to the fax machine. They're sure to start asking questions if you're hanging around sending an inordinate number of faxes. If you do get asked a bunch of questions, just say that you're faxing the doctors at the mental-health

facility where your violent sibling is incarcerated, and you'll probably be left alone.

3. PHONE CALLS—Why have a line put in at home if you've got a cell phone and an office phone? This holds particularly true if you're in sales and have to be on the phone all day. In sales, no one really knows who you're talking to or why. This may be the only redeeming feature of a phone-sales job, so take full advantage of it. The same holds true if your company issues you a cell phone; just make sure that the bill for your phone isn't being reviewed or approved by a manager.

4. OFFICE SUPPLIES—Nearly 40 percent of all office theft is constituted by the pilfering of office supplies. That includes pens, folders, paperclips, Liquid Paper, printer ink, pencils, paper, Post-its, and anything else you might find in an average office supply closet. Why is such a high percentage of all stolen items from this category? Because they're portable and can be used at home. Carry a roomy bag, take small amounts at a time, and don't tell anyone what you're doing. This is so common, it isn't even worth much of a reprimand if you get caught. In the meantime, think of new and interesting ways to use all those extra rolls of tape at home.

5. SURF THE WEB—If you don't have to have an internet connection at home, there's no need to incur the extra cost. You can do all your emailing, surfing, and online shopping at the office. Keep your monitor turned away from general traffic and have a very official-looking document minimized and sitting in your toolbar at all times. If anyone comes by, pop up the document and look busy.

6. DEFUNCT MACHINERY—Is there an old monitor sitting in the supply closet? Has it been there for over a year collecting dust? It may

be time to take it home for repurposing or sale. There are always buyers for slightly out-of-date machinery so long as the price is right. Considering that anything is the right price if you didn't have to pay to get your hands on it in the first place, you can really clean up this way. If you are going to take a large item, make sure it's something that's no longer in use and no one is keeping track of. Removing the new plasma TV from the conference room guarantees that you'll draw attention to yourself. Stick to old keyboards and fax machines.

7. WEIRD AND INVENTIVE APPLICATIONS— There's no shortage of crazy and inventive ways to find hidden perks at the office. If you're really desperate to save money, the manner in which you do it could be so strange that no one really believes it (or even understands it), thereby insuring that you'll escape detection. Or perhaps if your desperation is sensed, you'll be left alone out of sheer wonder and pity. Either way, you're saving money. Which is tantamount to making money, so don't hold back. One example of inventive savings is to bring every small appliance that needs its batteries charged to your cubicle to get juiced up. Doing this several times a week will definitely reduce your electricity bill. You might be the office weirdo, but if you're willing to do this sort of thing, you probably aren't really reined in by convention.

8. PROMOTIONAL EXTRAS—A lot of companies have T-shirts or mugs with their logo on them. While you might not be caught dead wearing your company's logo on your off-hours, others may not feel the same way. Collect as many of these promo items as you can when you're in the office alone and load up the car or minivan with your loot. You can use this stuff for gifts, school raffle items, or even try to sell it. Who know what's considered a collector's item? One man's trash is another's treasure.

MOST LIKELY TO SUCCEED

You'll definitely succeed at this cheat if you don't really care that much about your job. That doesn't mean that you don't want to keep your job; you should, as the end of the job means the end of your cheating ways. Not caring about your job in this case means not feeling overly invested in the company or what it stands for. It's that type of disassociation that allows you to chip away at the company's bottom line on a daily basis without much pause.

It also helps if you work alone most of the time. Having a lot of interaction with colleagues or heavy supervision doesn't leave much room for you to improvise with this cheat. Solitude allows for innovation, not to mention ample opportunity to shove stuff in your bag unnoticed. If you're constantly in the company of others, best not to tempt fate.

CATCHING OFFICE THIEVES
AT THEIR OWN GAME

First off, you've got to know if items are missing from your office. Assuming that you're a company owner or manager, it's probably in your best interest to know how money is being spent. It's also in your best interest to know if what you're spending it on is leaving the office at an alarming rate. Interestingly, this sort of accounting doesn't always get done, and office theft can go undetected for a long time, thanks to inertia on management's part. If you want to catch an office thief, make sure you know how much is being spent and on what.

If you suspect it's your accountant or office manager who's doing the cheating, plan an outside audit, and let your employees know it is happening. Fear will help things to quiet down for a while.

Don't ever sign blank checks to be used in your absence. This is too tempting for the cheaters you've hired. Don't ever let the lunatics run the asylum. If you do hand over checks, you won't do it twice.

Finally, check people's cubicles for items that look out of place. If someone's charging their car battery at their desk, you'll easily spot it and nip overreaching behavior in the bud.

⤙ *Would I Lie?* ⤚

.... **1** ....

A 2002 study by American DataBank found that office theft totaled $120 billion annually and contributed to 30 percent of all business failures. When asked whether or not they had ever taken office supplies, most people responded that they had, many even taking small items regularly. The prevailing belief among the office burglars was that as long as they didn't take any expensive items or things in bulk, they weren't really hurting their company. Many felt that they deserved the extras due to working overtime or being underpaid.

.... **2** ....

Ethics researchers have a few theories as to why normally upstanding citizens don't feel that it's wrong to skim from the office pot. Some believe that it's because a company is not the same as a person, in that it doesn't have a face. Most people would take something from the company's supply cabinet before taking the same item off of their coworker's desk. Other ethics educators think that people feel entitled to things at the office because of all the hard work they do. They may be underpaid, they may feel undervalued, but whatever the case, they think it's their right to take things from the hand that feeds them. The most interesting observation along these lines is in offices where the staff feels mistreated and where workers don't respect their employers. In these cases, employees will actually try to hurt the company by committing subversive acts whenever they can.

<hr />

3

In downtown Shanghai, theft in office buildings went up 17.6 percent from 2003 to 2004. With stolen goods totaling over $30,000 (U.S.) per year, Shanghai officials are concerned with how to stop this growing problem. Most of the thieves don't work for the company that is victimized; however, they often work in the same office building, be it for another large company or in a service position such as repairs or cleaning. One thief stole three laptops in 2003, and then still managed to get into the building in 2004 to steal four more laptops, along with a cellular phone and some cash. There have also been cases of fired employees stealing electronic devices on their last day. Officials say that too many companies don't lock their office doors at the end of the day, or they need new antitheft equipment that will not malfunction.

THROWING A GAME

YOU BET YOUR LIFE

The love of the game is what's supposed to motivate young athletes who get involved in sports at school or after school at the local park. The sheer joy of running around with a ball, a bat, a hockey stick, or whatever floats your boat is what attracts so many young boys and girls to the sport they play. If one of these young athletes is lucky, he or she can make a career out of the game they love and clean up big by playing pro. As everybody knows, if you make it to playing professional sports, you'll probably earn a ridiculously large paycheck. And more power to you. If you can earn millions of dollars a year for chasing a ball around a court or around a field, why not do it? You may not be able to do it forever, but with a good accountant and investment banker behind you, you'll do all right. If, however, it doesn't look like you're going to the big show, or you're just not sure if you will, the big money may not be there for you. What's an athlete to do in that situation? How can you insure that you'll still see some cash?

Thankfully, betting on sports can rake in some big bucks. This isn't lost on the players, and they make the regrettable decision to get involved in betting on their own games. Pete Rose famously did that in 1989 by betting on the Cincinnati Reds while he was manager. Apparently this is a major gaffe, as Rose has since been banned from any involvement in baseball and has also been declared persona non grata at the Baseball Hall of Fame. Pretty harsh punishment considering that he is the game's all-time leader in career base hits. Even though Rose exists as a living example of what happens if you get involved in gambling as a player or manager, a recent report offers startling information. It shows that 35 percent of male student athletes bet on sports, which is not good. College sports authorities frown on athletes betting on their own sport, and it can certainly be argued that if they're doing it at the college level, they'll continue this questionable behavior if they make it to the professional level.

But there's something that a player can do that's even worse than betting on his or her own team, and that's throwing or fixing a game. It's one thing to bet on a game, it's another to alter the outcome of how your own team plays. To throw or fix a game means that as a player, you play in such a way as to insure the final score or outcome of the game. That could mean that you throw the game, or lose it intentionally. You could win the game by doing damage of some kind to the other team. You can also fix the point spread by making sure that the score shows a certain difference in points between the two teams playing.

Why would anyone do this? Why engage in activity that's so antithetical to the spirit of competition and excellence? Money, of course. Players who alter the course of a game do it to benefit gamblers. The gamblers, who are high rollers and can afford to bribe players, are willing to pay the price to insure a huge win.

So if you need the money, and you're an athlete, one way to secure the cash you need is to throw a game. You could struggle to make it from college sports to a professional league. If you are a pro, you can work hard to get a good contract, attract endorsements, and manage your money wisely. Or you could add to your nest egg by throwing a few games. Considering that gambling on sports is a multi-billion-dollar business, why not cash in if someone's offering?

THE UPSIDE

There's only one real upside to throwing a game, and that's getting paid. For the most part, college students are targeted by gamblers now for this particular cheat. While it was once possible to manipulate professional athletes with the promise of a payout of this kind, they are less inclined now, as they have more to lose. Back in the days of Shoeless Joe Jackson (who, along with seven other members of the Chicago White Sox, threw the 1919 World Series), players made very little money and had to supplement their incomes in the off season. Clearly that isn't the case anymore. One endorsement deal for anything from foot powder to corn chips, and you could be set for life. College kids, on the other hand, play for no pay. That is, until the gambling world finds them. Waiting to see if they get drafted by a major league team, of which there is no real chance for a lot of players, can be too much to bear. A bird in the hand (or in this case, a wad of cash in the hand) can be worth two in the bush.

THE DRAWBACK

There are a lot of drawbacks to this cheat. The key to deciding if you're going to do this particular cheat or not lies in whether you're a gambler yourself. The upside is that you could make enough money by throwing or altering a game to make a real difference for you. The downsides could take you out of the game forever. The gamble is determining whether or not you think you can get the money without being found out. The specific drawbacks all revolve around the cheater's ability to remain a college or professional athlete. If you get caught, you don't stand a chance. First, you'll get kicked out of the game, and if you're a college athlete, you'll be banned from a future as a pro. If you're a pro, you're also out of the league. Forever.

Next, you'll have to pay a fine. That goes for both college and professional athletes. The fine can be crippling, depending on your income. If you're a college athlete, this can ruin you.

Depending on the circumstances of the betting that was done on your game, and as a result of your actions, you could even go to prison. That happened to Stevin Smith of Arizona State University in the early 1990s after he shaved points on a basketball game. Oops!

Regardless of whether you play for your school or you're a pro, once you've been banned from the game, you've got a real problem. If playing your sport is your only real skill, what can you do to earn a decent living? Your only recourse is to keep playing, but you'll have to do it overseas. Essentially, the downside is that you wind up living in exile. Stevin Smith is stuck playing in Russia. If you do this cheat, consider your desire to live outside the U.S. seriously.

Finally, if you cheat at sports and bring your team down with you, you won't have many fans. Public censure will be immediate and devastating upon the discovery of your cheating ways. If you care about being liked and having fans look up to you, this is not the cheat for you.

TOOLS OF THE TRADE

Your skill at your sport of choice is really the tool that's needed for this cheat. Not only do you have to be a player who would attract the notice of the gambling community, but you have to be good enough to have your actions really affect the outcome of the game. Beyond that, there's very little that you need. In the most basic sense, the tools that you need to pull this cheat off are:

1. A spot on a college or professional team
2. Skill
3. Cash flow problems
4. Gambler's instincts

WAYS AND MEANS: HOW TO PULL IT OFF

Although the principle behind this cheat is a simple one, there are a few ways to pull it off. If you're a player, you can change the outcome of a game in a few different ways, depending on whether or not you're acting alone. If you're a gambler, there are also a few different ways to approach the challenge of getting a player to do your bidding. Here are a few ways to get the job done:

1. BRIBERY—Money talks. It can speak very loudly if you're desperately in need and someone is waving what looks like a lot of it in your face. Gamblers and odds setters who approach athletes know that and will do what they need to in order to make it worth an athlete's while to affect the outcome of a game. The definition of *worthwhile* has certainly changed over the years. White Sox pitcher Eddie Cicotte was supposedly offered a $10,000 bonus if he won thirty games back in 1919.

That's $333 and change per game. If you're going to bribe an athlete, you'll need to produce a little more than that these days.

2. READ ALL ABOUT IT—If you're trying to figure out who to bribe, check out the tabloids and sports blogs. If anyone is down on his or her luck and really needs a financial boost, you might pick up that vital information if you're paying attention to the gossip surrounding the team. If someone made a bad investment, lost an endorsement, or simply comes from compromised circumstances, they're easy targets for this cheat.

3. I'VE GOT AN OFFER YOU CAN'T REFUSE—If money doesn't work, good old-fashioned violence might. Snuggling the butt of a pistol into an athlete's back or temple might be all the incentive they need to make the score look the way you want it to. If you're not already handy with a firearm, don't start now. But if you have one hanging around anyway, and you're comfortable waving it around, why not? You could save some real money that way.

4. WINNER TAKE ALL—If you're an athlete, and someone has come to you with money or a weapon to entice you into making their bets pay off, you have a few ways you can make it work. The most difficult method is insuring that your team wins. You'd have to be pretty sure of your abilities, your team's abilities, and that your opponent stinks before you agree to this. If, however, you have some way to make everything line up properly (like hobbling the best player on the opposing team—calling Tonya Harding!), give it a shot.

5. GOOD LOSER—While it's very difficult to insure that you'll win, it's pretty easy to make sure you lose. This is the real definition of throwing a game. If you lose deliberately, you've thrown the game or "taken a

dive." Either way, you're letting down your teammates. This move is the antithesis of teamwork, and if your fellow players find out what you're up to, you're in serious trouble. It could be worse than what any bookie has in store for you.

6. SPREAD IT ON THICK—Another method for an athlete-cum-cheater is to help a bookie's point spread along. Betting on the spread means that all people placing bets are wagering that the difference in points scored by each team will be above or below a certain number chosen by the bookie. If you're helping the spread, you're assuring that the bookie will be right about his prediction for the game. This can be done by messing up your team or finding a way to hobble the other team. It was shaving points that brought down the City College of New York basketball team in 1951, in a scandal that rocked New York college sports for the rest of the decade.

7. TOURNAMENT TROUBLE—Another cheat for athletes to pull for their bookie friends is to fix the outcome of a tournament. The way that teams rank in tournaments is more fodder for bookies, and tying or losing a game to affect a team's advancement can affect everyone's bottom line.

8. MISERY LOVES COMPANY—Sometimes you just can't go it alone. That's when you get your whole team involved. If you can't make the scores turn out the way you need them to all by yourself, get your teammates to collude with you. When you've got a bunch of gamblers pushing you to perform, there's safety in numbers. Never go down alone.

MOST LIKELY TO SUCCEED
If you're a star athlete who can affect the way your team scores all on your own, you'll succeed at this cheat. You'll also succeed if you can

keep your mouth shut. This cheat is considered really dastardly by sports fans (a rabid bunch to begin with), and if you're known to shave points or take a dive, you'll have terrible press and get bounced from your team faster than you can imagine. If you can keep your counsel and lay low, you stand a chance of keeping the rumor mill quiet, and your cheat will remain a secret.

CATCHING SPORTS CHEATS AT THEIR OWN GAME

Athletes perform somewhat predictably. They have certain quirks that are known by their fans and anyone else who follows their sport. If they suddenly begin performing erratically, and the ups and downs of their performance coincide with sudden good fortune, you've got a cheater on your hands. New cars, houses, flashy clothing, fancy watches, and tuition paid in full are all signs of an athlete who's throwing games for cash.

⚜ Would I Lie? ⚜

············ **1** ············

In the 1919 World Series, baseball experienced its largest scandal in history, resulting in eight Chicago White Sox players being banned from the game for life. Local gamblers thought up the scheme, but most believe that the connections and resources that brought it all together came from a New York gangster named Arnold Rothstein. The players, later nicknamed the "Black Sox," were supposed to receive

(continued)

$100,000 from the gambling ring for throwing their World Series against the Cincinnati Reds. The grand jury tried the case in 1920, and while all of the men were acquitted of criminal charges, they were forbidden to play baseball after the scandal broke. The eight players involved were Arnold "Chick" Gandil, "Shoeless" Joe Jackson, Buck Weaver, Fred McMullin, Charles "Swede" Risberg, Oscar "Happy" Felsch, and pitchers Eddie Cicotte and Claude "Lefty" Williams.

.... **2** ....

In 2004 a former captain of the Kenyan cricket team was banned from the game for five years after being charged with accepting bribes to fix matches from an Indian bookie. The International Cricket Council (ICC) held a hearing and convicted Maurice Odumbe after an investigation by the ICC's anticorruption and security unit. The presiding judge, Ahmed Ebrahim (formerly of the Zimbabwean supreme court), had nothing nice to say about Odumbe. He called him greedy and bold in his actions, adding that it did not appear that Odumbe was particularly desperate for money. There was even evidence that the former cricket captain was living a life of luxury and overindulgence.

.... **3** ....

In December 2006 three Israeli soccer players were arrested for accepting bribes to throw an important game. Yehiel Tsagai, Evyatar Iluz, and Miki Atiya played for the team Hapoel Beer Sheva. The team was about to play its rival, Hapoel Raanana, when the Israel Football Association postponed the game on account of receiving knowledge that the three players had been given $2,400 and told not to play their best at Saturday's game. One player allegedly had a gun held to his head. The Israeli sports lottery had an estimated payout of $9 million at the time of the incident, and as a result, investigators are focusing their investigation on a gambling ring that had the most to benefit from a Hapoel Beer Sheva loss.

GETTING OUT OF PAYING YOUR WAY

A PENNY HERE, A PENNY THERE

Everyone knows that paying retail is for suckers. Consequently, bargain shopping at outlet malls has become one of the most popular ways to find all the fancy goodies we love at prices we can tolerate. The popularity of consignment stores, thrift shops, home shopping networks, and bulk grocery stores are also signs of the times. Our willingness to search out low pricing for premium goods shows how tightly we hang on to our hard-earned money and really understand the value of the dollar.

These are certainly excellent and well-considered ways to save money while avoiding ascetic denial, but is that all we can do? Definitely not. There are infinite small ways that we let go of our cash that we never really think about and that can be avoided with a little crafty thinking.

Most people have experienced some sequence of events in their lives that causes them to acknowledge that, yes indeed, little things can add up to something big. That could be a series of personal slights that result in a huge argument, or it could be a casual accrual of local art that results in a big, beautiful collection. Needless to say, it's the same thing with saving money. A little bit socked away every day can add up to big savings. But what do you do when you just don't have anything left to save? How can you get a leg up? What can you do to find that extra financial wiggle room?

The only reasonable answer is that you can cheat your way into solvency. Find ways to get what you want and not pay for it. This is not out-and-out stealing, it's more like a shift in perspective. If you don't *have* to pay for something, or there isn't an identifiable individual who will get hurt by your cheat, what's the harm? Sure, you could get another job or cut back on the spending you already do, but what if you can't cut back any more? What if you just don't want to? By instituting a series of small changes in the way you look at goods and services, and the way you've paid for them thus far, you can save thousands of dollars each year. All you need to do is think creatively and with a fabulously enhanced sense of entitlement.

THE UPSIDE

Saving money is great. You can lift yourself out of debt, have available resources for your kids, even go on a vacation. The sky's the limit when you have a nice wad of cash hanging around.

What's even better than having extra cash is getting it without having to endure any hardship. Normally, we all have to scrimp and save to create a nest egg of any real size. It can be really depressing and debilitating to forgo the pleasures in life just to pay the bills and save a little something for retirement. If you can save your pennies by getting out of paying your way, the solution to your problems lies before you! No hardship of denial and no depleted bank account. Essentially, you get to have your cake and eat it too.

In addition to staving off a punishing and austere lifestyle, this cheat is great because if you do it carefully, it's hard to catch you in the act. The key to doing this cheat properly is that all of your actions are low profile, so you're avoiding drawing attention to yourself. If you can control yourself and pull it off, you can keep this cheat going indefinitely. Then it makes the leap from cheat to lifestyle. Let the good times roll!

THE DRAWBACK

The downside to getting out of paying your way raises its ugly head if your conscience gets the better of you. To have a serious effect on the way you spend and save money, you have to do this cheat a lot. That's why it's best if this really becomes a lifestyle choice. Some people can't handle this kind of long-term commitment to cheating, so if you're not in it for the long haul, don't bother.

You might also have a problem with family and friends if you're not artful with this cheat. There are definitely ways to get out of paying for stuff that aren't directed at people you know, but some of them are. If they catch on, it can cause a lasting rift between you. People try to assume that their inner circle isn't going to turn out to be a bunch of grifters. No one wants to be conned by his or her intimates, so be sure to be sly or don't do it at all.

Finally, while you won't think of any of the cheats that get you out of paying for stuff as stealing, others might. Don't let mall cops catch you, and most certainly don't try anything while the real police are around. If there's room for ambiguity, law enforcement probably won't see things your way. Keep an eye out for who's watching you and be prudent, unless you feel like hiring a lawyer.

TOOLS OF THE TRADE

This really depends on which cheats you feel are right for you. Each cheater will probably come up with his or her own repertoire of easily accomplished cheats, so let your list of tools flow naturally from that. The cheats listed below are intended to get you started, so here are a few tools that are also a good starting point:

1. Reversible jacket
2. Big sunglasses
3. eBay
4. Black-tie outfit

WAYS AND MEANS: HOW TO PULL IT OFF

Let your personal circumstances and imagination guide you to finding access to quick cash all around you. The methodology represented below can and will reward you handsomely, but remember that your situation is unique, and you must tailor your system to take advantage of the loopholes that present themselves in your daily routine.

1. KEEP THE CHANGE—If you do all your daily shopping with a check card, you're leaving very little room for human error, and human error is the key to getting your hands on extra cash. In our digital age, fewer and fewer cashiers are accustomed to handling paper money and coins, particularly if they're young. When grocery shopping, picking up a prescription, or doing any other daily shopping, find the youngest cashier with whom to do your transaction and pay cash. It's a good

chance that 25 percent of the time you'll get the wrong change, and it will be in your favor. Say nothing. Take the change and walk away. You've benefited, and you didn't do anything overt to make it happen. Put this extra change in a jar and see how it accumulates at the end of the year. Perhaps a nice pair of shoes will take away that nasty guilt?

2. ONE NIGHT ONLY—Want a new outfit for that fancy dinner you need to attend? How about a new dress for an old friend's wedding? Sounds great, but who wants to spend a few hundred dollars on an outfit you'll wear once a year? Save the money by keeping the tags on the outfit and only buying from stores with good return policies. Most department stores let you return anything as long as you've got the tags and the receipt. It's an oldie but goody—keep your closet uncluttered, look great, and save the expense. This is frugality at its finest.

3. HEY KIDS, LET'S PUT ON A SHOW—Going to the movies is great. You can't beat the in-theater experience. You can, however, beat the prices. At over ten dollars a ticket, going to the movies is no longer the cheap treat it once was. You can avoid the high cost of entertainment by choosing a multiplex and taking the whole day to see as many movies as you can. Just buy one ticket and sneak into as many shows as you like. Wait until the previews are over and theater staff has moved away from the doors. You may have done this as a kid, but now is a great time to fall back into old habits. Why pay to see three movies when you could cough up for just one?

4. REGIFTING—If you're lucky enough to get invited to gala openings, premieres, or even product launches, you've probably already been the recipient of a swag bag. Swag is the promotional stuff that companies give away at high-profile events so they'll get listed as a sponsor, or simply get their name in the press thanks to the extravagance of what they're

giving away. If you can get yourself invited to these events, you too can be on the receiving end of everything from makeup samples to jewelery. You can keep this stuff for yourself (which may not cut down your basic living costs, but it is nice to have luxury goods), or you can make some cash by selling your swag on eBay. No need to feel cheap or low-rent if you do this; high-profile celebrities are already supplementing their incomes this way. Then again, behaving like a celebrity may be just the thing to make you feel low-rent and cheap. Whatever the case may be, swag can be your ticket to big savings and better living.

5. HARDWIRED—No need to pay for a cable internet hookup or broadband if you live in the right neighborhood. Before you rush to make arrangements to get online, make sure to configure your computer to have wireless internet. Then check if there are any open networks you can connect to (your computer will probably prompt you on its own). If you find one, hop aboard and never look back. You've got a regular (albeit insecure) connection, and you won't have to pay a dime for as much surfing, browsing, or emailing as you can handle. Do be aware that the insecurity of the connection will leave you vulnerable to other cheaters who may want to help themselves to your personal information.

6. *MI CASA ES SU CASA*—If you're not a giant misanthrope and have extra room in your apartment or house, you could consider getting a roommate. The twist with this arrangement is that you've got to find someone who will pay enough monthly rent to actually cover the entire rent or mortgage payment. While this seems improbable, it can be done. If you live in a city that has enough big businesses to create a flow of well-heeled people who need temporary housing, you can find people willing to throw cash at housing as long as its decent. Frequently, a law firm or bank will even pay the rent for an employee from a foreign

office. Under those circumstances, no one's minding the store, and you can really charge what you want. In the event that you can't find transient business types, you might just get lucky. Try to find someone fresh off the Greyhound bus.

7. FORGET THE FORMALITIES—Looking for all the food and booze you can handle without paying a dime? Look no further than your nearest banquet hall. Weddings, bar mitzvahs, sweet sixteens, and even funerals can keep you in free scotch and cocktail wienies until you've had your fill. The bigger the event, the better off you are. Make sure no one's checking invitations or names at the door, and you're home free. Wear the right clothing, such as a suit, tuxedo, or cocktail dress, don't make a lot of noise, and try to blend in. Go with a friend so you don't look lonely. If you do, people will approach you, and your cover will be blown. Doing this once every few weeks will cut down on grocery and bar bills, not to mention give you a swinging night out on the town.

8. PRESS PASS—Journalists can always call any company to say they're writing a story about them. It is then customary to request a sample of the product you are going to review. If you are creative enough to concoct a publication that you're writing for (best to stay away from saying you're with an established magazine, in case anyone checks), you can make the calls and let the swag roll in. Just like the swag you get at an event, this review fodder can be useful to you in its original form or as material to sell on eBay.

MOST LIKELY TO SUCCEED

These are cheaters who love to act. They love the thrill of getting caught and the unexpected. If you were ever in an improv group or did summer stock, you'll do great with this cheat. The ability to talk your way out of getting caught sneaking into the movies without a ticket, or claiming you're rightfully at that bar mitzvah is key here. If you can invent a colorful background story without batting an eyelash and have a little poise and aplomb, you're going to succeed at this cheat.

CATCHING MISERLY CHEATS AT THEIR OWN GAME

As long as you're not the one paying this cheater's way, this is actually not a bad sort of cheater to hang out with. The nonpaying cheater can actually drag you into his or her orbit and expose you to a few unpaid gifts or items that you wouldn't have been able to get your hands on otherwise. So long as your cheater pal is generous, you've got a good thing going. If, however, you're the one who's handing cash and opportunities to the cheater, the situation's not so good. You can catch this cheater by noticing repetitive behaviors. The cheater who finds a cheat that works for him will do it over and over until it doesn't yield a payoff anymore. For example, if a cheater can make a ton of cash by posing as a journalist for swag, it'll be hard to catch him the first time. By the third time, when there are no articles he can produce and no good reviews for your product, the game is over.

❧ *Would I Lie?* ❧

················· 1 ·················

Most people would never dream of shoplifting, but some of us don't feel bad about taking small things we haven't paid for here and there. After all, we work hard and *deserve* that brace-

(continued)

---

let for free—and it's totally overpriced anyway. If this sounds like you, be careful, or your sense of entitlement may inflate to such a degree that you develop WRS, or Winona Ryder syndrome. In 2001 Ryder was convicted of shoplifting for pocketing thousands of dollars' worth of designer clothing and accessories from the Saks Fifth Avenue store in Beverly Hills. In an entertaining aside, one of the items found on her was a $140 Frédéric Fekkai hair clip, which enjoyed skyrocketing sales after Ryder's case broke.

.... **2** ....

Have you ever needed an outfit for a black-tie affair when you were completely broke? Here's a good trick: Buy that expensive dress you love, wear it to the event and soak up the compliments, and then return it the next day. Just make sure the dress isn't soaking up anything more than compliments! A 2002 report on CNN about stores cracking down on their return policies included an interview with *Wall Street Journal* reporter Jane Spencer. According to Spencer, an estimated 1.5 percent of all store returns are scams, and when it comes to women's fashion, 30 percent of apparel that is purchased is returned. Most retailers have wised up and overhauled their return policies, so make sure you know what you're getting into before pulling this stunt.

.... **3** ....

When free food and booze are what you're after, crashing a party is usually the way to go. One host will think you know the other hosts or vice versa, and you'll probably get away with it. Of course, it may not be the best idea to crash a party if you're an instantly recognizable celebrity: Paris Hilton crashed one of British singer Siouxsie Sioux's private parties in 2002 by sitting down at Siouxsie's table uninvited and beginning to gab on her cell phone. Siouxsie would have none of it and told Hilton, "You are being rude and ruining my party. Take that incessant, vapid conversation away from here." Let's hope she set a precedent.

ART FORGERY

ART FOR ART'S SAKE
(AND A FEW DOLLARS)

Art forgery is the creating and selling of any work of art that is erroneously credited to an artist who did not actually create it. This particular cheat has a long and illustrious history, and an equally long and illustrious history of experts trying to catch the cheaters in the act. If you can pull off a forgery—although there's not much fame that can accompany your success, as only anonymity will allow your work to retain value—you can certainly find fortune. The art market has become crazier and crazier, with prices soaring into the multimillions for pieces by high-profile artists, sometimes even for a preliminary sketch or model. Any scenario where big money can be made is a perfect target for the con artist or cheater. It's even better when the subjects of the con are so ego driven that they're not likely to admit they were conned. Hence, low incidence of reporting the cheat; or in this case, forgery.

The first forgers, although they weren't known as such, were Roman sculptors who ripped off original work by the Greeks. No one cared much, as the point of those statues was to be aesthetically pleasing, not to drive up an art market. On the heels of this Hellenic imitation came forgeries from the Renaissance, when apprentices proved their mettle by imitating the works of their teachers. Even though the apprentices were signing the masters' names to the works, the masters had the last laugh on this type of forgery, as the faux works were theirs to sell. Contemporary painter Mark Kostabi and his assembly-line art had nothing on these guys.

Eventually, forgery morphed from a get-rich-quick scheme by clever artists with willing pupils to the kind of scam we have today. There was a big upsurge in art forgery in the nineteenth century, when moneyed but untitled collectors started buying artwork and recognized that certain artists were worth paying more for. This was the watershed moment for the modern forger.

So for every talented but starving artist out there, this is the cheat for you. Got talent? Have classical training? Know a little art history? Don't feel like starving much longer? Get out there and start forging. Yes, of course, you can stand by your artistic vision. You can scrimp and save to express yourself through paint, metal, wood, whatever. Or you could come down off your high horse and make in the sale of one forgery what you could in a lifetime.

THE UPSIDE

Money makes the world go around. And it buys a lot of new art supplies. The major motivator for most forgers is the financial gain to be had from the sale of their work. Not a hard concept to grasp when you learn that Jackson Pollock's *No. 5, 1948* was recently sold by Sotheby's for $140 million. If the art market can command those kinds of numbers, any artist has to figure there's a piece of that pie just waiting for them to snap it up.

Another advantage to this cheat is that if you can pull it off, you're effectively thumbing your nose at one of the snobbiest, exclusionary, self-referential industries around. How fabulous to get a roomful of Italian-suited snots to agree that your bogus Klee is the real thing?

Even if no one knows you're doing it, you're getting one in for the little guy. Damn The Man!

THE DRAWBACK

As beneficial as it can be to successfully forge and sell a work of art, it can be equally horrific if you get caught. Unlike a lot of other cheats that are small potatoes and just help you get through the grind of your everyday life, this cheat is all about the big time. People don't like it if they've been defrauded out of millions of dollars and had their reputations tampered with. If you get caught passing off your work as a Picasso, a Pisaro, or a Pollock, you could find yourself facing jail time and a hefty fine. Jail is bad enough when you're in there for something tough and menacing sounding. Think about how bad it's going to be when your cell mate (who's sharpening his toothbrush-cum-shiv) asks what you're in for. You definitely don't want to say, "Oh, my Impressionist style wasn't good enough; I should have stuck to Dadaism."

Also unfortunate, but not as bad as hanging out in jail for poor forging skills, is that getting caught means that your reputation in the art world will forever be sullied. Once you're known as a bottom feeder (which you may or not be, but that will be your reputation), you'll never find a gallery to take your own work. If they do, you'll be a novelty item whose moment in the sun will be brief at best. So if you really want to build a career in art, stay away from forgery.

TOOLS OF THE TRADE

This all depends on what kind of artwork you're going to forge. Most people stick with painting, although photography forgery is becoming more and more popular. If you're a traditionalist, you'll need:

1. Canvas
2. Stretchers
3. Pencils
4. Paints
5. Brushes
6. Palette knives
7. Projector/camera obscura
8. Chemical treatments for aging materials
9. Antique materials (any of the above)

WAYS AND MEANS: HOW TO PULL IT OFF

Art forgery techniques are increasingly sophisticated, but there are some basic tried-and-true techniques to getting your work to pass muster. If you want to get your work past at least the first wave of historians and critics, here are a few of the fundamental methods to employ:

1. BEG, BORROW, OR STEAL—Get your hands on the original you intend to copy. It's nearly impossible to forge a piece accurately if you're not intimately familiar with it, so a reproduction from a book is not sufficient source material. Find a way to borrow the original from the owner or get close enough to it to study it sufficiently. Some wily forgers have borrowed the original and given the forgery back to the innocent owner. Whether you're able to do this or not, be sure to get up close and personal with your subject.

2. ART SCHOOL CONFIDENTIAL—It almost goes without saying, but you've got to be a talented artist in the first place to pull off this cheat. If you've never held a paintbrush in your life, or you've done it only to slap another coat on the dining room walls, this is definitely not the cheat for you. A healthy dose of training and natural talent will set you up nicely to cheat your way into the museum or gallery of your choice.

3. REVOLVING DOOR—In their eagerness to turn a profit, art dealers and auction houses have been accused of agreeing to sell forgeries as the genuine article. If they can get them in the house and back out quickly and quietly, the attitude seems to be that all is well so long as no one's the wiser. Let this work for you. Make sure that you rip off artists who have a reasonable level of demand for their work, but not so much in demand that the average person would know if the work is forged.

4. PRIDE AND PREJUDICE—Let the egos of the art mavens work to your advantage. If someone's career is based on being able to spot a good painting or a great sculpture, the last thing he or she wants is for anyone to know that they were taken in by a forger. It is believed that, thanks to this ridiculous level of pride and self-importance, 40 percent

of the art that's being bought and sold by collectors is forged. If that's true, this is clearly not that hard a party to get into.

5. PAPER TRAIL—If anyone does decide to check the background of the art you're trying to unload, it's best to have your papers in order. The paper trail that authenticates a work of art is known as the provenance. Be thorough when you create the provenance for your work. Research where the original is supposed to be and who owns it. Make sure you don't make claims that are easily refuted. If you create a work that isn't a direct copy but is an original in the style of a particular artist, you can really go the distance and get it referenced in articles and archives by art historians. Remember, the more people you drag into your cheat, the less likely they are to bust you. If you look guilty, they look stupid.

6. WHAT ARE YOU MADE OF—If you're setting your sights on creating a faux Rembrandt or a Dürer knockoff, don't be a giant boob and use modern materials to create a fifteenth- or sixteenth-century painting. Make the investment in materials that date to the period you're ripping off. If your work ever does get investigated for forgery, dating the work is one of the first things that art experts will do. You'll be found out and thrown in the pokey faster than you can say "Man Ray." The only artwork you'll be doing for the foreseeable future is prison tattoos. Don't make this rookie mistake.

MOST LIKELY TO SUCCEED

Not only is talent essential to pull off this cheat, but so are connections. If you're already at least on the periphery of the art world, you'll have a decent chance of safely getting your forgery on the market and sold. If you're coming out of left field, it's going to be an uphill battle to get the clubby, cliquish members of the art scene to pay attention to you.

You'll also do well to be a decent salesperson. No matter how fancy the trappings may be, art dealing is selling. It may not be the Willie Loman variety, but it's sales nonetheless. You've got to be persuasive, slick, winning, and not too desperate. If you can project the attitude that you can take or leave the sale, you'll have a better chance of placing your artwork with a willing mark. A successful sale is just like successful dating. Never let the person you're targeting know you want them, or you'll lose them in a heartbeat.

CATCHING ART FORGERY CHEATS AT THEIR OWN GAME

There are amazing techniques and technologies that are employed to catch art forgers in the act. If you're a forger, you'll have to be on top of your game to successfully avoid the debunkers. Here's what they might use to expose you:

1. MISTAKES—A good forgery expert knows so much about the artist you're imitating that they'll know if you slip up in even the smallest way. Art historians will look for signature details the original artist might use, or extra signatures of the forger's that she isn't even aware she's adding to the mix. A single brushstroke out of place, and the forger's subterfuge is over.

2. COLOR PALETTE—It may seem like all colors and pigments have existed as they are from the dawn of time, but they haven't. Colors are just as manufactured as anything else we use in our daily lives. It's a common mistake of forgers to use colors that were not used during the lifetime of the artist being imitated. Catch a wrong color, and you've caught the forger.

3. THE DEVIL'S IN THE DETAILS—Some forgers decide to get tricky and do too much to make their work look like an antique. Aging techniques or even details like wood rot on the frame are frequently simulated in forgeries, but if they're not done right, it's a dead giveaway that the work is not authentic. Look for little touches that are slightly off-kilter, and your cheater will be exposed.

4. CARBON DATING—Just like archaeologists, art historians will use carbon dating to determine the age of a particular object. If you show up with an onyx statue of a cat, claiming it's Egyptian from the era of Ramses II, you'd better be right. You don't want to be the guy who gets busted for trying to pass off a knickknack you found at Khan al-Khalili while you were vacationing in Cairo.

5. X-RAY SPECS—There are a few different ways that X-rays are used to discredit art forgeries. A regular X-ray can be used to find an earlier work lying beneath the image that's visible to the eye. This can be used to verify a true masterpiece or reveal that beneath the supposed Matisse lay a sixties-era sad-eyed clown. X-ray diffraction can analyze paint components, while X-ray fluorescence can even uncover an artist's fingerprints. Unless you've got a canny forger who wears gloves to paint or sculpt, you might be able to nab him using this technology.

.... **1** ....

In May 2000 New York's two most famous auction houses, Christie's and Sotheby's, were preparing to release their spring catalogs when they discovered a problem. Both houses were showing the same painting, *Vase de Fleurs (Lilas)* by Gauguin, and each one thought it had the original. The paintings were immediately flown to a Gauguin expert in Paris, who determined that the Christie's version was the fraud. Christie's contacted the Gallery Muse in Tokyo, which had sold it the painting, and the shocked owner led the auction house back to New York art dealer Ely Sakhai. The FBI got involved and was surprised to discover that Sakhai was also the owner of the original *Vase de Fleurs.* Upon further investigation, they found that Sakhai had been pulling this scheme for years; he bought cheaper, lesser-known paintings from such famous Impressionist and Postimpressionist artists as Monet, Chagall, and Gauguin, forged them, and then sold the forgeries to buyers in Asia. He then sold the originals in London and New York to make twice the profit.

.... **2** ....

In 1991 Sotheby's auctioned the Kuhn collection of African objects, the flagship piece being a terra-cotta ram that sold for $275,000. In Mali, where the piece came from, rumors abounded that the ram was a forgery. Through a five-year investigation, it was discovered that almost 80 percent of the so-called antique terra-cotta works from Mali have been copies. The original pieces have become very scarce since the eighties, so Malian dealers commission local potters to create forgeries of every original that's discovered in the region. It is believed that many of the terra-cotta sculptures in museums all over the world today may be counterfeit.

.... **3** ....

Elmyr de Hory has been called one of the greatest art forgers of the twentieth century. The Hungarian artist was a master when it came to forging the masters, everyone from Matisse, Dufy, and Derain, to Picasso, Monet, and Modigliani. De Hory's forgeries have become so well known that there are even artists who forge his forgeries! His paintings today sell for upward of $20,000, but before he was discovered, he sold his counterfeits to galleries, collectors, and museums. After his scams were exposed in 1967, he began signing his own name on the back of his copies, no longer hiding the fact that they were not authentic. De Hory overdosed on barbiturates in Ibiza in 1976. It's believed that he committed suicide in order to avoid facing fraud charges.

FALSIFYING A WORKERS' COMP CLAIM

I'VE FALLEN AND I CAN'T GET UP

An office, or any other place of employment, can be a very dangerous place. Every day someone falls off a ladder, lifts something they shouldn't, or inhales toxic fumes. This results in millions of Americans sustaining injuries on the job, and thousands of even unluckier workers suffering an untimely demise. There are innumerable ways to get hurt while working, and if it does happen, there is recourse for you.

Workers' compensation law was written to protect you and all the other klutzy workers who make up the approximately fourteen million people who are bonked on the head (or worse) every year while at work. The law varies from state to state, but its intent is always the same. Workers' comp is designed to allow employees who were injured in the course of their duties to receive medical attention and financial compensation. That's excellent news. The less excellent news is that these benefits are received without having to prove that the employer was at fault in the accident. That means you can't receive workers' comp *and* sue your employer.

If you are injured and want to get workers' comp, you have to prove that the damage done to you did indeed happen at work. You've got to prove that you didn't have a preexisting condition, which simply came to light while you were at work. If you want to receive compensation beyond reimbursement of your medical bills, you've also got to prove that the injury has lasting effects. Sometimes it's hard to prove all that stuff. Sometimes you just feel that you're ready for a little time off. Sometimes you do get hurt, but then you get better. And the thought of going back to work is just too much for you. That's when it's time to cheat.

Falsifying a workers' comp claim can require a bit of planning and creative subterfuge. It can, however, be worth it. If you've got a horribly strenuous job that puts you at risk, it's reasonable to interpret any injuries you sustain as a warning to get out of that line of work. Workers' comp can keep you safe and decently compensated for the rest of your life, if you play your cards right.

So you could get medical attention, rest, take a little time off, and go back to your dangerous job. Or you can play it smart and let your injury become a get-out-of-jail-free card. No more work, no more worries.

THE UPSIDE

Let's see. What could the upside be of not working a job that could get you grievously injured, and still getting paid? True, you're getting paid only two-thirds of your original salary, but it's tax free, so everything evens out.

As is usually the case when you're doing some kind of cheat that takes you out of the workplace, you're benefiting because you're getting a break. Everyone needs a break, and we so rarely get them. Unlike our European friends, we don't get four weeks or more of vacation per year. A measly two doesn't do much to take the edge off. This way, you can have a paid vacation until you feel truly rested.

If you work construction or some other kind of job that puts you at risk, you won't be exposed to that inconvenience anymore. How nice not to worry about falling beams or breathing asbestos. Considering that a lot of law firms have made their fortunes from employees who have been harmed in the course of their duties, it's not a bad idea to get away for a while.

Provided that you like your family, you'll get to spend more time with them. You might actually be able to see your baby's first steps, snap a photo of your daughter going to her prom, and see your son catch the winning pass. If your family's not so picture perfect, maybe you can be around for your teenager's first intervention. Either way, it's better to be a present parent than an absent one. Let your family know you care.

You could learn new hobbies heretofore completely closed off to you. Maybe a few weeks around the house will result in you finding your inner artist. Perhaps you'll realize your dream of creating a woodworking shop in your garage. You could even learn to knit. Whatever it is you're into, this could be your time to discover it.

THE DRAWBACK

If you're supposed to be hurt and incapacitated to the point where you can't work, it's not a good idea to let anyone know that you're really just fine (or close to it). The number one drawback to this cheat is all the hiding and skulking required. If you've always wanted to see what a life of espionage would be like, this is your moment to experience it. You will have to remain indoors (can't let the neighbors know what's up; they always talk when it's least appreciated), and when you do go out, you'll have to behave like you're really suffering from whatever you've claimed has felled you. All that cloak-and-dagger stuff can be ridiculously tiring.

Cameras are not your friends. This means every type of camera, from your cousin's point-and-shoot, to the camera at the traffic stop, to the video camera at the 7-Eleven. If at any point a claims investigator from your company or the insurance company decides to poke around, photos will expose you for the fraud you are. Unless you can manage to leave the house in whatever bandages and braces you're supposed to be sporting, avoid the paparazzi at all costs.

If things get a little too close for comfort, and you think anyone's onto you, you may have to disappear for a while. This is a bummer, as the whole point of your cheat is to take a little time off (or a lot of time off) to relax. Going on the lam is not relaxing.

TOOLS OF THE TRADE

You want to make sure that you're convincing in your performance. You have to appear to be hurt, to be a sympathetic character, and that there's no way on earth that you could be expected to work. Obviously the level of injury you're faking demands a different level of performance and commitment to creating your damaged alter ego. Whatever you do, just make sure you've got some of the right hardware. It's very hard to be instantly suspicious of someone who claims a heavy beam hit them and is sitting (with assistance) in a wheelchair. Organize it so the person who doubts you will look like a heartless bastard. Some useful tools are:

1. Neck brace
2. Crutches
3. Knee/wrist/back support
4. Hospital bed in your home
5. *Merck Manual of Medical Information* for descriptions of symptoms

WAYS AND MEANS: HOW TO PULL IT OFF

Now that you've got your tools lined up, here's the methodology to follow to make the cheat really come together:

1. WHAT HAPPENED?!?—It's a good idea to make your injury fit your job description in some way. For example, if you're a computer programmer, it makes sense if you develop carpal tunnel syndrome. No one's going to give you a knee-jerk response that what ails you just doesn't make sense. Similarly, if your job calls for you to deliver washing machines, a back injury doesn't require a stretch of the imagination. Avoid insane claims like "wild animal bite" if you're a paralegal.

2. I WAS JUST STANDING THERE AND . . .—You can fake an injury to get workers' comp in either one of two ways. You can sustain an actual injury and then proceed to make a mountain out of a molehill. In other words, you can have a little stiffness in your wrist but then claim crippling carpal tunnel syndrome. Or, if nothing has happened at all, you can be an opportunist. Keep on the lookout for falling heavy items or hazardous conditions. If something dangerous or destructive happens, rush to the scene and claim that you were in the line of fire. So

long as no one saw it happen, you've got a claim that a refrigerator weighing several hundred pounds squashed you like a bug, and you must be attended to. Yell for help and let the good times roll.

3. KEEP ON TRUCKIN'—If you are interested in this cheat as a way to make more money, not to relax, you will not be disappointed. After you've set up everything so that you can receive your workers' comp, wait a few months and then move to another state. In your new digs, no one will know you, your neighbors won't know that you're supposed to be incapacitated, and you can pick up a new job to supplement the money you already have coming in. You're best off if you get paid under the table or use a new name in your new job.

4. NO WITNESSES—We've covered this a little bit already, but it bears being emphasized. No one can know what you're up to. You can't tell your best friends, neighbors, cousins, poker buddies, *anyone.* You never know who a claims examiner will decide to speak to, and the shallower the pool of possible sharks who can reveal your game, the better.

5. CONCEAL INJURY OR ILLNESS UNTIL YOU GET TO WORK—Another way you can get injured on the job is to actually be injured or ill before you show up. If you fell off the roof of your house over the weekend while you were clearing out the gutters, why not hold off on going to the doctor until Monday? Just climb up to a high shelf or do something else that will take you to significant height, then fall off. Or don't even do that. Just drop something heavy and lie on the floor moaning. When you're found, explain that you fell trying to do inventory (or something similar) and that you're ready to go to the doctor.

6. ORCHESTRATE AN INJURY AT WORK—If you aren't already injured before you show up on Monday, and you can't find a way to fake

an injury, you can always orchestrate an injury at your job. This is advisable only if you can control the environment enough to insure that you won't wind up seriously messed up.

7. DROP-DEAD BRILLIANT—If you're clever and know how to cover your tracks, you may be able to collect workers' comp long after the injured party dies. Just keep collecting the checks after your spouse/roommate/tenant dies. If a claims agent ever comes to call, get someone to fill in as the injured party. It's best if they bear some resemblance to the original claimant in case the agent has seen him or her before. Just make sure that you're not claiming that the person who's collecting has now reached some absurdly advanced age. That is, unless you can verify that they've used the techniques described in cheat #32.

8. GET A DOCTOR TO COLLUDE WITH YOU—There's no shortage of people who aren't willing to mastermind a cheat but are more than happy to get cut in. If you can find a doctor who will claim that you're legitimately all messed up (despite your apparent good health) and will sign his name to it on the insurance papers, you're good to go. Don't be greedy. Give the doctor a good percentage, and you'll ride the gravy train indefinitely.

MOST LIKELY TO SUCCEED

If you're a good actor, you'll do well with this cheat. You'll also do well if you can plan ahead a bit and put all the necessary elements of the cheat in place ahead of time. Having good backup is no less important. If you have family that will help with the subterfuge, you're in good shape. If you are lazy and don't mind hanging around inside the house away from prying eyes, you're doing well. It's when you want to get up and start using all your spare time to play golf, go tailgating, or go to the community pool that you're in trouble. You need a support system that will cover for you and remind you when you're overstepping your bounds.

CATCHING WORKERS' COMP CHEATS AT THEIR OWN GAME

No matter how hard people try to do all the necessary things to pull off this cheat, it's really quite hard to do. At some point, you want to get up, get out of the house, and start living a normal life again. That's when you get caught.

Here's a laundry list of some of the characteristics that can give away the workers' comp cheat on a dime: The cheater moves to different locations frequently; has an arrest record; the cheater has already requested time off for the dates during which he or she winds up being injured; the cheater doesn't have any health coverage; there's a history in the cheater's family (of big fat cheaters) of pulling the same scam; the cheater shows up after his or her "confinement" with a glowing tan; and, finally, no one is home when the claims agent checks in on the "incapacitated" claimant.

❧ *Would I Lie?* ❧

.... **1** ....

Ramasamy Subramaniyan, an Indian national, was convicted to three months in a Singapore prison on January 27, 2005, for falsifying a workers' compensation claim. The case was referred by the Ministry of Manpower (MOM) to the Commercial Affairs Department (CAD) in 2004 after its investi-

(continued)

gation into Subramaniyan's claim exposed it as a probable scam. His claim was that he had accidentally chopped off his finger while using an axe to clear cement away from a mixer. Upon looking into the details of the claim, MOM discovered that the axe was too blunt to be able to sever a finger, and there was no blood on either the axe or the cement mixer. Further searches found the severed finger in a toilet cubicle with a chopper nearby, and the DNA of the finger and blood on the chopper matched that of Subramaniyan.

2

One roofer who filed for workers' compensation in San Rafael, California, actually exposed his boss's insurance scam and got his boss convicted of workers' compensation fraud. Kenneth Scott Cooper paid half of his workers' wages in cash, filed false tax returns, and failed to list his employees as roofers, all in order to avoid higher insurance premiums. The worker who filed the claim was legitimately injured upon falling off of a roof; however, he received less money than he should have. It was because of the low payment that authorities looked into Cooper's records and discovered his scams.

3

In 1976 a claim for workers' compensation filed by Irving Zilbert set off alarms that ended up exposing the entire Ohio Bureau of Workmen's Compensation as corrupt. Zilbert's claim that he had injured his back and neck while remodeling a house was granted $5,600. The only problem was that Irving Zilbert had died of a heart attack six months earlier. Upon looking into his employer's address, investigators found an abandoned barbershop. It turned out that there were more than one thousand suspicious claims out there. At the head of the state industrial commission in charge of the program was the since-ousted Gregory Stebbins, who had also approved a $20,000 payment to a claimant who used the money in a real-estate deal, yielding $7,445 to Stebbins.

ENHANCING ATHLETIC PERFORMANCE

WE CAN BUILD THEM FASTER, BETTER, STRONGER

A serious debate has been raging in the athletic community for the last forty years or so and doesn't show any signs of abating. No, it's not debate over athletic prowess, or who holds the title for "fastest 100-meter dash" or "freestyle swimming champion." What has both fans and athletes alike in such an uproar is the subject of "doping," or taking drugs to enhance one's performance in any given sport.

Athletes have a very narrow window in which to peak at their sport, win competitions, gain notoriety, and win prize money or endorsements. Their physical powers are at a height for a short period of time, which usually corresponds to youth and good health. For the obvious reasons, an athlete has to make the most of their skills and cash in while he or she can.

But thanks to the appearance of a variety of drugs on the legitimate and black markets, athletes are finding ways to make that window of opportunity stay open longer than ever before. Starting in the mid-1960s, athletes and their trainers have been experimenting with concoctions that can make the athlete stronger and more resilient for a longer period of time. As a result, more people can stay in the game longer and earn more doing it. That goes for coaches, trainers, and sponsors, too.

The concept of taking substances to enhance one's physical performance isn't a new one. The ancient Greeks would chow down on a tasty meal of sheep testicles before a sporting event, claiming that it gave them a competitive edge. Not a surprise, considering that those testicles were chock-full of testosterone, the same hormone that first found its way into athletes' regimens in the 1960s. Thankfully, twentieth-century athletes got their testosterone in pill or injection form, and could forgo the Rocky Mountain oyster dinner the Greeks choked down.

Even though performance-enhancing drugs can lead to grand slam home runs and incredible feats of human achievement, there are a lot of people out there who are vehemently against it. They claim that sports are supposed to be about training and challenging the human body to do the most that it can naturally. Therefore, any enhancements are against the pure nature of competitive sports.

They also claim that drugs of this kind can be bad for the athlete, not to mention gateway drugs that lead the users to take other, more dangerous recreational drugs. Once that happens, athletes' position as role models is destroyed, and their young fans will be led astray.

These are interesting and compelling arguments, but they don't really address why doping is (or isn't) bad for athletes and sports. So what if everyone has to dope just to level the playing field? What's the inherent problem with that so long as the drugs are regulated? Who says that athletes have to be role models? Are rock stars role models? When did anyone put Keith Richards on a cereal box? Why should kids' role models be anyone but their parents?

At the end of the day, doping is all about being an outrageously successful athlete, no matter what the cost. It's too bad that the women on the East German Olympic swim team all had little moustache problems to contend with, and there are probably a lot of baseball players with tiny gonads. Even so, it's up to them. As an athlete, it's your choice to do something that gaming officials frown on. Then again, you could cash in while the getting's good, so long as you are discreet. It's up to you: Stay clean and struggle to make a living while you can, or dope up, cash in, and wow spectators. Ball's in your court.

THE UPSIDE

Should you decide to take performance-enhancing drugs, there are a handful of great upsides to enjoy. Obviously, the first is the life-changing kind of money you can rake in from prizes and sponsorships. If you can get a sneaker company to back you or a nutritional bar to put your likeness on the wrapper, you're golden. Invest wisely, and you're set for life.

You'll also get a lot of personal satisfaction from knowing you're the best at what you do. Athletes are, of course, competitive by nature. Knowing that you're the best is frequently enough reward.

If it isn't enough, there's also the fact that with your enhanced physique, you can break records and set the bar for other athletes around the world. Not only will you know that you're the best, but everyone else will know it too. Setting a record will secure your place in the history of your sport for all time. Beat that!

THE DRAWBACK

While the upsides to doping can be a bit ephemeral, the downsides are not. Considering the disapproval that all sports-related agencies feel for doping, the first downside is that any athlete who's caught taking drugs will face serious consequences. They can have their medals taken away, prize money and endorsements revoked, and possibly even be banned from their sport.

If the rumors are true, another problem is that doping really is a gateway drug for other non-sports-related drug use. Athletes who are accustomed to taking drugs to win may not have any problem taking recreational drugs to help them relax, cope with adversity, or just have fun.

Testosterone-based drugs such as steroids can lead to serious hormonal problems for both female and male athletes. Even though their bodies are enhanced to do well in competition, they may wind up having negative side effects on their secondary sex characteristics. Women will become masculine, and men and women could suffer liver damage, mood swings, baldness, and for men, breast development. Other drugs can lead to strange physical side effects such as rapid heartbeat, infertility, baldness, overgrowth of hands and feet, or even an enlarged tongue. The fame will be fleeting, but an enlarged tongue can be forever.

TOOLS OF THE TRADE

Athletes need just a few things to get themselves on the doping track. Aside from the drugs, if you want to take performance-enhancing drugs, you'll need:

1. Trainer
2. Coach
3. Team physician
4. Private sports-medicine physician
5. Access to black market

WAYS AND MEANS: HOW TO PULL IT OFF

Now that you've decided to shoot up or take the necessary pills to be the über-mensch of the sports world, you'll need to decide exactly which drug you need to do the job. The ways and means to pull off this sports cheat are really focused on what your drug of choice turns out to be. Here's an overview of the drugs available to you and how or why to take them.

1. ANABOLIC STEROIDS—Anabolic steroids are used to build muscle mass and increase strength. Anabolic steroids are derived from cholesterol (is that the good kind?), and work to build muscle and bone mass by stimulating the cells to create more protein. If you take these hormones, you can train harder and push yourself further. You'll also be angry a lot and get into a lot of fights. And generally be annoying to be around.

2. HUMAN GROWTH HORMONE—HGH also works to build up muscle and bone mass. It is a naturally occurring hormone, and will not only bulk up your muscles, but help you shed fat. This drug is increasingly popular because no drug test can detect it. Even though

you're getting away with enhancing your performance, you might suffer an enlarged heart and liver. If you're into becoming human foie gras, this is the cheating method best suited to you.

3. EPO—EPO is the abbreviation for the commercially produced protein hormone erythropoietin, which increases the oxygen in your tissue (muscle mass, not Kleenex) by increasing the red blood cells in your body. This is essential to endurance athletes, as the best ones need lots of oxygen in their bodies to sustain their exertions. The only downside of this enhancement technique is a possible heart attack. Or stroke.

4. BLOOD DOPING—If you can't wait for the effects of the HGH to take hold, you can always opt for a blood infusion. This increases the amount of oxygen in your blood very rapidly and will help with endurance sports. In addition to a heart attack, you could enjoy blood clots and viral infections. Then again, you'll also take home a medal. Sweet!

5. MORPHINE—If you're in terrible pain from the exertions of your sport, or you just want to stage a private production of *Long Day's Journey into Night,* you can take morphine to help with the agony. You can also try methadone, heroin, or other opiates to dull what ails you. Not only will you blunt the pain, but you might also become disoriented during competition and try to do something crazy, like run off a cliff or bounce a discus off your head. Although athletes do try this pain management technique, it is ill advised.

6. EPITESTOSTERONE—Instead of enhancing your performance, this natural form of testosterone will mask other drug use. It's the Trojan horse of performance-boosting drugs. It works by tricking drug tests into not properly reading the amount of testosterone in an athlete's blood or urine. Only use this if you're taking a testosterone-based drug.

If you're doping with something else, and you decide to take epitestosterone, you're an idiot. Or you've taken the morphine route.

7. GENE DOPING—Gene doping is all the rage because it's impossible to test for. It involves using gene therapies that are intended for people with degenerative diseases that waste muscle tissue, and builds muscle and bone mass. Even though the use of gene therapy in sports is questionable, what's even more questionable is the fact that there is a limit placed on research that would help nonathletes with degenerative diseases. If ever an athlete were to be a humanitarian, he or she would gene dope and offer himself or herself as a guinea pig for this worthwhile medical cause. If you can't make it to the Olympics, why not leave your mark in another way?

MOST LIKELY TO SUCCEED

Are you a risk taker? Are you driven to win at any cost? Do you fear nothing so much as not being remembered? Then this is the cheat for you. Add a dash of cash (or a desire for it) and a dollop of ruthlessness, and you've got the ideal candidate for doping. It helps if you're already at the top of your game, as doping can't make a lousy athlete great, but it can make a great one a legend.

CATCHING DOPING CHEATS
AT THEIR OWN GAME

Two words: Urine test. Testing someone's urine is the best way to tell if they've been doping. It's the tried-and-true method to test what foreign substances are floating around in a suspect's system, be they steroids or narcotics. It also helps to have an eagle eye for weird side effects (like women with Adam's apples). Soon you'll be catching cheaters left and right.

If you want to go one step beyond the urine test, a blood test will help too. Be warned, however, that no test is foolproof. Doping for sports is a constantly evolving field, and what you really have to do is second-guess anyone whose performance seems superhuman. A lot of athletes will slip through the cracks, but excelling beyond normal human potential is the first sign of the committed cheater.

✦ *Would I Lie?* ✦

············· **1** ·············

The 2006 winner of the Tour de France, American Floyd Landis, tested positive for elevated levels of testosterone in his body. Just four days after finishing first in the race, Landis failed the mandatory drug test for Tour de France cyclists. He claims that he did not take any testosterone and that his body naturally produced the higher-than-normal levels found in his sample. He was required to take a second test a week after the first, and failed that one as well. He faces a two-year ban from professional cycling if the International Cycling Union decides to charge him.

············· **2** ·············

U.S. sprinter and former gold-medal favorite Kelli White was suspended from the 2004 Summer Olympics in Athens after admitting that she had taken performance-enhancing drugs. She had won the 100- and 200-meter races at the 2003 World Track and Field Championships, and thanks to her steroid use, she was banned from the sport for two years. BALCO, the Bay Area Laboratory Co-operative, was charged

(continued)

with conspiring to sell illegal drugs to athletes, with the most famous athletes involved in the case being several players from Major League Baseball. The U.S. Anti-Doping Agency (USADA) received evidence against Kelli White during its investigation into BALCO, and when the agency confronted White, she confessed that she had used both steroids and a blood-boosting agent.

.... **3** ....

During the height of Communism in East Germany in the 1970s and 1980s, the government administered steroids to all of its athletes so that they would be able to win world championships and Olympic medals. Between 1972 and 1988, East Germany won 384 Olympic medals thanks to the government's distribution of an estimated two million steroid pills called Oral-Turinabol. The pills were produced by the state-owned and Communist-run pharmaceutical company Jenapharm, which has since been sued by over 150 former East German athletes. One of the athletes, Andreas Krieger, was once the 1986 European shot-put champion—he also used to be a woman named Heidi. He blames the East German Communist regime for Heidi's death, because they gave her so many steroids that she was essentially forced to have a sex-change operation. He still requires testosterone injections (administered by his doctor) to this day or, as he puts it, his body "starts going berserk."

CHEATING DEATH

I'LL BE SEEING YOU IN ALL
THE OLD FAMILIAR PLACES

The ultimate cheat, and the only one that has any real meaning, is cheating death. What good is immortality achieved through masterful literature, music, or art if you can't be around to enjoy the accolades? It's all well and good to live on through our children and to have our genetic lines continued, but that isn't *really* living on, is it? No. That's just having your last name continue to exist for a while. And the name may not even last that long. Considering the propensity in the modern era for couples to hyphenate their last names upon marriage, or to take on an entirely new name, living on through your kids is really becoming a thing of the past. Case in point: One couple recently took the last name Skywalker. While George Lucas may have been thrilled, their parents were not.

All these notions about achieving immortality through great contributions to the arts, acts of bravery in battle, or even giving birth to your standard-issue 2.5 kids is really just a way to soften the greatest blow of all. One day, every single one of us, from the lowliest ditch-digger to the most celebrated Nobel Prize winner, will die. Everyone we know and everyone we care about (and who could we really care about more than ourselves?) will bite the big one, kick the bucket, and be greeted by St. Peter with a hearty hello. If you don't subscribe to notions of Christian theology, it may be Charon or a shaman who escorts you to your final reward, but that's beside the point. You're dead, and that sucks.

This is a very heavy concept for most people to wrap their heads around, and there's good reason. It's pretty bleak news. To soften the blow, most people subscribe to the idea that there is some kind of final reward to be found after death. As Prince famously instructs us in "Let's Go Crazy": "Electric word life, it means forever and that's a mighty long time. But I'm here 2 tell U, there's something else . . . The afterworld. A world of never ending happiness. U can always see the sun, day or night." Let's hope he's right. Then again, this is the man who also instructs his listeners in the same song to "look 4 the purple banana, 'til they put us in the truck." So, then again, he may not be the spirit guide we're looking for.

So for those of us who, like Woody Allen, don't want to achieve immortality in any figurative way but by living in our apartments forever, what can be done?

THE UPSIDE

Cheating death has its obvious advantages. If you're the type of person who always wants to know late-breaking news, be it gossip or a CNN report, avoiding death guarantees that you'll always be in on the latest scoop. Hate to leave a party? Find yourself staying until the bitter end for fear of missing out on the fun? Once again, cheating death guarantees that you'll party on . . . and on . . . and on . . . You'll literally be the life of the party, no lampshades on heads required.

Another major upside of living on in perpetuity (to the chagrin of your landlord, should you have a rent-controlled apartment) is that you'll miss out on what waits for you after death. If you believe in the afterlife, and you happen to be a self-aware sinner, meeting your final demise and fiery downfall probably doesn't seem too appealing. Who wants to baste to tender-fleshed perfection in the big barbeque pit of hell? Chances are, a not-so surprisingly small number of people are lining up for that opportunity. If, on the other hand, you believe that after death you are faced with the gaping maw of nothingness and that death is nothing more than an opportunity to decay underground, you'll likely enjoy avoiding this fate as well.

True, population control may have to be addressed sooner than we think if we wind up having people living indefinitely. But consider the benefits! All these old people wandering around with incredible resources and knowledge to share—it's like a living, breathing, very wrinkly think tank at our disposal!

THE DRAWBACK

If you believe in the afterlife, and you see it as a filmy, wispy world of cotton candy dreams and unicorn rides, cheating death is definitely a bad idea. Why miss out on the glorious second act to the play that is your life? Another popular vision of heaven is that along with the Elysian fields, you'll see all your friends and family once you cross to the other side. Provided that you actually like these people, it would be ill advised to give this up, right? You'll be surrounded by people who love you, for all eternity, and you'll never know another day's sorrow. Sounds great! The trick, of course, is knowing that after death you're taking the elevator ride up, not down to the boiler room. So if you're sure about the afterlife, and you know that you're joining the spirit in the sky, by all means do not delay your journey. This cheat is definitely not for you.

Other drawbacks to the cheat require imagining a world filled with ancient people. These folks will have cheated death and then wander around the planet exhibiting all the usual old-people quirks that can be so annoying. Think about it, there will be a population boom of people over eighty, who will still insist on driving, get cranky after 3:00 p.m., talk loudly in movies, crinkle hard-candy wrappers in quiet places, and repeat the same stories ad infinitum. This will require a lot of patience on the part of younger people. Which is not necessarily a truly bad thing, it's just irritating.

Finally, there could be negative implications in the afterlife for cheating death. If you're a believer, this is another solid reason to seriously consider how far you'd go to avoid the reaper. Let us not forget Sisyphus, for example, whose attempts to stay out of the underworld so angered the gods that he was forced to roll a boulder up a hill for all eternity. Not a good way to spend a Saturday night, much less every night.

TOOLS OF THE TRADE

How do you get motivated to live your life so that you can live forever? It doesn't hurt to be overwhelmingly afraid of dying. You've also got to be driven to get online and research new life-extending techniques, potions, and supplements at all times. The methodology below will spark your creativity, but it helps to start off having the following:

1. Anxiety
2. Fear
3. Access to the internet
4. Ouija board

WAYS AND MEANS: HOW TO PULL IT OFF

Cheating death can take many forms, from ingesting odd extracts and supplements to subjecting oneself to physical rigors. Whatever it is you choose to do, choose wisely. Your choice could mean the difference between life and death.

1. DOCTOR, IT HURTS WHEN I DO THIS . . .—Extreme hypochondria is not a comfortable psychological realm in which to live. Even so, it could be argued that it's the most prudent state of mind anyone could have. If you are constantly worried that every ache, pain, twinge, or instance of fatigue is an indication that you're on death's doorstep, chances are you'll check out the source early on. By visiting the doctor with regularity that is simultaneously comforting to you and deeply annoying to your doctor, you'll be on the cutting edge of the news about your own health and in a great position to nip any life-threatening illnesses in the bud. So remember, heightened anxiety means longer life.

2. HUNGRY FOR LIFE—Several studies over the last few years have shown that people who eat less live longer. By eating a calorie restricted diet that doesn't sacrifice nutrition but does keep calories very low, you can theoretically exceed the maximum human life span of 120 years and possibly even increase it to 160 years. While this isn't exactly living forever, it's definitely living a long time. A long time that feels even longer because you're eating a steady diet of kelp and vitamin supplements. That's not to say that a life without Twinkies isn't worth living, it's just

that with all the weird stuff you'll be eating, you'll probably be really crabby from all that self-denial and smell like mulch.

3. ONE FROM COLUMN A, TWO FROM COLUMN B—Traditional Chinese medicine has long espoused that the secret to long life lies in the three elements that lie within every person: your essence (*jing*), your energy (*chi*), and your spirit (*shen*). If these three elements are not strong and in harmony, you don't stand a chance. Although all three are clearly important, it's your jing that specifically rules the longevity part of the picture. So here are a few rules to follow to beef up your jing: Eat organic foods, get eight hours of sleep every night, sleep with socks on, wear a warming vest, and don't overdo sex. Certainly don't have it more than once a week, and when you do, try to avoid having an orgasm. In other words, join a secluded order and wish you were dead. If you can hack the monastic lifestyle, try to make sure that you eat a hearty dose of ginger, ginseng, pearl powder, yams, and prunes. You'll live a zillion years, but you'll suffer from crippling gas the entire time.

4. IT'S FREEZING IN HERE—The first urban legend almost everyone in the United States is exposed to is the "fact" that Walt Disney had himself frozen to be revived at a later date and cured of what ailed him. This is totally untrue. It is true, however, that there are people out there who will very happily freeze you solid as last week's meat loaf and promise to thaw you out when your rare and debilitating illness can be cured. This is the science of cryonics. What these pioneers in immortality actually do is infuse your body with a freezing liquid at the moment of legal death (most of them will do it right before for an extra charge) and then bring you back "when the technology to do so is perfected." This is an interesting dilemma. For the true believers, this is a passport to future happiness. No more disease, no more worrying about death; you'll just make sure you get revived when all the mysteries of eternal life have been ironed out. For those who think it all sounds a little

sketchy, this is not the path for you. Zeal is required to go this route. Try the pearl powder instead.

5. WINE, WOMEN AND SONG—Hidden deep within the common grape (and blueberry, bilberry, raspberry, peanut, and cranberry) is a tiny fountain of youth called resveratrol. This compound can be ingested as a pill or powder and is said to fight cancer and extend life by up to 60 percent. Amazing. You're particularly in luck if you're a fruit fly, yeast, or worm, as you're the only creatures to have reaped and demonstrated the benefits of resveratrol so far. The good news for longevity seekers of the human variety is that red wine contains resveratrol, and regular ingestion may yield major health benefits. A word to the wise: Mixing copious amounts of red wine with a calorie restricted diet will likely lead to a lot of unfortunate falling down. Which can lead to loss of life. Pick one or the other.

6. TWO HEADS ARE BETTER THAN ONE—In the event that it turns out to be too difficult to truly cheat death by living forever, what are the alternatives? Right now, the best we can hope for is the stuff of countless late night horror movies. That's right, folks, it's never too late to consider cloning. But what to do if you can't locate slimy human-generating pods or a mad scientist with sparking Tesla coils in the background? Find your way to a lab that specializes in genetic engineering and donate your DNA. A few eggs and implantations later, and presto! You've got a mini-you to love and tend to—and whose organs you can safely harvest to replace your own as they start to fail. You may not live forever, but you can get an extra good fifty years or more this way. Needless to say, there are some major moral issues that arise with this particular technology and use of human clones. Then again, you can always argue that when it comes to survival, it's every man (and clone) for himself.

7. THAT'S THE SPIRIT—In the event that all your best efforts fail, and you do indeed shuffle off this mortal coil, there is one last thing you can do to shoot for immortality. Should you wind up as a spirit entity hanging around the ether, start haunting people. You can communicate with kids at a slumber party through a Ouija board, scare the bejesus out of a boardwalk psychic by making him or her actually hear voices, or talk to people through the static on their TVs and radios (aka electronic voice phenomenon, or EVP). In other words, haunt the living and make yourself heard as much as possible. You can even pull a Houdini and establish a code with a living friend or relative by which to identify you when you make your spectral return. Your pseudo-immortality will last as long as you can keep up your ghostly visitations.

MOST LIKELY TO SUCCEED

To be honest, anyone who succeeds at this cheat, or comes close to it, needs to have the right combination of genetics, luck, and sheer will. To even come close to pulling off this cheat, you need to be incredibly motivated and have steely determination. Cheating death requires a massive shift in the way you live, and considering the discomfort and inconvenience this might cause, you've got to be ready for it. If, however, you do manage to escape the bony clutches of the reaper, be sure to share your secret and don't forget to charge for it.

CATCHING DEATH CHEATERS
AT THEIR OWN GAME

If you have determined that someone else has enjoyed an unreasonably long life span, chances are you've lived longer than your own normal allotment as well. Why spoil the party? Just clam up and keep it to yourself. If, however, you've caught on to your ancient pal's secret in some other way, don't try to thwart them! Just squeeze them for the secret and share it selectively. Discretion is key here. There's nothing worse than spending eternity with a bunch of bores. Then again, you'll have all the time in the world to make new friends, and isn't that what life is about?

❧ *Would I Lie?* ❧

.... **1** ....

The fountain of youth has been a popular myth for hundreds of years, the story being that the magical spring will stop the aging process and restore youth to those who drink its waters. Spanish explorer Juan Ponce de León was credited with coming to the New World in search of the fountain. Instead he discovered Florida, which, ironically, is not the locus of the fountain of youth at all. It is more commonly referred to as "God's waiting room," thanks to the enormous number of retirees who enjoy its balmy weather. Sadly, the fountain has yet to be discovered.

.... **2** ....

To this day, the longest life ever recorded belonged to a French woman named Jeanne Calment, who lived to be 122 years old. She was born in 1875, before the invention of the lightbulb or phonograph, and died in 1997, after outliving her husband, only child, and only grandchild. She used to say that she was still alive because "God must have forgotten me," and on her 110th birthday, she claimed, "I've only ever

(continued)

had one wrinkle, and I'm sitting on it." So what was her real secret to cheating death for so long? Well, take your pick among these: She smoked well into her hundred-teens, drank a glass of port a day, and ate more than two pounds of chocolate a week. She also treated her skin with olive oil, rode a bike until the age of one hundred, and people close to her say that she seemed to be completely immune to stress. Now that sounds more like it!

.... **3** ....

Hormone therapy is a new and controversial method for longevity enhancement. There are several hormones that can be administered in this type of treatment. HGH, or human growth hormone, is the body's hormone responsible for human growth, and it decreases in our bodies as we age, leading some people to believe that HGH can be used as an antiaging supplement. It has also been speculated that hormones like DHEA (converted by your body into the sex hormones estrogen and testosterone) and melatonin can be used to fight the aging process by protecting against serious diseases and enhancing sexuality. The body also needs antioxidants such as vitamins A, C, and E to neutralize free radicals and cleanse the system, so some scientists think that ingesting enough antioxidants will help prevent chronic diseases and lead to longer lives. The bottom line is that so far there is no one magic pill or approach that has been proven to increase your life span or keep you healthier for longer.

ACKNOWLEDGMENTS

Many thanks to all the friends, family, and colleagues who were so instrumental in getting this book published. Special thanks go to Anthony Ziccardi, without whom this book wouldn't have seen the light of day, as well as Mitchell Ivers, Erika Burns, and all the other good eggs at Pocket Books. Special thanks are also in order to my fellow D&J Book Packagers, Laurie Dolphin, Tonia Samman, and Allison Meierding. You're the best wingmen around, not to mention the brilliant Alison Seiffer. Finally, thanks to my family and friends who supported me and made sure I brought the funny. These decidedly left-of-center souls are: Jim Hubbell, Terry Deal, John Dorfman, Anthony Jones, Nathaniel Marunas, CJ Gedeon, Nina Peek, Sandra Dorfman, Bertrand Dorfman, Gerard Lynn, Bascha Satin, Bronwen Epstein, Kim Fields, Maggie Rosen, and last but never least, Nick Nicholson.

I also have to thank all the terrific blogs and websites that provided so much fascinating information about the nefarious exploits that people get up to. They were invaluable in providing endless amounts of food for thought as this book came together. What follows is (what I can only hope is) a complete list of the websites that proved to be so helpful: aalbc.com, abcnews.go.com, www.about .com, www.accuracyproject.org, akak.essortment.com, www.alcor .org, allafrica.com, www.allheadlinenews.com, www.alwaystest clean.com, www.amazon.com, www.anecdotage.com, www.answers .com, antipolygraph.org, arts, guardian.co.uk, blog.fastcompany .com, www.blueoregon.com, www.bodybuilding.com, www.body language.net, www.bookkeeperlist.com, www.bookreporter.com, www.boredatwork.com, www.boston.com, www.bsm.bmj.com, www.businessweek.com, www.cabinetmagazine.org, www.calgary sun.com, www.calorie-count.com, cannabisnews.com, cardshark.us, www.careerbuilder.com, catalog.hsn.com, www.cbc.ca, www.cbsnews .com, www.citizenworks.org, www.celebritywonder.com, www.cfo .com, www.chicagohs.org, www.chinadaily.com, www.chron.com, chronicle.com, www.cnn.com, www.cnnsi.com, www.columbia tribune.com, www.complete-review.com, cornell-magazine.cornell .edu, www.crimelibrary.com, www.cryonics.org, www.deadspin .com, www.detnews.com, www.detoxforless.com, digg.com, www .digitaljournalist.org, www.divasthesite.com, www.drug-testing-solutions.net, www.educationalissues.suite101.com, www.electronic-school.com, en.wikipedia.org, encarta.msn.com, english.people daily.com.cn, www.erowid.org, www.eschoolnews.com, espn.go .com, www.ex-designz.net, www.famousplagiarists.com, www .farshot.com, www.fbi.gov, www.findarticles.com, www.fitness .com, www.fldfs.com, www.fno.org, www.forbeginners.info, www .forbes.com, forums.govteen.com, www.foxnews.com, galleryofthe absurd.typepad.com, gettingdownfraud.com, www.glass-castle .com, www.heidirice.com, www.hiphopmusic.com, www.home poker.com, www.homepokertourney.com, www.ifb.org, www.imdb .com, www.indiana.edu, info.interactivist.net, ins.state.ny.us, insurance.ca.gov, insurancefraud.org, www.insurancejournal.com, www.investigation.com, www.iol.co.za, www.ishouldbeworking .com, www.it-director.com, www.jamesriser.com, www.joebobbriggs .com, www.keepmedia.com, www.kvbc.com, www.launchpoker .com, www.law.umkc.edu, www.laweekly.com, losangeles.broowaha .com, www.markhofmann.com, www.marwen.ca, www.mayoclinic .com, www.medialine.com, www.michigandaily.com, www.mom .gov.sg, www.mrmike.com, www.msnbc.msn.com, www.museum-security.org, www.mystudios.com, www.nationalvanguard.org, www.nbc4.tv, www.nerve.com, www.netribution.co.uk, news.bbc.co.uk, news.com.com, www.newsdissector.org, www.newstatesman.com, www.nutrasanus.com, nymag.com, www.nytimes.com, www.oddjack.com, www.onlinedatingmagazine.com, www.passdrugtest.com, www.passyourdrugtest.com, www.pbs.org, www.playwinningpoker.com, practice.findlaw.com, www.prairienet.org, www.prospect.org, www.queendom.com, www.rbs2.com, www.rd.com, www.realitytvworld.com, www.reason.org, www.rendezvousradio.com, www.rotten.com, rpv.blogspot.com, www.santacruzpl.org, www.salon.com, www.science.org.au, www.sexinfo101.com, www.sfgate.com, www.sfsu.edu, www.signonsandiego.com, simplyappalling.blogspot.com, www.slate.com, www.smeal.psu.edu, www.smh.com.au, sniggle.net, www.spherion.com, www.swamppundit.powerblogs.com, www.taxabletalk.com, www.taxfables.com, taxprof.typepad.com, www.tcm.com, www.tech.mit.edu, technoculture.mira.net.au, www.telegraph.co.uk, www.thedoctorwillseeyounow.com, www.the-scientist.com, www.thesmokinggun.com, www.thesullivangroup.com, thinkjss.wordpress.com, www.tightpoker.com, www.time.com, www.tv.com, www.usdoj.gov, usmagazine.com, www.usnews.com, www.vanityfair.com, www.warholstars.org, www.washingtonpost.com, www.webgrrls.com, www.web-miner.com, whyfiles.org, www.wikihow.com.